TOWARDS A WORLD THEOLOGY

LIBRARY OF PHILOSOPHY AND RELIGION

General Editor: John Hick, H. G. Wood
Professor of Theology, University of Birmingham

This new series of books will explore contemporary religious understandings of man and the universe. The books will be contributions to various aspects of the continuing dialogues between religion and philosophy, between scepticism and faith, and between the different religions and ideologies. The authors will represent a correspondingly wide range of viewpoints. Some of the books in the series will be written for the general educated public and others for a more specialised philosophical or theological readership.

Already published

William H. Austin	THE RELEVANCE OF NATURAL SCIENCE TO THEOLOGY
Paul Badham	CHRISTIAN BELIEFS ABOUT LIFE AFTER DEATH
Patrick Burke	THE FRAGILE UNIVERSE
William Lane Craig	THE *KALĀM* COSMOLOGICAL ARGUMENT
	THE COSMOLOGICAL ARGUMENT FROM PLATO TO LEIBNIZ
Lynn A. de Silva	THE PROBLEM OF THE SELF IN BUDDHISM AND CHRISTIANITY
Padmasiri de Silva	AN INTRODUCTION TO BUDDHIST PSYCHOLOGY
Ramchandra Gandhi	THE AVAILABILITY OF RELIGIOUS IDEAS
J. C. A. Gaskin	HUME'S PHILOSOPHY OF RELIGION
H. A. Hodges	GOD BEYOND KNOWLEDGE
Hywel D. Lewis	PERSONS AND LIFE AFTER DEATH
Eric Lott	VEDANTIC APPROACHES TO GOD
Hugo A. Meynell	AN INTRODUCTION TO THE PHILOSOPHY OF BERNARD LONERGAN
F. C. T. Moore	THE PSYCHOLOGICAL BASIS OF MORALITY
Dennis Nineham	THE USE AND ABUSE OF THE BIBLE
Bernard M. G. Reardon	HEGEL'S PHILOSOPHY OF RELIGION
John J. Shepherd	EXPERIENCE, INFERENCE AND GOD
Patrick Sherry	RELIGION, TRUTH AND LANGUAGE-GAMES
Wilfred Cantwell Smith	TOWARDS A WORLD THEOLOGY
Robert Young	FREEDOM, RESPONSIBILITY AND GOD

Further titles in preparation

TOWARDS A WORLD THEOLOGY

Faith and the Comparative History of Religion

Wilfred Cantwell Smith

First published 1981 by
THE MACMILLAN PRESS LTD
London and Basingstoke
Companies and representatives
throughout the world

Printed in Hong Kong

British Library Cataloguing in Publication Data

Smith, Wilfred Cantwell
Towards a world theology – (Library of Philosophy and religion)
1. Religions
I. Title II. Series
291 BL80.2

ISBN 0-333-27605-1

Contents

Acknowledgements

This book is a revision of the Cadbury Lectures given at the University of Birmingham, under the auspices of the Theology Department there. My thanks are warmer and deeper than I can readily say, to Professors J. Gordon Davies and John Hick, my hosts: for the honour of the invitation, the graciousness of their hospitality, and the challenge to try to articulate clearly a position on this momentous topic. My gratitude goes also, in no merely formal way, to the Cadbury family.

Part I

The History of Religion: Historical

I A History of Religion in the Singular

The vision to be set forth in this presentation is of the unity or coherence of humankind's religious history. At one level, this unity is a matter of empirical observation. It is an historical fact. At another level, it is a matter of theological truth. It is of ultimate significance, for each one of us personally (whether 'religious' or not), and for any interpretative theory of reality, or of the human condition. Since neither of these matters, the historical unity or the theological, has been clearly recognised in the past, however, they must be argued, demonstrated. This study attempts that. Any significance that the work may have will lie in its success in making evident these two realities, and the link between them.

I betray my own orientation by starting with the historical matter. One might say that I am an historian first, a theologian afterwards. That would be important, yet it oversimplifies. I betray my orientation also not merely by moving on to the second level, the concern with ultimate significance; but also by coupling the two in the same exposition. I hold that history, since it is human, therein has transcendent (shall we say, metaphysical) overtones. More inductively, let me report that I have found this, and keep finding it, in the course of historical studies. In human lives as lived over the centuries and around the globe lies the empirical base of metaphysical truth. I also hold – the same studies increasingly illuminate for me – that in turn truth has an historical dimension. It, including ultimate truth, or shall we say, God, is actively involved in the historical arena. It is, surely, altogether fitting that a Christian theologian should take history seriously; and hardly improper that he should begin with it. It is equally fitting that a modern academic theorist and inquirer should do so. The history of religion, by which I understand the history of men and women's religious life, and especially of their faith, lived always in a specific context, is intrinsically the locus of both the mundane and the transcendent, unbifurcated.

Accordingly, in the later chapters of this study, I shall endeavour to speak theologically about the unity, the interrelation, that I discern in the religious history of our race. Here, on the other hand, I begin more concretely, and perhaps more incontrovertibly, with an attempt to exhibit that unity itself; hoping to illustrate it in such a way that my readers too will see, and even will feel, at least its historical dimension.

Those who believe in the unity of humankind, and those who believe in the unity of God, should be prepared therefore to discover a unity of humankind's religious history. We are not so prepared, however. Neither preconception nor observation has conduced to our discerning it, or applauding it. Doctrine has inclined us to think of world religious unity sometime in the future, conceivably, but not in past or present history. Empirical awareness, as it has recently grown, has, vividly and properly, been of religious diversity. Personally, I find the religious diversity of the world almost bewilderingly complex. The more I study, the more variegated I find the religious scene to be. I have no reason to urge a thesis of unity among 'the religions of the world'. As a matter of fact, I do not find unity even within one so-called 'religion', let alone among all. The unity that I see and whose vision I am advocating is not of religion, which is varied, but of religious history – a different matter.

It is not the case that all religions are the same. The historian notes that not even one religion is the same, century after century, or from one country to another, or from village to city. So much is this so, that I have found myself pushed to dropping the word 'religion' as a concrete noun altogether, and also terms such as 'Hinduism' and 'Christianity', since I find nothing on earth, or in Heaven, that will consistently answer to those names; and have argued at length that modern awareness requires – and rewards – dropping them[1]. To take one example: forty years ago I set forth to find out what Islam is; and the more I learned, the more impressed I was by a discovery of a rich and marvellous diversity. The richness, the diversity, are of what Islam has been, in the minds and hearts of Muslims throughout history; and in the forms through which this has been expressed, and by which, elicited. Similarly, of the Christian Church only the uninformed can now imagine that it has sung but one tune in diverse times and places. It is only the historian who can hold all the evolving diversities of any one religious community's developments in interrelated intelligibility; and *a fortiori*, all the evolving diversities of all religious communities.

I repeat: it is not the case that all religions are the same. Moreover, if a philosopher ask (anhistorically) what they all have in common, he or she either finds the answer to be 'nothing', or finds that they all have in common something so much less than each has separately as to distort or to evacuate the individual richness and depth and sometimes grotesqueness of actual religious life. If every Christian man and woman throughout history is to be requested to renounce whatever in the fullness of their Christian living and aspiration they do not share with every other Christian, of other denominations and other centuries, let alone whatever they do not share with a Jewish scholar of the Law and a Hindu villager and a Muslim mystic, what violence is not being done to the integrity of their personal faith? The historian must stand guard against a vitiation of man's actual religious living by enthusiasts for emaciating abstractions. He or she must stand guard, in the name of actuality and of the unique, and of human dignity.

History is the domain of the specific, the multifarious; of recalcitrant fact; of the human. It is the domain of personal faith, in its depth and vitality and diversity. For the historian, then, unity is not at all to suggest that *A* equals *B*, or even resembles it. Rather, it is to affirm that they are historically interconnected; that they have humankind's religious history, which is the vision of this presentation, is not to propose that all men and women have been religious in the same way. That would be absurd. No two centuries have been religious in the same way; certainly, no two communities; in the end, no two persons. It is, rather, to discern that the evident variety of their religious life is real, yet is contained within an historical continuum. To say that *A* and *B* share a common history is not at all to suggest that *A* equals *B*, or even resembles it. Rather, it is to affirm that they are historically interconnected; that they have interacted with the same things or with each other, or that one has 'grown out of' or been 'influenced by' the other; more exactly, that one can be understood only in terms of a context of which the other forms a part.

What all Christians have in common is that they have shared a common history. They have participated in a common process: namely, the Christian Church in its ever-changing multiformity. They have in common also, no doubt, at the theological now rather than the historical level, something transcendent. Yet to say in words what that transcendent reality is – the Real Presence, Christ, God; or to say that the Church, in whose on-going life they variously participate, is itself the body of Christ; or however one conceptualise it – is to employ formulations that in turn are themselves not transcendent, and that are historically not stable. This dimension we shall be considering in our later chapters; also, whether the diverse religious communities of the world too have something in common at the transcendent level, despite their conspicuously disparate formulations. For the moment, I am arguing only that on earth what the communities have had in common is that their several histories, individually already complex, can be understood, and indeed can be understood better, and in the end can be understood only, in terms of each other: as strands in a still more complex whole. What they have in common is that the history of each has been what it has been in significant part because the history of the others has been what *it* has been. This truth is newly discovered; yet truth it is, truth it has throughout been. Things proceeded in this interrelated way for many centuries without humanity's being aware of it; certainly not fully aware of it. A new, and itself interconnected, development is that currently humankind *is* becoming aware of it, in various communities.

Let us turn from general principles to some specific illustrative examples.

My task in this introductory chapter is to help us become more aware of this truth; or simply to remind us of it. The unity of humankind's religious history is obvious, once one sees it. We have, however, been assiduously trained not to see it. Even more strongly, we have been pressured not to think it; and not to feel it. Yet today it beckons our minds. I cannot, of course, at best do more than hurriedly suggest it and partially illustrate it, in one brief presentation here. An ambition of mine has for some time been to try my hand, before I die, at writing a world history of religion in the singular: century by century, rather than in the more customary fashion of system by system[2]. For the moment, we must content ourselves rather with a perspective opened up by two or three, I hope illuminating, examples.

First we turn to Russia in the nineteenth century, to the figure of Leo Tolstoi. As is well known, this intense and brilliant aristocrat underwent in mid-life a drastic spiritual conversion. After a somewhat dissipated youth, and then for a time the career of an army officer, he had become a relatively well-to-do landlord and illustrious writer; then, in what seemed a sudden right-about-face, he turned, in a dramatic renunciation, from worldly success to an ascetic life of non-violence, poverty and social service. It was a religious conversion of a fairly classic pattern. Behind him lay sufficient fame, and within him sufficient power, that the move had considerable repercussion.

This shift by Tolstoi from the worldly life to the spiritual, by which his personal religious crisis was resolved, appeared sudden. Yet it may be recognised as the product of profound forces that had for long been operating in his mind and personality. In his subsequent *Confession*[3], widely circulated, he indicates that the conversion was crystallised rather suddenly by his reaction to a transparent fable from the Lives of the Saints. Clearly the entire process was enmeshed in the large context of his ambivalent but deep relations to the Church and to the whole Christian complex, most conspicuously his study of the Gospels, as he makes clear in his powerful writings produced at about this time: his attacks upon institutionalised Church and State and his exalting of the humble and meek. This one particular fable, however, seems to have served as a catalyst. In this tale, the human condition is portrayed as like that of a man who, fleeing from a furious beast, falls into a well and is held from dropping into the jaws of a devouring dragon below only by clinging to a bush that will, he sees, presently inevitably give way, since it is being nibbled at by two mice, one white and one black, that go round and round and slowly but relentlessly gnaw at its roots. The two mice are day and night; the bush, which tastes sweet at first but soon loses its savour, is one's worldly position; man knows that he or she must in due course die.

This myth, or parable, evidently made a profound impression on Tolstoi, quite changing the course of his existence. He had come to find his life hauntingly vacuous: meaningless despite his position, wealth and fame. His readiness to turn his back on his worldly goods, and to start afresh by going forth into the world in ascetic piety, was given form by this particular fable and triggered as he accepted it for himself. Of it he writes in his *Confession*, 'This is no fable. It is a real unanswerable truth'[4].

Our reason for noting this tale is that it formed part of a complex that had indeed had an altogether remarkable power; not only in Tolstoi's life, but in that of many thousands, if not millions, of others. It came to him from Christian hagiography, in an account of the lives of Saints Barlaam and Josaphat, to use their Latin names. This story, still alive and effective in nineteenth-century Russia, had there and elsewhere a striking – one could almost say, stunning –

history. Throughout mediaeval Christendom it had been extremely popular: more influential than nowadays we can readily conceive. Indeed, it is hard for our non-ascetic and literarily cluttered minds to credit the onetime widespread prevalence of such a legend. The Russian tale was taken from an early Greek version, from which had come also a Latin, which in turn spread of course in Western Europe. Among other Slavonic languages into which the tale was rendered, and in which it became popular, were Czech and Polish. The West had vernacular versions not only in Italian, Spanish, French, German, and the like, as well as Swedish and Norwegian, but also in, for instance, Icelandic, in which there was a translation as early as about 1204[5]. The mediaeval Christian consciousness was in no negligible part formed by this story. Its central theme is the renunciation of worldly power and wealth by a young prince, Josaphat, who, under the influence of the preaching of an otherworldly hermit, Barlaam, is baptised a Christian, abdicates his throne, and goes off into the wilderness in ascetic piety. He has left the world of pomp and pelf and worldly power to seek instead moral and spiritual truth.

Although the story as presented is explicitly Christian, the scene is set in India. Josaphat is portrayed as an Indian prince, converted by Barlaam, a Sinai desert monk.

The Greek version, underlying, as we have said, virtually all the Christian mediaeval ones, east and west, was for long attributed to John of Damascus. It is now known, however, to have been produced rather in the eleventh century on Mt Athos by a Georgian monk; and to have been taken by him from a simpler Georgian rendering, of the tenth or more probably the ninth century[6].

It was the Georgians – that 'Christian nation of the East' – who had turned the story into a Christian tale.

Their original, however, was Islamic. They had taken the story from a Muslim source, circulating in Arabic. The motif was the same: Muslim piety also at that time was receptive to an otherworldly spirituality articulated in a tale of a wealthy prince who turns his back on the material world to go out in search of salvation in devout asceticism. The Arabic version itself maintained a long and widespread popularity in the Muslim community[7]. For example, in the nineteenth century an edition was lithographed in Bombay[8]; and the new Ahmadiyyah movement in Islam took it up and adapted it for its own purposes[9]. One may note in passing also that, alongside the continuingly prevalent popularity of the Muslim

Arabic version, from the Greek rendering of the Georgian Christian modification of this tale there came also later a Christian Arabic version[10], which circulated among Christians in the Near East.

The story was not, however, original with the Muslims. Rather, they gave it an Islamic form; but they had got it in Central Asia from the Manichees – that fascinating community which for some centuries in Western Asia established itself, grew and flourished, and looked for a time as if it might prove to be one of the most expansively successful of the world's religious movements. Theirs was a syncretising movement; and it is not surprising to discover that they in turn had incorporated into their spiritual lore from Sogdian, Middle Persian and old Turkish sources this particular story, along with others, from the Buddhist movement, which in the first half of the first millennium A.D. had in missionary zeal firmly penetrated Central Asia[11].

For the legend is indeed a Buddhist one. It was fundamentally the story of Siddhartha Gautama and his setting forth from his palace home, having turned his back on family, wealth and worldly power to go off in search of enlightenment. He became 'the Buddha' on gaining that enlightenment under the Bo tree; at the time of his Great Renunciation he was, not yet a Buddha, but a future Buddha, or 'Bodhisattva'. This word appears then in the Manichee versions as Bodisaf, in the Arabic version as Yudasaf, in the Georgian as Iodasaph, in the Greek as Ioasaph, and in the Latin as Josaphat.

The particular form of this Buddhist story that gave rise to the wide-spreading tale is itself an amalgam, partly found in a text known as the *Lalitavistara*, composed in Sanskrit in the fourth or perhaps the second century A.D. The Mahayana movement had picked up the motif, and presently carried it also to China and Japan.

The story of origins does not stop here, however. The particular fable with which we began, that of the man in the well with the circulating black and white mice nibbling away at his precarious hold on life, a tale that had become incorporated into the Barlaam and Josaphat legend, and which struck Tolstoi with symbolic force, the Buddhists had added to the story of their own saviour. They picked it up for incoporation from either a Hindu or a Jain source. For both these communities are known to have made use of the fable, in their own spiritual teachings[12].

There is some suggestion that it may ultimately have had a pre-Aryan origin[13].

Let us, next, supplement our following back of the complex and rather astonishing career of this story by retracing our steps, forwards. From its prevalence in the Muslim world it spread then also to Jewish circles. Abraham ben Hasdai in Barcelona in the early thirteenth century produced from the Arabic, with appropriate adaptations, a Hebrew version, and this became widespread in the Jewish world[14]. Of the Jewish tale, the sixteenth century saw a Constantinople edition, and an Italian; the eighteenth, German and Polish. Also in the eighteenth century a German translation appeared, followed by another German paraphrase; and as recently as the nineteenth century it re-emerged in a Yiddish version[15].

We may, however, push the matter still further. Although it is entrancing to discover that Tolstoi, in nineteenth-century Russia, had his spiritual life given shape by a story that we can trace from the Jains, and perhaps from pre-Sanskritic India, and although it is also significant that his writings about his conversion, although suppressed for a time within Russia, were published in Geneva and translated into most Western languages and circulated far and wide, none the less the story does not end there. It is not merely a question of the West's being influenced from the Orient, a situation that has marked its religious history for long. Also striking is that at the turn of this century, in London, a young and brilliant Westernising intellectual from India, who had come there to study British law, met such works of Tolstoi's and was in his turn profoundly stirred by them. His name was M. K. Gandhi.

The impact made on the young Gandhi by reading Tolstoi was great; not only in the sense that it hit him hard at the time, but also in that it changed the course of *his* life also, with consequences ramifying throughout his career[16] and ultimately throughout the world. He did not immediately abandon 'the world'. He did turn to a concern for service to others; for spiritual inwardness; and for moral purity and ascetic discipline. He read the Bhagavad Gita first in London, in English. In South Africa, somewhat later, when the welfare of his fellow Indians took precedence for him over his own career and other concerns, he established near Johannesburg as the embodiment of his then vision what he chose to call Tolstoy Farm. For a time, Tolstoi's influence was perhaps as decisive in Gandhi's thinking and feeling as that of any one thinker. No doubt over the years, not least after he left England and later South Africa and settled once more in India, he turned more and more back to his own Indian tradition, in a complex way both Jain[17] and 'Hindu';

and there (and in the influence that of course he had consciously and unconsciously absorbed from it as a child) he rediscovered nurture for, deepening of, and elaborations from, his in one sense new spiritual and humane orientation. Yet, as with Tolstoi, and with others, a particular matter had served as a catalyst for spiritual capacity deep within him, long tacitly developing, and for spiritual response to an ancient tradition round about him. One might almost say that he spent the rest of his life as it were repatriating to India and exploring the Indian basis of and articulations for the impetus and aspiration of a style of moral living that India as a whole had never lost but for which Europe had at a given moment supplied him with the activating symbol – a figuration that Europe itself a millennium or so earlier had borrowed for its own spiritual life, and whose dynamic he was now, as it were, taking back home.

We should seem, then, to have come full circle: from India to India via Sogdiana, Baghdad, Georgia, Mt Athos, Kiev, Geneva, London and Durban.

The circle does not stop spinning, however. Gandhi's most important twentieth-century disciple, it has been suggested, is perhaps Martin Luther King, whose non-violence both as a formulated ideal and as a deep character orientation he learned in substantial part from Gandhi[18].

Our next example is a little different. Some while ago, on a visit to California, I was introduced by my host to a friend of his who was a Roman Catholic. On the same street as the latter's home there stood, I learned, a Japanese Buddhist temple, serving some of the local Japanese community as well as some interested Americans. This situation brought into somewhat striking exemplification a matter that has for some while now interested me: namely, the use of the rosary. Japanese Buddhists and American Catholics have many religious forms that differ markedly; the telling of prayer beads, however, they share.

October 7 in the Roman Catholic Church[19] is the feast of the rosary. This is a matter that one way and another is rich and elaborate. Most Protestants think of the rosary as a string of beads, of which the use religiously is a 'Christian' practice in the sense of being a Roman Catholic one. Historically, however, it turns out on investigation that that particular group of Christians have employed it only during part of the second half of the Church's history thus far. Christians lived for a thousand years without it, and then adopted it at about the time of the Crusades from the Muslims. As every visitor to the Near East knows, Muslim use of prayer beads is widespread.

Again, however, the Muslim practice, probably again via Central Asia, followed on a Hindu use. This, Buddhists also in turn took up, developed, and carried in their northeastward movement through Asia, including to Japan. In my California instance, therefore, the Buddhist usage had come to the west coast of America from Japan, by sea, just as the Roman Catholic usage there had arrived a trifle earlier, by land from the east coast of America and across the Atlantic from Europe. This history of the spread of the rosary is a good deal more complex, of course, in every case, than the above quick sketch perhaps suggests, or than we can go into here. I am simply making the point that we were witnessing on that particular occasion the closing of a circle that the historian can see has encircled the world, its two arms both beginning in India and moving out thence northeast and northwest respectively through intricate and variegated developments over a wide range of centuries – until they touched again in our day on a street in California.

The matter is again more complicated, however. Religiously, a rosary, or, as the Japanese call it, a *nenju*, is not merely a string of beads but the symbolism that goes with it. In differing religious communities this is in some ways similar, in some ways different. The number of beads used, for instance, diverges, not only between traditions but also within each. In the Christian case, for example, although a larger number is now standard, there was a time when thirty-three beads were used, and this symbolised among other things the thirty-three years of the life on earth of Christ; whereas the thirty-three beads on a Muslim string usually symbolise the names or attributes of God: ninety-nine, when gone over thrice. Similarly, the 108-bead *nenju* sometimes symbolises 108 names of the Buddha; though it may also signify passions of man to be overcome. (108 is the usual Hindu number of beads.) And so on. Of other similarities or contrasts, one may note that in India a rosary is called a *rudraksa*, which is the name of a shrub whose hardened berries are used for the purpose, the shrub being sacred to the god Rudra or Siva; whereas in the Christian case the name has to do with a different shrub: namely, the rose, sacred to Mary.

This brings us to a different matter: namely, that to think of the rosary as a string of beads at all is somewhat insensitive reification, the outsider's objectification of what to an insider is less tangible and more subtle. I can still remember my Protestant surprise when I first read in the *Enciclopedia Italiana* its opening definition of rosary as the name of a prayer. The history is complex, as ever. Originally the word had nothing to do with a string of beads (to which the name was later transferred by some, as that along with which the prayer is said; but this transference has been much less general than Protestants may suppose). Nor, in fact, had it to do originally even with a prayer; nor even with a chaplet, although the meaning of 'rosary' as chaplet is older than the other significations. The rose was a symbol of earthly joy, of love, of spring, and such matters; later, of heavenly joy, and therefore especially, it came about, of Mary. The concept rosary (in Latin) seems to be found first religiously about the middle of the thirteenth century in a mystical sense as Mary's rose-garden (in Latin that is what *rosarium* meant). The association of the rose with Mary, and the rosary as a chaplet specifically, is a European practice in continuity with the pre-Christian custom of certain bushes' being sacred to certain divinities: as, in Greece, the laurel to Apollo, the olive to Athene, the myrtle to Aphrodite; and this in turn can be traced back also to ancient Egypt, where the head-band or crown of a sacred tree was the locus for *mana*, which could then be carried by, or transferred to, priests and kings who wore it.

In evidence here is a rich and deep human capacity to symbolise, in this case with flowers: a capacity with a long and honourable history. When we say that the head-band of the leaves of a particular bush carried the *mana* of that sacred bush and the aura of the divinity associated with it, we are saying in part that human beings have been able psychologically and emotionally to have such symbols carry and articulate for them certain of their deepest feelings, and to focus some of their most powerful perceptions.

To be observed also at work in this is a process of change of symbolisation, not merely across religious boundaries but within them. Apart from the question of the rose's, or indeed anything else's, being a symbol of anything at all (a subtle and elaborate question, with its own world-wide history), there is the further point that the rose was apparently a symbol of joy in the twelfth, thirteenth and early fourteenth centuries in Christian Europe, but of sorrow in the fourteenth and fifteenth – in both cases linked with Mary; and it is interesting to note the history of the Dominicans' endeavour to maintain the two simultaneously.

In a decidedly superficial way, then, we are here simply touching lightly on the fact that during the last roughly one-third of Christian history thus far, some Christians, but not others, have participated through the rosary in a, to them, deeply meaningful complex, the various strands of which are historically continuous with several matters each of which links those Christians with various other peoples across the centuries and throughout the world, although the particular configuration into which they structured that complex has, of course, been their own – itself differing for Christians from century to century, and from place to place, in historical intricacy[20].

Let us take one more example: that of greeting cards. Those Westerners who have Muslim friends will for a number of years have been receiving through the mail, as have I, on the occasion of the great annual Islamic festival, ‘Id cards, with greetings of the blessed season. The practice of exchanging such cards among friends has grown strikingly of late in the Islamic world. Now a Westerner's first impulse is to assume that Muslims have copied Christians in this matter, the custom being clearly modelled on that of Christmas cards. One might interpret the phenomenon historically as a manifest instance of the influence of one religious system, the Christian, on another, the Islamic.

At one level, this would be accurate. At another, it would be misleading; for the historical fact is that the first Christmas cards are recorded as having been introduced in the mid-nineteenth century. (I have also heard that for a goodish while the practice was not only resisted but condemned by various Protestant groups, as un-Christian.) The precision of this account can, as a matter of fact, be impugned, depending on just how one interprets ‘Christmas card’; but, if the interpretation be significantly broadened so as to include various precursors, then the custom can be traced back – as, indeed, can Christmas itself – to pre-Christian Rome.

It is altogether too breezy, too anhistorical, to diagnose the religious-festival greeting-card phenomenon as a Christian one. Even in its typically modern form, there were no doubt a few decades during which such an interpretation would hold; but only a few. A more reasonable statement of the facts would be that the modern sending of greeting cards on a large scale at the season of the major religious festival has been a nineteenth- and twentieth-century phenomenon in the religious history of humankind, emerging first, but not without opposition, in Christendom but soon establishing itself among other communities also across the world.

This sort of interpretation will turn out to apply to a great many more phenomena in humankind's religious development than we are currently accustomed to thinking.

One might feel inclined to respond that this kind of thing is all very well, but that I have chosen rather peripheral and minor matters to illustrate my point: which is, that every religious tradition on earth has in fact developed in interaction with the others; not in isolation, in some watertight compartment. This point might seem obvious, or even trivial, did it not play havoc with much traditional theology – and even, more subtly, with traditional conceptualisations. To take elements theologically more central would have evoked more theological controversy; and I have said that I am deliberately beginning with historical and less controversial matters, postponing theological issues until later chapters. One should not imagine, however, that historical change and historical permeability are confined to minutiae, the negligible accoutrements in the various cases on some central core of each religious system which itself remains somehow unchanged over the centuries and untouched by man's common humanity. The practice of burial of the dead, and other rites of passage, for instance, including in the Christian case baptism, participate each in a large history; in the burial case this extends back to palaeolithic times. The world history of the idea of the Devil, to take another instance, is quite specific, and cannot be understood within any one religious framework; even though at one time it played in Christian thought and life a role by no means peripheral or incidental. The idea of Hell, also, which in our day has almost ceased to be one of the elements in the Christian complex so far as the religious life and faith of many are concerned, was once of utmost significance and centrality. It would be absurd to say that, over the course of several centuries, it was not a crucial item in the form of the faith of Christians, determinative, consequential, powerful; although it would also be incorrect not to see it historically as an item whose world history – whose career in the global sweep of humankind's religious life – transcends Christian history. It is an item that Christian history in the course of its development picked up; made central for many long centuries; and is currently to all appearances now in process of dropping again.

Let us take a still more crucial example. Little has been more central in Islamic religious life than the matter of scripture. The concept is so integral that most observers and virtually all participants would hold the Islamic system unthinkable without it. Yet a world historian of religion can discern the growth, development, spread, and varied crystallisations of this massively important conception over the course of global history now with some precision. The fact that the Islamic movement arose where and when it did within the total course of that global history is not unconnected, we can nowadays see, with its vividly bibliocentric orientation. On this last point both an historian and a Muslim theologian would agree, each in his own distinct way.

Finally: although I should not wish to make the naïve mistake of confusing God with the idea of God, none the less it would be difficult to deny that the idea of God has played a central role in Christian history. By this I mean, in the spiritual life, the moral action, the community practice, and every other facet of Christian being. The theologian might wish to recognise the justice of this historical observation by saying that God has mediated Himself to Christians through, *inter alia*, their idea of God. I myself have said something like this, on occasion; and we shall return to it below. Here I wish only to press the point that the Christian idea of God in its course over the centuries has been, the historian can now see, a part of the world history of the idea of God on earth, Christians receiving from, contributing to and participating in that total history.

We leave aside the question of the role of God in Christian life, for consideration in a later chapter; here we but insist that the role of the idea of God has been often decisive. (We leave aside until later also the question of the role of God Himself in East Asian life, where the idea of God has not been historically salient.) God has throughout not altered, most Christians would affirm; whereas the idea of God has never been unchanging, in Christendom or elsewhere. It has demonstrably varied, among centuries, among classes, ultimately perhaps between every two persons; if not grossly, anyway not negligibly. Every person's idea of God has been part of the history of that idea. (To believe in God is, then, to participate in that history, in a fashion that we shall subsequently be exploring.)

Obviously, this is an enormous topic. Let us touch, briefly, on only one illustrative example: mediaeval theology. Christian scholasticism, to take that instance, was what it was in significant part because of the historical context, including Muslim scholasticism, out of which it grew. So powerful and consequential a figure as St Thomas Aquinas gave his vision the formulation that he gave it, and articulated his concept of God as he articulated it, in ways that can be more fully and accurately understood, it is now recognised by the informed, in terms of many things including the formulations and articulations of an Ibn 'Aqil, a Ghazzali, and an Ibn Rushd ('Averroes')[21].

There are many profound differences, obviously, especially in substance, between the Christmas- and 'Id-card movement in the twentieth century, on the one hand, and the Aristotelian-based scholastic movement in the eleventh, twelfth and thirteenth centuries, on the other. In addition, though perhaps less obviously, between the two movements there are certain similarities, perhaps particularly of historical form. Mediaeval scholasticism, although it arose in the Islamic world, permeated also the Jewish (or by some reckonings this would be, rather, *vice versa*) and especially the Christian. The trilogue in mediaeval Spain is both an important and an illustrative phase of it.

In the perspective of world history – nowadays increasingly available – this view of mediaeval religious life and thought is conspicuous, and indeed is becoming almost inescapable.

Common to the Islamic, the Jewish and the Christian scholastics were not only certain forms, arguments, questions, categories, methods; but also a mood, an intellectual–spiritual outlook on the world, an orientation with common presuppositions, tastes, and goals. Similarly, in the case of the Bodhisattva story of Siddhartha Gautama's Great Renunciation, and the many variant and modified versions of it that took on Manichee, Islamic, Jewish and Christian forms, there was in common not only the particular motifs and formal elements in a tale that gave expression to the various ascetic pieties of those communities in that era. Common also, and much more important, was that mood of ascetic piety itself: the outlook and feelings and the form of human consciousness that envisaged virtue and 'salvation' in terms of a turning away from material concerns towards an otherworldly realm of saintliness. This mood, in many forms, obtained across much of the civilised world during a long phase in the total religious history of humankind. Its rise, its prevalence and its subsequent waning can, in a complex fashion, be discerned. It will make an important chapter in that world history of religion that will some day be written. The mood has not yet vanished; but as a dominant phase it has everywhere receded. Western Europe entered a different phase in that world history, a phase characterised by a different mood, earlier than did Eastern Europe; although both were Christian. Similarly modern Buddhists and modern Muslims, and not only modern Jews and modern Americans, tend currently to evince another era of religious consciousness.

Remarked above was the aspiration towards constructing someday a scholarly presentation of the religious history of humankind as a global continuum. One is not alone in such a dream, of course: in America the sociologist Bellah[22], the philosopher Burtt[23], the late brilliant historian Hodgson[24], and in Britain the comparativist Trevor Ling[25], have also, among others, thrown out feelers in this direction. This involvement on the academic scene has its counterpart in the fact that young people today not only are, but are beginning to see and to feel themselves as, heirs to the whole religious history of humankind. They are developing a new outlook in this realm, nowadays as early as at the secondary-school level in some cases; and a new consciousness, at the college and university level, or even outside these institutions. Some would see in this sort of development one more divergence, even conflict, between the academic vision and the theological. Not so I, as will appear below.

In the meantime, one need only observe that evidently the new way that we are beginning to be able to see the global history of humankind is presumably the way that God has seen it all along.

This much at least we may say: that the new empirical awareness of historical interrelations approximates more closely to the truth ('the way God has seen') than did the older, less well informed notion of disparate entities, each either given statically or developing, if at all, in sharply boundaried compartments. To the theological dimension of our new awareness we shall be attending later in our study. Here we may but note that those who would dissent from some such formulation will be drawn chiefly from two overlapping groups: those who dichotomise between theology and other knowledge, and those who anachronise. To opt for a position that would somehow allow the academic historian to discern inter-involvement, inter-dependence, but would hold that the various theologies none the less rightly proceed in autonomous sectors and postulate independent concerns, is surely an unwarranted bifurcation – whether consciously isolating theology from the rest of what is seen as truth, or unconsciously accepting from the past a theological vision integrated into a view of reality no longer held.

To assert that God created the world has inescapably come to mean that He has created the kind of world that natural science is in process of depicting; and to affirm that God is active in history is to aver that He has been acting in the history that modern study is increasingly making known.

In the past, our inability to see the historical coherence was due simply to ignorance, now being slowly outgrown.

More mundanely, there is a further point on which one may insist. Not only has God seen world history in total conspectus all along: the religious vision of history has tended to be unitary also. For in fact until quite recently Christians also – and Muslims, and the rest – saw the global history of humankind in integrative fashion. I would submit that, to take only the Christian instance as illustrative, Christians have traditionally seen themselves, and their religious truth, as within the total history of the world, in a way that came to be infringed only recently, and that we are now in process of becoming able to recapture. Later on we will touch on the theological aspect of this fact; but here on the historical.

The matter could be established from Japanese, or from Islamic, history; I will clarify it only from Christian. Two illustrations of the point are the first chapter of Genesis, and the Barlaam and Josaphat story that we have cited. Of late, the Christian Church has come to think of the accounts in Genesis of creation and of early times as particular myths and legends arising from a particular time and place in Palestinian history. Before the nineteenth century, however, the story served rather to give Christians the feeling – the consciousness, we might say – that they stood religiously in a continuum that went back to the emergence of man on earth; that their religious life was not a fragment of, but co-extensive with, the divine–human drama on this planet. It is important for us to reflect on those ways in which they were more right in this than have been our more recent predecessors, their bewildered successors. Biblical criticism has for many purchased technical accuracy at the cost of spiritual insight.

Or take the Barlaam and Josaphat story. The nineteenth-century West made the *faux pas* of imagining that to discover the true origin of this legend was to debunk, and to impoverish; rather than to enlarge and to enrich. This fear of recognising one's religious solidarity with all humankind still persists. Yet it need not; and, surely, must not. Speaking of the Georgian version of this particular tale, a recent editor wrote that in the latter half of the nineteenth century 'the authenticity of this Christian cult was challenged, and definite proof produced to show that Barlaam and Josaphat were not . . . Christian saints at all, but legendary figures whose image was based on ancient Indian stories about the Bodhisattva prince and his Great Renunciation'[26]. He is, of course, right that they were legendary figures based on the Buddhist original (although we are not so sure that the tale is not legendary also of Siddhartha. Does that matter?) Yet he was wrong, I would suggest, in inferring from that that they were not Christian saints. I am an historian, and I take historical facts seriously: we must accept them, in all their stubbornness, their richness and their uncancellable truth. Historical facts may not fit into our conceptual patterns; but they remain facts, thus to be accepted and revered. The historical fact is that, through this story, for a thousand years the Buddha *was* a Christian saint. This fact we can now acknowledge. Will others not join me in then affirming that it was inept history, as well as inept theology, that during a few embarrassed decades in Western Europe and America this kind of universalism lapsed? Surely we should now look forward to its being reinstated; though no longer in an unconscious, but now in a conscious, a self-conscious, way.

We have all along been participants in the world history of religion; although we did not know it. More accurately, until recently we knew it only imaginatively, mythically, in the form of legends and of tales. The breakthrough is that now we do know it, accurately. I, for one, rejoice.

2 Religious Life as Participation in Process

The presentation thus far has led us to a recognition or reminder that it is no longer possible to understand each 'religion' as a stable system. Any pattern that may exist or be conceived at any given time or place is in process of historical change. Of the elements out of which that pattern is formed, some transcend the disparate religious traditions, historically; while others emerge and disappear within each.

I suggested further that, rather than disrupting our spiritual life, this new awareness enlarges it, restoring our Christian, or shall we say our human, capacity to feel at home in the world – the whole world. We can once more see that Genesis was right that our religious life goes back to the very beginning of human history, and Tolstoi right that India, for instance, has something to say to Christians that can help us to turn outward Church doctrine and precept into inner personal truth. In this, as should be expected, a truer knowledge of history leads in the end to a greater awareness of spiritual truth. The Muslim, similarly, can see that the Qur'an was right, or the Japanese that the Shinto myths were, in positing the same thesis of primordiality, although in differing ways.

Does this mean that there are then no problems? Hardly. An awareness of the history of religion helps us to know, but not automatically to understand. The history of man's many religious forms turns out to be different from what we have been brought up to suppose – or, if we were Christians, to believe. And the history of religion must be taken seriously, by Christians of all people, in relentless accuracy. Yet by the same token, surely Christians, of all people, should not fear it. Obviously, our difficulties stem not from an enhanced knowledge of the facts (though it seemed that way to many, at first blush); rather, from our having attempted to cope with those facts by means of inappropriate concepts and theories. The ideational framework within which we have been asked to interpret what we see has become awry. If we go about trying to understand the flux of change in terms of notions that postulate or require static religious entities, or trying to understand global interconnections in terms that postulate or require discrete religious entities, independent of each other, then clearly we shall be in trouble.

This has indeed been the case with many. Having inherited from a more stable era a set of ideas that perceived reality in relatively fixed patterns, and from a more parochial era one that perceived it in relatively limited ones, such persons were in danger of losing sight of the truth framed within those patterns, once the patterns themselves began to be seen to crumble or to overlap. What has been shown by modern historical scholarship to be inadequate, however, in religious people's perception has been not their traditional apprehension of ultimates, particularly; but, rather, their interpretation of how religious life on earth in its historical development has in fact been working in making that apprehension possible. It is the understanding of religious history that needs refining; especially for a community such as the Christian, which has made a point of perceiving transcendent truth in historical forms. And of course it is specifically that that our modern knowledge makes possible. Here again it becomes clear why we begin this study on the historical plane and shall move on only later to the theological.

Our task in this present chapter, then, is to wrestle with the historical in religious life. I shall insinuate that it is not only an intellectual but a spiritual mistake to shy away from it, in some false feeling that the religious, spiritual or Christian task is to try to salvage something permanent from the flux of historical process so as to give our allegiance to that, or to try to construct something impermeable and uniquely our own so as to cut ourselves off from other groups and their allegiances. Modern historical awareness, austerely imperious, can save us from becoming that idolatrous or that immoral.

Might one perhaps protest that it is all very well for erudition to descry larger patterns and global involvements historically transcending the particularities of, for instance, Christian life; but that Christians themselves have in fact lived spiritually not in that wider vaguer world but consciously and deliberately in the context of their specifically Christian patterns? Admittedly, until recently Christians have been unaware of how ramifying beyond

Christendom, in both time and space, were many elements of the pattern of their faith. Yet today they are in process of becoming informed not only of that external largeness, but simultaneously also of an internal smallness, as it were: becoming aware of how particular, and almost contingent, their specific Christian pattern has been, within the flux of many such Christian patterns that in their multiformity, and ceaseless evolving, together constitute Church history thus far. The actual form of Christian truth or practice that any given Christian or Christian group in the past has consciously perceived, and may have regarded as 'Christianity', a modern Christian can see as, to a notable degree, particular as to time and place.

The context of religious life in the past, we now know, has in fact been in some ways larger and in some ways smaller than older concepts can well accommodate. Pluralism, and the need to come to terms with it conceptually and spiritually, confront us in our day in the intra-religious level also, not only globally. Religious diversity is a problem within, as well as among, communities.

Our immediate task is to understand it. Since it is a fact of religious history, this means to understand that history: to apprehend it and to that end specifically at this stage to construct concepts in terms of which that can be accurately done. I shall argue in due course that the concepts that render the history intelligible have the added bonus (and corroboration?) of serving also theologically; but that comes later. For the moment, our task is simply to see clearly what has been going on in humankind's religious life.

Let us look first at the Buddhist movement, and then at the Islamic. The one has been in some ways the most proliferating, expansive, fluid of all the great human enterprises that have been called religions; the least systematic, the least reified. The other, in contrast, has shown itself in some ways the most systematic, coherent, consolidated. Both turn out on inquiry to lend themselves well, I will suggest, to the notion of process in which persons of faith participate.

In the Buddhist case it is apparent almost at first glance that the life of Buddhists across the centuries cannot in fact be analysed in bifurcating fashion in terms of persons each of whom on the one hand has a secular context to his or her life, historically determined, particular, diverse, dynamic, and all of whom on the other hand share an additional entity *x* that may be termed the Buddhist religion. Indeed, it is not helpful to think in terms of their each 'having' a 'religion' at all. If one ask what it has meant to be Buddhist, the only possible answer from anyone even reasonably informed is that it has meant different things at different times and places.

This truth is firm and stark. It is fundamental for any understanding of the religious history of our race, the religious life of our fellow human beings (and then of ourselves).

This being so, if one ask why then we call them all 'Buddhist', the logician may be perplexed, but not the historian, who sees them all linked in the dynamic processes of history. 'Buddhist' is an historical term – as, in the end, are all human concepts[1].

Of course, it has taken historians a little time to attain this awareness; and only now are they providing it to others. Until last century the West had never heard of 'Buddhism'; it then became gradually aware of what it first thought of as a religion, to which it gave that name; it soon replaced this with two strikingly different species of the genus, Hinayana and Mahayana; it presently found that this in turn over-simplified, there being somewhat more than two – and moreover that even within these, and especially within the latter, a wide congeries of sects was to be recognised, with a further differentiation soon between, for instance, Chinese Ch'an and its Japanese version Zen; and then the historian subdivided each of these, in turn, into a series of consecutive periods, while the sociologist subdivided each into strata of classes, and the psychologist into an array of types; and our doctoral students today who write their theses on, for instance, various Japanese sectarian leaders analyse each figure's religious development into a succession of stages in that particular person's life.

It is not that the thing has become fragmented; but that it is not a thing. The *Oxford English Dictionary* enters the term 'Buddhism' as in use since 1801, and says that it means, 'The religious system founded by Buddha'. That was in 1888. We now know that it is not a system, but a religious movement; and that he did not found it, he inspired it. The analysis that I have elaborated elsewhere is that we have here an historical involvement, a complex: formed by a continuing interaction of personal faith, on the one hand, and, on the other, of certain things which I call dynamically a 'cumulative tradition', meaning by 'tradition' quite literally that array of observables that is handed on. I choose that word, and its epithet, in order to recognise its continuing variety without fragmenting it: to see its successive moments as differing yet interconnected. That segment of the cumulative tradition that is available and germane to any particular Buddhist person or group constitutes the Buddhist context of their life.

Such an analysis hopes to make clear at least that the significant overt elements in any person's or group's religious life, the operative part of the religious environment in which their faith is generated and sustained, is not only what can be traced back by modern critical scholarship to some early beginning. That person's or group's faith is what it historically is. Significant are all those elements that nurture it; operative is all that process in relation to which it lives. (The rosary has been an important part of the religious context of some Buddhists' lives; a less important, of others'; and not at all, of still others'. Certain ideas, similarly.)

Thus from Sri Lanka to Japan, and at one time from Samarqand to Sumatra, by interiorising it, each Buddhist has added to, subtracted from, or in some way modified some part of the Buddhist tradition that he has inherited from his forebears and that in turn he passes on to his children; or she, from and to hers. Our task is to study not simply the teachings of the Buddha, but rather what men, women and children – many millions of them – have done with these teachings, or through them, or because of them, in interaction with them; have done or felt, or realised, or become. Every Buddhist who has ever lived has added his or her own particular brick to the structure of the continuingly growing Buddhist movement.

Not every one has been brilliantly creative, or even significantly so: in many cases the bricks have been small, and remarkably like previous bricks in the structure. On the other hand, from time to time persons, or groups, have come along who have introduced new types of brick, or new types of architectural pattern altogether, or new windows or doors or balconies or towers. As the movement in its geographic spread reached new areas, persons added to the growing structure bricks in a new style: often the traditional style of their locality, perhaps quite different from those in other Buddhist countries. Yet in each case these men and women would not have been able to add their particular innovations, however novel, had they not had the previous structure to build on, and had the previous structure not inspired them to feel that taking part in this project was worthwhile.

And of course the picture of a structure, even one that is continuously and still today in process of construction, breaks down.

Like all pictures, it soon proves inadequate. For it is too static, too impersonal, too structured. The analogy of a river would be better, for conveying something of the idea of flow. Yet it too remains impersonal, and external. So far as the static quality is concerned, it is of course true that after a book has been written or a statue sculpted, after a person has died, after a generation has passed away, after a century is over, after, maybe, a particular part of the world has ceased to be Buddhist, then these contributions are fixed, are given solidly, like the bricks on the lower floors of a building, even if on the top floor one has to change one's metaphor and to think rather, let us say, of people dancing. One does not 'have' a dance; one takes part in it. The pattern one may learn from others; but a dance pattern does not become a dance until someone dances it.

Siddhartha Gautama in the sixth–fifth century BC in northeast India launched a movement; but no historian familiar with that movement can see him as the last creative figure in it, or can imagine that the many shapes that the movement has continually taken across Asia were somehow already given either in him or in what he launched, were latent only waiting to be uncovered; nor can suppose that anything new subsequently added must be either negligible or false.

(And some Buddhists, of major stature, for instance in Japan, have held that Siddhartha Gautama in India was a figure of quite negligible significance.)

Living life religiously – for Buddhists as for all human beings, even if in the Buddhist case it be a little more obvious – has been a complex interaction among four things:

(i) the accumulating religious tradition that, in one or another particular limited form, each inherited;
(ii) the particular personality – with its own potentialities and its own quirks – that each brought to it;
(iii) the particular environment – new every morning – in which each happened to live (this and the first above include the community in which each participated); and
(iv) the transcendent reality to which the tradition pointed, and in relation to which the life was lived.

Without the fourth component here, human history cannot be rendered intelligible. Those who would omit it altogether are empiricist dogmatically, rather than observers empirically of what has been going on. None the less, we leave it aside until later. Of the other three, so far as the first is concerned, every Buddhist who has ever lived has been born into and has lived within a particular religio-historical context constituted by one particular sector and phase of the wider, and withal rather kaleidoscopic, Buddhist movement. His or her religious life has been what it has been in relation to, in interaction with, one particular complex of items within the on-going movement, a complex that differed according to time, place, language, social milieu. In India, Sri Lanka, Thailand, Burma, Tibet, China, Japan, in this or that century, as a member of this or that sect, the religious or Buddhist quality of every Buddhist person or group is to be perceived in terms of the person or group's participation in some part of a process, one that we may call Buddhist because of its evident continuity and its self-affirmation. I would not wish to belittle the historical Buddha's active inspiration; it was awesome. Yet I would insist that by him the process was indeed inspired, rather than determined.

Few are likely to dispute a thesis of the extravagant richness of the Buddhist movement historically, even if some might wish to ferret out, more resolutely than I find necessary, some common thread running through it all. The point that I would urge is that the faith of each Buddhist has to be seen not in terms of that common thread, even if it exist: some least common denominator, some original or minimal 'essence' of the Buddhist complex hidden within the various parts of its historical elaborations. It is to be seen in terms rather of the full roundness of that particular sector of the whole process in which he or she in fact historically participated. It was this, in its colourful exuberance and its historical actuality, and not the black-and-white truth of some abstract 'Buddhism', that gave that person's life its religious quality. So, at least, the historian must insist; and so, in a later chapter I shall argue, the theologian must recognise – and may delight in.

The matter is important. We shall never be able in the sequel to attain a theology of the comparative history of religion unless we can discover here first what it is that that theology will be a theology of. The religious life of man in its multifarious variety has been the life of persons whose *faith* – whose Buddhist faith, to keep that one example – has been in each case generated and sustained and shaped not by Buddhism as something that he or she can share with all other Buddhists (however central may well have been a sharing with some), and about which one may abstractly theorise; but by the particular context constituted by that one historical phase of the on-going Buddhist process in which he or she personally participates. That person's faith is to be seen as a function not of the context, but of his or her participation in that context.

Some have participated more richly, more deliberately, more devoutly – or more obstreperously – than have others. Also, the notion of process must not be reified or precisely delimited. Each person was aware of, concerned with, only a part, whether large or small, of the total process that we may call Buddhist. His or her life was formed by only a part, and he or she in turn affected only a part. This is inherent in the notion that we are here postulating: to participate in a process means to be affected by, and to affect, a phase – whether great or small – of the total development. This is fundamental for the whole conception, as will become apparent when we later move on to consider persons' participation in the total process of human religious history.

One may conceptually give a specific historical instance any desired degree of particularisation; by speaking, for instance, of a person's participation in the sub-process of the Nichiren sect's history, or the sub-sub-process of that one development in the early twentieth century in a particular quarter of Tokyo – remembering, however, that that sub-sub-process cannot itself be understood except in part in terms of the larger process out of which it comes, and into which it feeds – just as this last participant may be and doubtless is participating also in the multi-religious world-wide process in our day of the interaction between religious tradition and technologised secularisation.

Well and good, might one respond; yet the Buddhist instance may be too easy for illustrating our theme, given, as I have said, its notorious fluidity. The Hindu, also, has been cheerfully uncoordinated, an unabashedly variegated enterprise; even though, in distinction from the Buddhist case, the Hindu complex may be thought of as in some degree boundaried at least within the geographic limits of the sub-continent (not without historical exception), and as rendered in some degree cohesive by accepted social patterns which are interdependent or at least mutually recognisant.

Let us turn, therefore, to the other extreme: the Islamic case, which in fact I happen to know better, apart from its being the least obviously calculated for this interpretation. It has had among its informing ideals *tawhid*, unification; and in several ways has been, as we have remarked, the most systematic of the world's religious traditions. If Muslims too turn out to be religiously not carriers of a pattern but participants in a process, then all men and women are. Or, put another way: if I can show what I mean in the Islamic case, I shall have succeeded in elucidating my thesis.

It may not be out of place to refer to the route that I myself travelled during the twenty-five years or so that I devoted to a fascinating and delightful and rewarding search for an understanding of Islam. I began with the usual notion that Islam was the name of a religion; the religion that the Muslims have, or more sensitively, aspire to have. Gradually I discovered that it is subtler than that; more fluid, more infinite, more dialectical, more personalist – more faith-like.

I had the good fortune to live in a Muslim community, and to have many Muslim friends. A good part of the zest of my search for understanding derived from the fact that many of my Muslim friends, mostly intellectuals but some of them also gradually moving into more active positions of formal and even political responsibility, were also engaged in such a search. Theirs was no academic or purely theoretical quest, but a serious wrestling with the issue of what is God's will in the novel, perplexing, ever-changing world of our twentieth century. What does it mean, they were concerned to know, to be Muslim in the challenging vicissitudes of modern life and thought? Beyond their classical heritage from the past, with its historical approximations and deviations, its good and its not so good, its variety, and amid the welter of modern interpretations by no means unanimous, what is true Islam?

My studies over the years were reasonably vigorous and always entrancing. They were the studies of an outside observer yet one not totally outside, and certainly not dispassionate, not unconcerned. Pursuing them, I gradually came to have on the one hand a lively sense of Islamic vitality and personal life, and an appreciation particularly of its mightily theocentric orientation and its deeply moral quality. On the other hand, there was also an increasingly full and focused sense of the mundane facets of Islamic evolution, of which I found interesting first the contemporary and very recent developments, but then also the classical and mediaeval. Here were institutions, structures, books; but also nuances, orientations, suppositions – and challenges to these, and questions, counter-actions, specific uncertainties. I was pursuing an answer to the question of what Islam *is*: a resonant and haunting question, certainly a religious question, and for Muslims a cosmic one. In the course of that pursuit I found myself with increasing material for answering the rather different question of what Islam has been. This latter is an historical matter; including, of course, contemporary history, where it becomes the fascinating and marvellously important question of what, today, Islam is in process of becoming, on its mundane and human side.

There was also the recognition that my Muslim friends, as persons, were not captured within any forms.

To reduce what Islam is, conceptually, to what Islam has been, historically, or is in process of becoming, as some outsiders have been tempted to do, but no Muslim, would be to fail to recognise its religious quality: the relationship to the divine, the transcendent element. Indeed, Islamic truth must necessarily transcend Islamic actuality.

A Christian may readily appreciate this. The history of the Christian Church has been a history of a congregation of sinners, as any Church historian knows all too poignantly; and yet the history of the Church would not have been there at all were the sinners not inspired by a greater truth than they were able to embody, or even adequately to understand. Similarly, the Islam towards which men have reached out has been greater than the Islam that the observer encounters. Since this is *human* history, the perceptive historian must and will recognise that the actual Islam that he or she observes is an approximation to an ideal Islam, by which Muslims across the centuries have been inspired and towards which they have at times grandly and at other times haltingly, gropingly, often ineptly, humanly faltered.

None the less, for all its unrealisedness, even that ideal Islam turned out to have had a history. The ideal that Muslims have conceived, their interpretation of that to which they did or ought to aspire, has changed; and in part it still changes. It has in some measure been different things in different centuries, in different countries, among different strata. It too has been not a system but a flowing stream. Not so fluid as the Buddhist, the historian recognises; yet alive.

It turns out that the situation has in fact been across the ages what both their theologians and ours have always said was the case: namely, that religion is a response to a divine initiative. Islam has been a human activity; and even the Muslim's ideal of Islam has been an evolving human vision. To see this does not entail holding that Islam has been a *purely* human activity, without transcendent involvement; since it would not have been what it historically has been at any given moment if those involved in it had not at that moment seen more in it than that. Yet it is a human activity for all that – human, and an activity. Islam has been something that people do, or dream of doing. It names something that people are, or aspire to be. And since those people have been people, each one different, and also living in varying places and times, it has been variegated, and dynamic; a living tradition, interacting with men and women of living faith.

I am proposing, then, to answer after my years of study the question with which I began – what does it mean to be a Muslim? – with an answer whose form can apply also to the Buddhist and to other cases. To be a Muslim means to participate in the Islamic process, as the context of one's religious life. To be a Buddhist means to participate in the Buddhist process.

As the sequel will make clear, I am not unaware of the magnitude and seriousness of what I am here suggesting. For this becomes not merely an historical or sociological observation, although it is those; but also a theological asseveration, ultimate and cosmic. It is also (but in the end delete that 'also') the only statement of what it means to be a Muslim, I suggest, on which both Muslims and outsiders might agree.

To be a *true* Muslim, those within the community might well respond (and others of us might well concur), has been to participate with faith; and it will matter on the Day of Judgement whether one have participated so, or only as a nominal Muslim. So far as this world and its affairs are concerned, however, both the Islamic theorist and the modern observer agree, that final question is held in suspense. (We shall be treating it theologically in our later chapters.) At the historical level, to be a Muslim has been and is to participate in a particular form of history.

This is true at the most casual level. Even for the marginally pious, the insouciant, the heretic, the debonair, to be a Muslim is to be engaged in the historical–cultural–social Islamic complex. And complex it is: it may mean to wear one kind of dress, to talk one kind of language, in Indonesia and in another area, to wear different clothes, to speak a different tongue, even in some degree to accept (or to fail to accept) slightly different doctrines, to observe or to flout slightly different legal–moral traditions.

At a more serious level also, the tradition has been cumulative and dynamic. If for virtually all times and places it has meant to see the Qur'an as final – to see transcendence in and through its resonant proclamations – even so it has never meant only that (the context has been more elaborate: the Qur' an has been one item, however major, in a slowly changing pattern); and also the interpretation of the Scripture has had, and continues to have, a history. What the Qur'an has in fact meant to any given Muslim or group of Muslims has inescapably varied, in ways that an historian (and indeed, even a biographer) can trace. To be a Muslim has been to take some part in the pulsating process of the Qur'an's actual meanings to real men and women in history. There is also a striking history of the role of the prophet Muhammad, and of the way that he and his sayings and doings were conceived and honoured, in the Islamic community. Of such fundamental concepts in Islamic life as *shar*ʿ and *sharīʿah* ('moral enjoining' and 'law'), even *islam* itself, there is coming to be a modern entrancing awareness of long-range development.

If the fourteen centuries of Islamic history thus far have evinced richness, variety and creativity, and, indeed, have been not free of conflict, similarly Islam in modern history also is animated. For good or for ill, and with wide latitude for regional and personal variation, even individual reaction, to be a Muslim today is to participate somewhere in our twentieth-century phase of that elaborate Islamic process in the world whose past history is now given, whose present vitality is open, whose future it is the witting or unwitting role of the participants in part to determine.

This is true for every Muslim, however secular we may call him or he may call himself; or her. The casual, the wilful, the obtuse, the destructive Muslim participates casually, wilfully, obtusely, destructively. Religiously: at a more serious, more pious, more dedicated and deeply involved level, to be a Muslim is to participate self-consciously, responsibly, spiritually, in the on-going religious heritage and process of Islam. However conservative or radical such a Muslim may be, whether the past tradition elicits from him blind allegiance, or warm affection, or critical assessment, or reforming zeal, or motivating drive, or emulative aspiration, the religious Muslim too is that person who participates, deliberately, piously, joyously, in the Islamic religious stream. He or she does so both as a member of the community at large, and perhaps more or less closely as a member of that minority within it whose special task is to cherish, to formulate, and to guide the evolution of, its institutions and norms.

At the highest mystical level, also, to be a Muslim (as distinct from being a Christian mystic or a Buddhist or a Hindu one) is to have communion with God through participation in those forms and patterns, channelled through that poetry and those institutions, that constitute on earth the historical process of the specifically Islamic peoples.

Let me generalise my thesis. I am proposing the conceptualisation of historical process as the context of religious life, and participation as the mode of religious life.

This way of perceiving has the conspicuous advantage of providing a manifestly more accurate apprehension of what has been observably going on around our planet over the centuries. It avoids the distortions introduced by ideational patterns generated by and inherited now from eras prior to our contemporary awareness of world history and of change; and avoids the incapacities of these to cope with present knowledge.

The new perception has what might seem further advantages as well. They are not really 'further': inherent in intellectually more accurate consciousness of the facts of man's religious history, and not additional to that consciousness, are theological and moral gains. One advantage is that the new discerning lays the foundation for a more adequate theology, as we shall later explore. Another advantage is that it supersedes the previous dichotomies in one's understanding of the life of humankind. Among these dichotomies has been that between one's own community and others: the complex religious history of the world is now able to be seen as variegated and yet coherent. The interpretation may be seen as cohering, also, with modern secular rationality. Self-understanding as well as an understanding of others is conjointly implied in a truer awareness of the human scene. There is made available a superseding at the level of intellection not only of the polarity between Islamic and other (for Muslims), between Christian and other (for the Church), and the like, but also, on the other hand, of the polarity between humanist–rationalist and religious: between academic observer and religious participant. This last we shall note further in our next chapter. Here we turn to the matter of Christian self-understanding in history-of-religion terms. The verifiability of a thesis about others is in part whether it can be applied also to oneself.

'Do unto others as you would that they should do unto you' is an injunction that we Christians have on the highest authority. In the comparative study of religion, I have found it a good rule to suggest for the interpretation of others' religious affairs only such theories and principles of interpretation as may be applicable, or at the least intelligible, for one's own case. The conceptualising principle that I have propounded is, I submit, of universal validity. 'To be a Hindu' means, in this vein, something that it has traditionally been almost despondently impossible to define, so ebullient and unrestrained has been among Hindus the variety of historical development; and yet all variety, all creativity, all seriousness are subsumed if one interprets it as meaning to participate religiously in the historical Hindu complex, which has in the past surged through India, and is still surging, is still creative. Again, 'to be a Christian', I am happy enough both to propose for others and to accept for myself, means – has always meant – to participate in the Christian Church: to take on its past, perhaps not without criticism yet, for all its aberrations, without ultimate embarrassment, and indeed with decisive appreciation; to take on its present, again certainly not without criticism, even not without tears, but in the end also not without hope; to contribute what one can to its future, in full seriousness and responsibility and with a devastating sense of one's own inadequacy and yet leaving the outcome to God.

Those of us who plunge into the tumults of the present with a profoundly grateful, if sober, acceptance of the past tradition, seen as instructive but not binding, may perhaps call ourselves Christians with full humility, full freedom, full commitment. We choose to participate in the historical Christian process because through it we find God; more strictly, of course, because through it God finds us. Because of its history over the ages, and through its institutions inherited from the past and currently being overhauled, through its images, its evolved and evolving doctrines, its foibles, its shortcomings and its splendours, and through its community both of saints and of other sinners like ourselves, God finds us and calls us to serve Him and His world.

To be a Christian means to participate in the Christian process, just as to be a Muslim means to participate in the Islamic process; to be a Jew, in the Jewish; and so on, and on. My own considered view, and I am prepared to argue for it later in our study, is that each of these processes has been and continues to be a divine–human complex. To fail to see the human element in any would be absurd; to fail to see the divine element in any would, I shall argue presently, be obtuse. (To fail to see the interrelatedness of all is, I suggest, old-fashioned.)

To put the matter in another way: the historian, looking out over the history of the world, sees what used to be called the various religions – including one's own – as a complex of historical processes wherein the several religious communities on earth have been carrying out *sub specie aeternitatis* the on-going task over the centuries of extrapolating within and for each age as it has come along the particular tradition that each inherited from its own past.

To be Christian or Muslim or Buddhist, to be religious, is a creative act, of participation in a community in motion.

At first blush this historical answer to what has usually been taken as a theological question, 'What does it mean to be a Christian?', may seem to some to omit too much. I would argue that in fact it omits nothing. (The point is important: the validity of our analysis turns on this.) The seriousness of the question I fully accept – and its searching depth, its moral demand, its personal commitment, its cosmic implication. Such Western readers as might have been willing to agree just now with my characterising the meaning of being a Muslim (or, *mutatis mutandis*, Buddhist, Hindu, Jew) in these historicist terms, were not, I trust, omitting from their perception of those Muslims' participation in their Islamic process an awareness of the seriousness of *that* question: of the searching depth, the moral demand, the personal commitment, the cosmic implication. My answer is not calculated to reduce the doctrinal, or ethical, challenge. It is calculated to disregard neither the commitment and transforming loyalty on the part of the person, nor the transcendence inhering within the changing context. To participate in the Christian Church is to participate in a process reverberating with doctrinal and ethical challenges; a process continued by and eliciting final commitment, and informed by its transcendent spirit. Some Christians (also, some Muslims) have brought to the matter *a priori* reasons for not perceiving that the same characterises others' processes (or some secularists, for not perceiving that the transcendent characterises all); and consequently have inhibited themselves from adequate understanding. Such understanding requires that we recognise that man, as an historical being, has been in interaction with the mundane; that, as a spiritual being, he and she have been open to the transcendent; and that the history of religion is the course traced out by this double involvement. To see human history and ultimate reality ('God') as disparate (or: as disparate except in the instance of one particular sector of the historical process) is to misconceive God, we shall suggest in our later chapters, and in any case is to misconceive human history (including the process even of one's own particular sector).

On this last point, let me briefly illustrate in the case of the Church a few facets of what is involved. First, the appropriateness of the concept 'context' may be stressed: the religious data of specific situations in history provide a sacramental environment in interaction with which persons' faith occurs – and takes on a particular form. To be a Christian is to join the Christian Church – at some one particular moment of its dynamic development, and in some one particular sector of its never quite unified life.

This clarifies in what sense the Buddha in the form of Josaphat is properly called a Christian saint. He was a Christian saint in the same historical sense in which Christmas has been a Christian festival, or Hell a Christian idea, or the book of Genesis part of a Christian scripture, or Luther's ideas a part of Christian theology. Siddhartha's legendary image became for a thousand years part of the context in which Christian life was lived, through which Christian life and faith were Christian.

That context is always in process.

To take a present-day illustration: many a modern Christian, living this side of the historical–critical interpretation of the Bible of last century and earlier in this, and the great controversies that it engendered, is ready to say and even to insist that an acceptance of the literalist interpretation of verbal inspiration of Scripture is not a necessary or perhaps even not a valid part of Christian life; is not a part of Christian truth. Fair and good. Yet, as in the Islamic case, for which the formulated law in one or other of its articulated systems once was (became) essential but for some few no longer is, so here let us not obscure the fact that at one time this more literalist vision of the Bible in Christian people's lives was *not* peripheral. Any theory is absurd that could hold that it was inconsequential in the meaning of *their* being Christian. I am not willing intellectually to let anyone define being Christian in a way that reduces the role of the Bible in my parents' faith; just as I am not willing to let anyone define it in a way that would exaggerate it in mine.

That we can now see the story in the Pali canon about Siddhartha's renunciation of his throne as maybe having been a later embellishment on the original biographical facts does not obliterate the further fact, a massive historical truth, that for millennia that story was part of Buddhists' religious life. The tale is a Buddhist tale, because for century after century it was part of the

Buddhist tradition. It was also a Christian tale for several centuries, for exactly comparable reasons: because during that long period it was part of the Christian tradition. In both cases there was a period in the tradition before the story became incorporated, and in both cases there is coming a period when its role will have to be reconceptualised, but in both cases in between it formed part of the historical religious process.

More on that subsequently, in our theological discussion. For the moment, we may perhaps agree that this is what is involved historically, at least, in being a Christian, or a Buddhist. Any person's faith is what it is; in interaction with the particular religious context in which that person actually lives. The context during any given century is different from that during any other, historians can now demonstrate for us; and, of course, the religious context for any person living in the latter twentieth century is in turn different from those that went before. The Christian pattern in which a Christian now participates is new (in the matter of theological teachings, forms, symbols, Church music, language of the mass, degree of denominational separateness for Protestants, and much, much else); the Islamic in which a Muslim does; and so on. It is different in other ways, but also, dramatically, in this: that the modern context includes a novel awareness of these very differences, a vivid sense of the dynamics of history, of unceasing change. Because of their preservative quality, every religious tradition has indeed been cumulative, has conserved some elements (not others) from its past. New are the recovery also of those that had been forgotten, the discovery that those preserved have changed, and the recognition that the only possible coherence now, or even intelligibility, and indeed enrichment, is historicising (a closer fusion of historical with transcendent truth). In what might at first seem an almost Hegelian sense, the on-going process is becoming self-conscious. To be a Christian has always meant to participate in the Christian historical process in one or another phase of its movement: today to be a Christian means to participate in it during that strangely new phase when it is becoming aware of itself, its participants are becoming aware of it, in a drastically new fashion as a flux.

Another novel item, less or more acute, less or more integrated, in the specifically religious context of every modern person is the awareness of the history of other communities, and of world history as a whole. The process of each is becoming conscious of the processes of all.

We hardly yet know how to think about the fact of our each participating in the total complex; this is one of the things that we must learn. There is another, correlated with it, which we noted in our opening chapter, and with which we are increasingly confronted as we look more closely. This, and it emerges as a somewhat formidable complication, is that persons play a part not in their own religious movements only.

They participate also, of course, in the remainder of the immediate historical process in which they live: what some would call its secular parts. There is the bustling courtyard of the profane outside the temple: *pro fano*. Our concern here, however, is to take note rather of another involvement: in a religious process other than one's own. This has constituted another kind, one might be inclined to say, of participation. Yet it is sufficiently different that there are difficulties in using the same word for both. It is a taking part in a religious process, indeed; yet not in it as the conscious and positive context for one's own religious life.

In our first chapter we observed that the diverse movements have proceeded not in watertight independence of each other, but at times in some sort of mutual interaction. (I took there a rather benign view of our mutual relatedness; yet one may make the case that historically we have affected each other's developments both for good and for ill.) The degree of separateness and independence has varied with time and place. Intermittently for some years now I have been conducting a graduate seminar at Harvard studying selected moments in global history where it would seem the case that the inter-dependence and inter-involvement of two or more religious histories have been markedly greater than usual. One such moment was the trilogue in mediaeval Spain, to which we referred above; another was the curious commingling of the San Chiao, the 'Three Teachings' (the so-called 'Three Religions') in mediaeval China, and Ryobu Shinto ('two-sided' Shinto) in Buddhist Japan; another, the age of Mani, and the entrancing role of broker played historically in world interreligious exchange by Central Asia. A while ago, also, I published an article on the interrelations of Sikh and Muslim religious developments in sixteenth- and seventeenth-century India[2].

It is an observable fact that what happens in the historical process of one religious tradition can be in significant part a function of what happens in the historical process of another. (Each can be a function of a larger development involving them both.) This has occurred in human history sometimes more markedly, sometimes less; but it does happen. In modern times, too, there are conspicuous examples: many, certainly, in India; many, certainly, in Japan; many, certainly, in America.

An acquaintance of mine teaching in a Christian theological college in Canada told me twenty-some years ago that each spring he assigned to his theology students an essay on the topic, 'Can I learn anything religiously from Radhakrishnan?' Some of those who wrote found, after reading this author, that they could. May one say that in this and in many other fashions Radhakrishnan has participated to some extent in the history of the Western Christian Church?

Similarly, *vice versa*.

The nineteenth-century Christian missionary movement in Asia, a world historian of religion or of culture can now see, was significant primarily not in the history of the Christian Church, whether in success or failure in its aim of making converts; but rather for the role that it unwittingly played, for good or ill, within the religious development of the non-Christian world. To Radhakrishnan's thought, to take that one small example of a very large matter, the fact that he was educated in Madras Christian College is by no means irrelevant. One might cite instances where the provocation has elicited a response vastly less irenic and less intellectualist. Most Westerners are unaware how caustic and how major was the onslaught; and how multivalent. More generally, the processes of Muslim, Hindu and Buddhist thought and development in the nineteenth century and on into this are in inescapably significant part to be understood in terms of the stimulus from and response to and reaction against that massive movement.

At one time the concept 'influence' used to be the standard way of interpreting these kinds of process. I have been unhappy with the term, ever since I began to ponder more closely how history actually proceeds, and I was interested to be reminded recently that 'influence' is in origin an astrological concept, not a scientific nor an historical one. To describe the development of an individual, it may perhaps serve (although even there it fails to discriminate between warm welcome and vehement rejection: we are influenced by those against whom we react, as well as those whom we follow). In any case, for larger social movements the word strikes me as altogether too externalistic, suggestive of too passive a role for the recipient of what it purports to describe, and it seems to postulate two separate entities in the very act of affirming that they are not quite separate. It seems somehow to leave out of account the more intimate appropriations, to underestimate interpenetrations, and perhaps to misperceive boundaries.

The thought of the Jewish writer Martin Buber, for example, has played an indeed striking role in Christian thinking in our century. It was welcomed and sought after, and actively incorporated. It is hard for the informed not to see him as a significant, indeed highly consequential, figure in the development of modern Christian theology. His *Ich und Du* was translated into English (as *I and Thou*) by a Presbyterian minister; another of his works was translated from modern Hebrew by an Anglican clergyman, subsequently archdeacon and canon. Much of the process of twentieth-century Christian thought would be distorted if perceived without Buber in its evolution. Early in his own career, on the other hand, he had in his turn done his doctoral thesis on two Christian mystics (Nicholas of Cusa, and Jacob Böhme), and later edited the writings of a third, Meister Eckhart; and in 1932 he published a volume having as its title the Christian as well as Jewish phrase *Königtum Gottes* and as its dedication a reference to two friends who had helped him 'to read the Scriptures': of whom one was a Jewish scholar and one a Christian. Do we not participate in the processes of each other's most intimate developments?

To speak of influence in the above cases seems a way of keeping the outsider out, at least in thought. Aristotle, to take a more mediaeval example, played so fundamental a role in the process of that period of Christian thought that we have forgotten to be awed by it. I find myself toying with the issues involved in seeing some sort of slightly jagged parallel, formally, between the way a Roman mid-winter festival became Christian during a certain phase in European history, and at a somewhat later stage the way Aristotelian thinking did so – or should we instead say, was incorporated into, took part for a time in, the on-going Christian process? Not all of us are Thomists; but then, neither did the Calvinist Scots take to Christmas as a festival.

Recent scholarship has discerned that Plotinus's thought played in mediaeval (and later) Christian theology a role comparable perhaps to Aristotle's; it is interesting to speculate whether this fact was less recognised for long (and more recently its awareness resisted) because Plotinus was not, like the Stagirite, a pre-Christian thinker but, troublesomely, a 'pagan' philosopher who knew of yet chose to remain outside the Christian Church.

We are just at the beginning of a phase in Western religious evolution in which the role of Asian missionaries, Buddhist and Hindu and Muslim, and certainly of Buddhist and Hindu ideas and motifs and art, is evidently going to be consequential in the development of Christian life, in one way or another. Few of us would care to predict what is likely to happen as a result; few, I guess also, would predict that nothing at all will. These new missionaries may make some 'converts', in the frontier-crossing, proselytising sense of that term; although this is not the goal of, for instance, the Ramakrishna Mission. The category that I am proposing is that whereby, in one fashion or another, for good or for ill, wittingly or unwittingly, little or much, Muslims, Hindus and Buddhists may be seen as participating in the future evolution of the Western religious tradition. Whether we applaud or not, the Christian Church will become what it will become, Christian theology will develop into what it will develop into, Christian worship will take the form that it will take, in part as a result of this Asian involvement in our affairs. (Or one might say: as a result of this growing Christian involvement in the larger human arena. The developments may be seen either as a participation of erstwhile 'outsiders' in Christian evolution, or as increasing participation by the Church within the encompassing global context.)

One may speak of the missionary, in either direction, as a deliberate or unwitting participant; but the rest of us also may – and, more than we recognise, do – become involved in each other's processes. Marx, Darwin and Freud have played a role, not quite unwitting, in the history of Christian theology. Obviously the activities of many sorts of person have impinged upon the religious history of the Christian world; and more narrowly, of the Christian Church; and more narrowly still, of Christian theology, liturgy, institutional structure, sacramental forms, and much else. This kind of thing happened in part through the doings, for instance, of emperors (as in the formation of the central creeds), and has happened in our day through the doings of scientists and technologists and urban planners and non-planners, both within the Church and without it, as well as through the specifically religious or anti-religious thinking and feeling and vision of persons beyond the Christian community. The degree to which Western ideas, techniques, institutions and processes are transforming the history, including the religious history, of the rest of the world as well as of the West is manifest, even if startling. The Wall Street banker and the Pentagon planner, as well as the technological innovator in agricultural machinery in Moscow or in the American Mid-West, are of course playing a role in the religious history of the Islamic and the Hindu and the Buddhist movements, however unconsciously and however ineptly. To build a dam in India is to take part in the religious history of Hindus.

A Westerner knowingly or carelessly may significantly affect religious thought and practice, sensibility and concern, in Asia – whether positively or negatively. Theodor Herzl is clearly an eminently significant figure in Islamic history. A Toynbee – or, as we have seen, a Tolstoi – has been consequential in not only Christian thought. At a more homely level, any local citizen who invites an Asian student at a Western university into his home, or fails to invite him or her, may thereby turn out to be playing some small role in the religious evolution of Asia. Human history, including its religious history, is an intricate and delicate web of human relationships.

I conclude this part of our presentation, then, by generalising the participation theme. First, I have suggested that in each community religious persons participate in that on-going historical process of which the contemporary life of their community is the current phase. As their community comes out of its inherited past and moves into an uncertain future, the present members constitute that present phase as each plays his or her part in the company of fellow members and in the constant presence, dimly or deeply perceived, of that transcendent power in whom we all live and move and have our being. It is the quality of their participation that gives their life its religious significance. It is through that participation that each finds his or her life opened to the divine; that each is, if one likes the term, 'saved'. We shall return later to this concept. Indeed, we shall contend in the sequel that through participation in a religious tradition each of us participates in the life of God.

Secondly, I have suggested that persons may, and many unwittingly and obscurely do, take part incidently or obliquely, for good or ill, in the on-going process of a neighbouring community. I have further suggested that a few may play this kind of role self-consciously and deliberately, constructively and graciously, joyously and humbly, with fear and trembling and yet with good rapport.

In the one case one participates in the historical process as self-consciously and positively the religious context of one's faith; while in the other case one is active in a process that is changing the context of other groups' faith. The question is delicate and intricate as to whether and to what degree the concept 'participation' may be used for both. Those who hear in the word certain notes, and would like to have them heard, of loyalty and reverence, and of self-conscious choice, may find the present a time of transition between an erstwhile phase of persons' being implicated, and an emergent one of their being *engagés*, outside their own historical borders. Involved in the transition is a shift from unawareness and insouciance to the new recognition of our global interdependence also in spiritual matters. Yet crucial also is a question of goodwill, responsibility, humility. Beyond unawareness and insouciance, there used on occasion to be also deliberate negativity: faith could at times take the form of a positive response to one's own tradition and of an hostility to others'. The faith of many persons in history has been given its particular shape in part by a rebound from his or her neighbour's divergent forms (or even, from that neighbour's person). The context of faith thus comprised both positively and negatively related elements. Or, more elaborately: that total context might, and regularly did, comprise elements from one's own and from other traditions, each or any of which might be related either positively or negatively. Participation has often been in more than one process, and in more than one way.

The same significant questions can be asked of one's own process, Christian or other, and of this newer kind: how far in any given instance is actualised the potentiality that each of us brings to it to respond to its challenges, to see beyond its externals, to be open to its grandeur, to take on its commitments; how far such faith is human capacity or divine gift; and so on. Christians, Muslims and the others who have asked themselves these and comparable questions within and about their particular movements severally may re-ask them now about human involvement on the larger scale that begins conspicuously to characterise the new contexts of our life. Traditional theology, as we shall see, does not preclude but rather is itself caught up in and enlarged by this new phase.

It remains perhaps debatable how one is to conceptualise the newly evident fact of our inter-involvements whereby a person or group plays a non-negligible role in the historical evolution of another group's religious life. None the less, we are reaching a further point where eventually each may see himself or herself or itself as participating in all. The new emergence is the recognition of the unitary religious history of humankind. Increasingly, the inter-involvement is actually happening, for good or for ill. The awareness of it follows. We may be frightened by it, or bewildered, or exhilarated. In any case, one has to try to understand. My suggestion is that we may aptly begin to understand it, and perhaps at the same time begin to enable it to be for good, if we see it as clearly not the same as and yet continuous with what has been the case in the religious past. This must mean, to participate with faith.

We noted above that on inquiry a static notion of an 'Islamic religion' gives way, once one looks more closely, to a dynamic notion of Islamic religious history, to the Islamic process in history in which Muslims have been participating. I may now add that on still fuller inquiry, as our knowledge and perception of the religious history of the globe increases, the notion even of Islamic religious history gives way to the truer concept of an *Islamic strand in the religious history of the world*. The same is even more obviously true for the Buddhist case, and is becoming increasingly visible for the Hindu, the Jewish, the Christian. Given the hostility among communities, ranging from open warfare on the battlefield to intellectual and emotional boundaries of stupendous rigidity, I am not unaware of the boldness of this concept. Yet I press it, as that towards which we are and should be moving. What is beginning to happen around the earth today is the incredibly exciting development that will eventually mean that each person, certainly each group, participates in the religious history of humankind – as self-consciously the context for faith.

I do not mean that Christians will cease to be Christian, or Muslims Muslim. What I mean is that Christians will participate, as Christians, in the religious history of humankind; Muslims will participate in it as Muslims, Jews as Jews, Hindus as Hindus, Buddhists as Buddhists. I am a Presbyterian; yet the community in which I participate is not the Presbyterian, but, at this level, the Christian. I participate as a deliberate though modified Calvinist in the Christian community, and the Christian process. In much the same way, I choose to participate as a Christian in the world process of religious convergence. For, ultimately, the only community there is, the one to which I know that I truly belong, is the community, world-wide and history-long, of humankind.

Part II

The History of Religion: Academic, Rational

3 Introductory: Conceptualising Religion and the Human

To understand the faith of Buddhists, one must not look at something called 'Buddhism'. Rather, one must look at the world, so far as possible through Buddhist eyes. One's ability to do this may be enhanced by familiarising oneself with Buddhist doctrines, Buddhist scriptures, Buddhist art, Buddhist practices, Buddhist history, Buddhists' languages, and all the rest. Yet that is at best only a first step: an important one, but one must not let it become a distraction. The faith of Buddhists does not lie in the data of the Buddhist tradition. Indeed, it is possible for an accomplished Western scholar to know much more about these than do many pious Buddhists. The data, or some few among them, serve the Buddhist by inducing in him or her a certain orientation to the world; and the skill of the comparative religionist then lies in the ability to use them to serve the observer also in a somewhat parallel capacity. One learns to use them to induce in oneself, by way of knowledge supplemented with appreciation – disciplined and precise knowledge supplemented with disciplined and precise, sympathetic, insight and carefully controlled imaginative perception, rigorously verified – to induce in oneself an understanding of the world as seen through Buddhist eyes, as felt through Buddhist sensibilities, as known through Buddhist faith. The faith of Buddhists does not lie in the data of the Buddhist tradition: it lies in the human heart; is what that tradition means to people; is what the universe means to them, in the light of that tradition.

It is not impossible for an outsider to come to know that faith, at least in significant part. One cannot comprehend; but one can apprehend. Yet to do so, one must know where to look. The locus of faith is persons.

(By 'person' I do not mean individual, as distinct from social. An individual becomes a person in community. And a society may be personal or impersonal.)

We read the Gita not simply to understand the Gita. Rather, if we are Hindus, we read it in order to understand the world; and if we are historians, in order to understand how the world has been seen by Hindus, to understand what the Gita has been doing to people these two thousand years as under its influence they have gone about their daily business, and their cosmic business.

There was a time when Western academic scholarship focused on the new overt material from oriental history that it was uncovering. More recently it has in addition turned to plumbing its human significance; the meaning that that material has demonstrably had, historically, for actual persons. Not the tribal dance, so much as what happens to the African dancing; not the caste system, so much as what kind of person the Hindu becomes within it, or without it; not the events at Sinai, so much as what role the recounting of those events has played in Jewish life over various centuries since.

Similar considerations apply also, of course, in the Christian case. No outsider would be credited with much awareness of Christian religious life who at the purely factual level did not know that Christians use a cross in their worship; yet it is one thing to grasp that fact, and another, to understand what the cross means to those Christians who worship under it. Again, the non-Christian historian of religion if he or she is a good scholar should know such facts as that at a given point in the ceremony of infant baptism the parents may receive the child back in their arms from the hands of the officiating minister or priest, and as well should know – understand, apprehend – the significance of this act, both potential and actual – in the lives of sophisticated and of unsophisticated Christians, in this century and in that, in this city and in that village.

The study of religion is the study of persons, as I have long urged; and indeed of human lives at their most intimate, most profound, most primary, most transcendent.

This principle, so obvious once it is recognised, although so slow in having become so, is revolutionising the outsider's understanding of Buddhists' religious life, and Hindus', and Muslims', and Jews'. This immediate point I shall not pursue here. It is the professional business of historians of religion to actuate the principle and thereby to illumine the various parts of the religious history of mankind. It is an exciting and almost breathtakingly rewarding task. Small wonder that students are proving responsive to the dramatic opening up of vistas of human, especially oriental, history that until recently seemed forbiddingly remote or bizarre, or at best 'irrelevant'.

That I leave aside. Yet I wish to suggest that the principle is revolutionary also in more sweeping ways, and nearer home. By taking seriously what religious systems are all about, one discovers not only that those systems take on a new vitality, but that life itself does. By recognising that the meaning of religious traditions lies not in themselves but in the life of men and women, one finds oneself embarked on a reorientation of one's own understanding, religious and other. Indeed, the dimensions of that reorientation are large. It is of one's understanding, one may repeat, religious *and other*: including, I will now urge, academic. We have seen, in our last two chapters, that there is involved in our modern vision a new understanding of history. We shall explore in due course what it involves of a reorientation in theology. In this chapter and our next I submit that this new enterprise involves also a new orientation even in our idea of knowledge, a new vision of the task of the university. The comparative study of religion turns out to be far too dynamic, too profound, too human, to remain pigeon-holed within traditional categories, or to leave ancient patterns of humane understanding untouched.

It is something new, that one civilisation should try to understand another; just as it is novel that one religious outlook should aspire to appreciate more than one. Now that we have begun to make progress in these tasks, nothing will ever be quite the same again.

We are being faced here with something as revolutionary intellectually as was science. The history of religion is vast; comparative religion is deep. The history of religion is the history of man (the humane history of man); comparative religion is the profound self-awareness of man in his and her unintegrated wholeness.

A whit rhetorical, that may sound. Let us try, in these two chapters, to explain. To understand humankind's religious life, in the global sweep of its age-long and multiform vitality, as the modern university has set out resolute to do, requires and provides, I am suggesting, a rethinking of what it means to know (to know things human, at least; science required and provided a rethinking of what it means to know the objective world of nature). It requires and provides, I would suggest also, a rethinking of what it means to be human.

We are here studying man most centrally, man at his and her most deeply, most fully, human. In this realm, therefore, especially (we have come to learn), it distorts to see an alien religious expression apart from man, passively, or as it is sometimes called, 'objectively'; and it illumines to see it humanely, actively, as a quality of personal living. In other realms also, however, if less conspicuously, yet no less radically, the same principle ultimately applies. It will help us to move towards our goal – of seizing the implications, for a religious outlook, of other religious outlooks – if we can recognise how this personalism, this humanism, operates first at the academic level. Let us first seize the implications for the rational mind of coming to understand multiple religious or ideological outlooks as such. For, although our focus is primarily on the religious, it is finally on man – and on truth; and I do not wish to perpetuate a dichotomy between the theological and the general intellectual.

Indeed, the bifurcation between these is part of what our new awareness helps us to overcome – just as in turn an overcoming of it helps us to attain a more effective awareness of what has been (and is) happening in human history. Of studying cultural diversity one reward is that we may gradually come to recognise the consequential particularities not only of others' outlooks, but of our own. Expanded consciousness becomes enhanced self-consciousness; and more critical self-consciousness. One's conceptual categories determine in some measure one's perception of the world, and are therefore difficult to improve. A critical awareness of them is probably the most promising route to their emending, to correlate with a fuller or more accurate perception. It is a major step forward when we can see ourselves as well as others, whom we study, as within the variegated process of the on-going human history of ideas and world-views.

I shall be suggesting in our concluding section that modern knowledge of comparative religion requires a somewhat revolutionary rethinking of theology, to carry it forward to a strikingly new phase – although some may be interested (or disappointed!) to find that, once the revolution is wrought, there turns out to be more continuity from the classical traditions discernible under the novel forms than perhaps superficially appears. Before turning to that, however, it seems helpful to explore something of how what is involved in this new knowledge is relevant to other current academic developments, and bears on the West's intellectual as well as religious crises and transitions. At the academic level, there is indicated a somewhat revolutionary rethinking of recently established orthodoxy, even though in this case too the revolution propounded turns out to be at heart markedly continuous with classical rationalist and humanist traditions, while startlingly at odds with certain present-day divergencies from these.

Of this new critical self-consciousness, and its consequent capacity to enlarge the framework of our thinking, and of our perceiving, we may consider here especially two facets. First, transitionally, the category of 'religion' itself, and its relation to the human (and, in passing, to the world); secondly, the category 'objectivity', and its relation to knowledge of the human.

We remarked above that the history of religion is the history of man. Such a sentence would seem bold to those who have not yet become aware that outside the West the history of religion is in fact the history of culture (and of philosophy). The implications of this fact are large, not only for one's understanding of religion but for one's interpretation of human life – that is, for self-understanding.

Western sceptics, in considering all religious life (but of course primarily Christian), and Christians, in considering the religious life of other communities, have both tended to perceive what they have thus labelled 'religion' or 'the religions' as a construct, an addendum that human beings 'have' over and above their prime humanity. Indeed, Western Christians nowadays live in a society in which secularity has gone so far that they themselves, as well as their irreligiously secular neighbours, tend at times to think of man as given in his and her secularity, so that religion then is something extra, a plus item that some people choose to adopt. As an historian might suspect, there are certain elements in classical Christian thought – for instance, by way of the Fall; and of faith as a supernatural gift of grace – that lend themselves to this sort of misinterpretation. Yet misinterpretation it is. The classical Christian position is that faith restores man, otherwise distorted, to his and her full humanity. Christ died that we might be truly and freely what we were created to be. One cannot understand the Christian vision unless one recognise it as envisioning not an overplus, additional to man's essence, but the restoring of man's essence, the removal of a subtraction from or distortion of it.

Now it turns out that academically also one cannot understand the religious history of humankind in general, quite apart from the

Christian case, if one goes at it taking for granted the Western dichotomy of religious and secular, as an unconscious conceptual framework within which to contain others' lives, an intellectual Procrustean bed. This particular pattern of thought is indeed particular. It has arisen for special reasons in Western history, and is part of the question at issue, not part of the nature of man. A just discernment of Asian religious history makes manifest that common modern-Western secularist mistake, of supposing that man is basically man but that for some strange reason he and she have here and there tacked on to their simple humanity one or another of these various bizarre addenda. To see things this way is to misunderstand the world, we can now see.

Indeed, it is to misunderstand even the West. For perhaps I should remark in passing that here I mean, by 'secularists', those of a certain modern type who have no use for faith at all. There is another, earlier reference for the word 'secular' in Western history, positive rather than negative, where it connotes one of the two great traditions of which jointly Western civilisation has been constituted: the Judaeo-Christian, and the Graeco-Roman. One of the unexpected results of our venture is that the historian of religion not only may, but I think must, come to perceive both these traditions as differing species of the same genus: that of the great so-called religious or spiritual traditions of the planet. The Greek philosophic tradition, Roman law and civil institutions, Western humanism and rationality, are a radically different complex from the Christian tradition; but no more different, it turns out, than the latter is from the Hindu, or than the Buddhist is from the Islamic. The Western humanist position is something to which people have given their loyalty (in which, to use an old phrasing, they have believed), in and through which they have had faith. It has constituted a framework for living in transcendence in the world. It has had its champions, its institutions and its martyrs. The Western faith in reason is one form, historically, of human faith; and what has seemed the reason-*versus*-faith debate has actually been a polarity between faith in reason and faith in God.

All the more clearly, then, one recognises both the validity, and the pathos, of affirming that modern secularism, in its nihilistic form, as distinct from (a later degenerate phase of) this secular humanism, has become an aberration. It remains to be seen whether it will prove possible for man to be fully human, or even tolerably so, in the negatively secularist fashion. There seem grounds for fearing lest a fully secularist society in this mode prove dehumanising, disruptive of man's humanity (although to hold that man has a humanity capable of being disrupted is already a metaphysical affirmation involving faith). However that may be, whatever the future hold for such secular developments – and, since they seem so prevalent, one cannot but profoundly hope that one's misgivings here be wrong – whatever new forms or lack of forms man may contrive for the future, the fact is that in the past, throughout human history until now, man has been man by his and her being in one way or another transcendence-oriented.

Men and women have not been human, and then Buddhist, Hindu, Muslim, rationalist–humanist, or whatever, in addition. Rather, there has been a Jewish way of being human, a Hindu way, a Greek-metaphysics way, a Christian way.

The new secular way, even if viable, is certainly not the only way; certainly not the foundational way; and not self-evidently the best – truest – way.

I do not mean that man is inherently religious. This way of putting it is an infelicity of secularist or exclusivistically Christian thinking. I mean rather that religion, and each of what used to be called 'the religions', is inherently human; and integrally so. If abstracted from man it wilts – abstracted from the men and women whose humanity it informs –, even if abstracted only for the purposes of intellectual scrutiny. It is not an entity to be postulated, one that can be legitimately conceived in itself or considered analytically. It is not a thing, but a quality; of personal life (both social and individual).

(The theological counterpart: 'religion' is not an idea in the mind of God[1]. Nor is any one concrete religion.)

With the secular–religious dichotomy paradigm of man (natural man as religious secondarily if at all) went along a similarly dualistic view of the universe. The Enlightenment developed its concept 'nature' grandly, and in contrast erected (rather uncritically) a concept of the supernatural, which has proven surprisingly persistent since. An attempt to avoid the dualism took the form of holding that 'the supernatural' does not exist. None the less, the concept was not dropped. (Even the concept 'nature' loses its meaning unless there be things with which to contrast it.) Few notions have been more fruitful of misunderstanding than the empirically absurd idea, common for a time among otherwise highly intelligent Western thinkers (including at first even scholars of Asia and Africa), that religion is people's views about the supernatural, a distinct realm. (Many added, 'distinct from reality'.) The Church resisted this distortion less than one might have hoped, because of its own mind's operating with not the idiosyncratic eighteenth-century concept of the supernatural, to be sure, but a seriously different one (also idiosyncratic, no doubt; but less vacuous) inherited from its own scholastic phase. Neither conceptualisation is apt for perceiving the history of religion in other cultures. Once again, a study of that history has the advantage of making possible (and in the end making necessary) a critical self-consciousness as to the particularity of these conceptual categories, and their problematic serviceability for interpreting the world of which today we are aware. (Less guardedly, one could say that to interpret other peoples so is a mistake.) It is not my intention here to pursue this major and subtle matter, however; significant though it be. I mention it only in passing, except in so far as it impinges on what is, rather, primarily germane for our argument: the conception of man (and therefore of human history), and the critical self-consciousness motif with regard to intellectualisation.

The bifurcation that secular intellectuals assumed in their thinking about religion tended to parallel or to converge with that of Church thinkers' isolating Christianity as if it were an entity (with metaphysical boundaries) segregated off from other religious (human) communities around the world and also, in recent centuries, from other intellectual activities at home. Such antinomies have tended to distort Western interpretation of religious matters, not only, but Western rationality generally, truncating its capacity to see human spirituality as a day-to-day dimension throughout man's world. Recent Western thought is having to struggle to enlarge its concept of history so as not to exclude *a priori* the transcendent dimension of human affairs that has been conspicuously integral to their on-going development. Modern intellectuals (tending at times to impose a naturalistic ceiling on their conceptualisation of human history at large) have sometimes had difficulty in discerning accurately, let alone adequately interpreting, the transcendent quality (interpenetrating with the mundane) of, for instance, Islamic or Buddhist history (as we had occasion to observe in our first two chapters above, on the historical). For many, the concept of history – as for Christians, that of history outside the Church – has been bifurcated from the otherwise virtually ubiquitous human awareness of involvement in a transcendent environment within and without. This was carried to the point where not only have theologians been slow in beginning to see world history as decisive, indeed foundational, for theology, but in addition historians, even 'historians of religion', are only slowly coming to recognise that an empirical understanding of human history involves, is in part constituted by, an understanding of the human spirit. This means, of our human spirit, as expressed, for instance, in its religious forms – but also in our studying of these.

The self-consciousness that this implies has been fended off for a time by a noble, but by now inadequate, device for keeping one's distance: the matter of objectivity. Through historical awareness, however, we may become critically self-conscious about this, as for Western thought recently a central category, a criterion for truth and a norm of inquiry. It would oversimplify drastically to say that therein – by that very becoming – we may recognise critical self-consciousness as a higher category: closer to the truth, and a more final norm of inquiry. I will, however, argue that given our new awareness we are in a position to recognise the concept of objectivity, developed in the natural sciences, and however appropriate there, as now to be subsumed and superseded in the study of man. The time has come, I submit, to move rationally beyond it, in what I will call the humane sciences.

Our consideration of this, as our second major instance of the new critical self-consciousness, will detain us longer. Equally radical, it is more novel; and academically more generic, since it seeks to clarify what we mean by knowing. To it we now turn.

4 Self-consciousness as the Mode of Humane Knowledge

(i) General: Objectivity and the Humane Sciences

At issue here are the content and the mode of knowledge in general and especially what I call humane knowledge. By this, as I shall elaborate in a moment, I mean the knowledge of man by man. In a nutshell, my thesis is that ideally all humane knowledge is self-consciousness. More historically: we have reached a point where we can – and, I submit, must – recognise this. Touched on herein are some of our more critical modern intellectual and spiritual, and certainly academic, problems. A valid understanding in this realm can perhaps contribute something to a solution.

My reasons for propounding the phrase 'humane sciences' are special; in part, historical. By it, as indicated, I intend all study of man by man. The current fashion has been to pattern intellectual activity in the Western university into three or four realms: the natural sciences, plus perhaps the life sciences; the social sciences; and the humanities. It is the last two that concern us here. The division between them has indeed become more than a fashion, with its particular institutionalisation, and its theoretical and as well deep emotional involvements – although in French, German and other European languages the dichotomy is not so sharp as in the English-speaking world. The phrasing 'humane sciences' is apt in so far as it may suggest a superseding of that dichotomising within the study of human affairs, and may suggest also a certain continuity (as well as difference) between man's study of the objective world of nature, in 'the sciences', and his and her study of those human affairs; between, that is, our study of the external world of things and our study of ourselves.

My phrase 'humane sciences' is not simply a translation from the French. For central to my thesis is a discrimination between human knowing and humane knowing. Our knowledge also of the material world is human knowledge, since it is we who have it. It is our knowledge of man that I am calling humane knowledge – that is, knowledge of man by man. All science is human science. All knowing is by man. (On this I side, therefore, with Polanyi against Popper[1].) It is important to recognise this and even to emphasise it, lest one succumb to an absolutising of science – with the feeling that '*our* way of knowing is the Truth, all others' are fanciful'. This constitutes a pattern with which the historian of religion is familiar. The natural sciences have for a few centuries been brilliantly successful (even more so in some ways than various other great movements have been in their early days). Yet they are human sciences, in the sense of human activities, human products: they constitute knowledge and study on the part of man.

Knowledge and study by man of the non-human are one thing; humane sciences, on the other hand, are knowledge and study of man by man. Manifestly, to understand man is to understand him and her as social. Manifestly also, our work does not deserve to be called scientific unless it be unrelentingly rigorous, critical, rational. I hold it equally manifest that an understanding of human society does not deserve to be called scientific if it omits the characteristically humane: if it does not see and interpret society and history as human in the fullest, deepest, most transcendent sense. We have then hardly yet attained humane sciences in these senses. Hence our fragmentation. Yet there are hopes of contributing towards such attainment if we rise to seeing the rational inadequacies of current patterns and the possibilities proffered by a new vision.

It may seem cavalier to assert that all knowledge of man by man is *ipso facto* self-consciousness. The assertion is true only in so far as all humankind is one. And it becomes operative (and salvific) in so far as that unity is seen, and felt; is willed. Otherwise, some men and women may have knowledge of others and may accordingly imagine that such knowledge is external. This is what has obtained in the recent past. It is not inherently false so much as simply a first approximation, only, to the truth – an approximation beyond which we now can, and sorely need to, move. It is here that 'objectivity' comes in.

External knowledge has, of course, been the triumphant paradigm of recent Western man's intellectual accomplishments. The spectacular success of the natural sciences illustrates this – and symbolises it. (Objectivity of knowledge has become for some an almost sacred concept.) In the humane sciences, however, a flaw in the procedure has begun to show up. To propose that we scrutinise the notion critically and recognise the rational and other inadequacies of the externality of the knowledge involved is an invitation not to a simple rejection of objectivity but to move beyond it.

Both Western secularists and Western Christians passed through a stage of dealing with oriental religious history in a subject–object way. More recent understanding has enabled us to move dramatically beyond this. Yet the implications elementally posed for the question of objectivity remain: the epistemological and other intellectualist issues that arise pertain to modern thought at large.

I know of no careful study, critically self-conscious, of the history of the notion of objectivity in Western thought. To attain this would for the West be to move from a cultural phase of objective knowledge to a new vantage point of self-awareness in this realm. The objective mode has seemed recently to many in Western civilisation to be the ideal mode of knowledge, or the only valid, certainly the only reliable, one, and above all the only academic one. We are, however, becoming aware that objectivity is, in more limited fashion, at best the proper, even the true, way of dealing intellectually with objects. In so far as what we would understand is not an object – for instance, is a person – or in so far as it is not merely an object – for instance, is a poem, a work of art, an African tribe – to that extent objective knowledge of it will prove at best inadequate.

To treat a person as if he or she were an object, or anything pertaining to the human as if it were only an object, is, besides being immoral, to misunderstand him or her or it; it constitutes an intellectual error. Accordingly, since it is foundational for scientific procedure that one use concepts appropriate to what is being studied, I contend that it is pseudo-scientific, is scientific in only an imitative and not a genuine sense, to apply to the study of human affairs the objectivity that is appropriate for the study of other fields. To claim that a procedure or a conceptual pattern is scientific, one must do more than demonstrate that it is has been fruitful in a quite different area of study.

A second element in the Western conceptual pattern regarding this matter has been the presupposition that the (only) alternative to objective is the subjective. On this polarity, I would submit, rather, that in addition to the subjective, my individual and internalist awareness of something or someone, or of myself, and to the objective, the impersonal, externalist knowledge, there is a third position, which subsumes both of these and goes beyond them; and that it is this that we should posit as our goal – in the humane field, man's knowing of man. I call it corporate critical self-consciousness.

In the 'corporate' concept here is subsumed and transcended a third element in the objectivity outlook. It is the point that an observer's knowledge of a given object is in principle available also and equally to any other observer. In the case of the natural sciences, as we shall later be noting, this means ideally all humankind; this does not work for objective knowledge of man, however, it being in principle limited not universal, since it is confined to observers, or outsiders.

By 'corporate self-consciousness' I intend knowledge that is in principle apt both for the subject himself or herself, and for all external observers; or, in the case of group activities, for both outside observers and participants. This does mean in principle all humankind. We shall be returning later to the logical flaw, and the consequent distortion of knowledge, involved in the theoretical limitation of the earlier pattern.

The transition from consciousness to self-consciousness is one of the profound, crucial moments in human evolution. Its first appearance represents the emergence of man. The transition from consciousness to critical consciousness was another extraordinary moment, marking the appearance of science, and its expanding development. The emergence of critical self-consciousness is the major transition through which the human race is perhaps now in a position to be about to go. Science, man's spectacularly successful intellectual achievement, will expand from the world of nature, truly to the world of man; and, moreover, man's awareness about himself and herself and their neighbour will expand to become truly scientific, truly rational; not when man's knowledge of man is objective, which is theoretically inapt and practically disruptive, but rather when human self-consciousness becomes fully critical and fully corporate, ideally embracing us all both in our diversity and in our personalism.

We are speaking of the study of man by man. By 'corporate

critical self-consciousness' I mean that critical, rational, inductive self-consciousness by which a community of persons – constituted at a minimum by two persons, the one being studied and the one studying, but ideally by the whole human race – is aware of any given particular human condition or action as a condition or action of itself as a community, yet of one part but not of the whole of itself; and is aware of it as it is experienced and understood simultaneously both subjectively (personally, existentially) and objectively (externally, critically, analytically; as one used to say, scientifically).

Introduced here is a decisive new principle of verification. The intellectual pursuit in humane studies of corporate self-consciousness, critical, rational, empirical, is scientific in various senses; including that of its being subject, and it alone being subject, in the deepest sense, to a valid verification procedure. In objective knowledge, that a first observer's understanding has done justice to what is observed is testable by the experience of a second and a third observer. In corporate critical self-consciousness, that justice has been done to the matter being studied is testable by the experience of other observers but also by that of the subject or subjects. This is important for various reasons. One is that, unlike what obtains in the world of matter, no human situation is truly repeatable. More fundamental is this: that intrinsic to human experience is that that experience appears differently, and in fact *is* different, from the inside and from without. No statement involving persons is valid, I propose, unless theoretically its validity can be verified both by the persons involved and by critical observers not involved. The proper goal of humane knowing, then, the ideal to which the human mind should aspire, academically, scientifically, is not objectivity but corporate critical self-consciousness. My submission is that this will yield truer knowledge; that with anything less we betray intellectual accuracy. Negatively: in this realm merely objective knowledge, like merely subjective knowledge, inherently involves major error, and the pursuit of it is irrational. It is also potentially immoral, and destructive, although that is a separate point. Positively: this new definition of our aim has opened up rich rewards of understanding (this can be demonstrated empirically) and – that matter of no small importance – of valid verification.

The argument rests both on theoretical considerations and on empirical observations. At the former level, of rational analysis, the basic premisses of the thesis are two. The first is that man is patently different, in ways highly significant, from material objects, and from all other forms of life known to us; so that any ideas about man that underestimate his and her uniqueness or downplay his and her humanity are *prima facie* inadequate, or worse. Human qualities such as self-transcendence, a sense of justice, a creative and destructive imagination, a capacity to respond to and to create beauty, a capacity for wickedness and also for dignity, freedom, compassion, rationality; a cunning capacity to deceive and also a drive or aspiration towards intellectual and moral integrity; the pursuit of truth; a sense of remorse, an ability to forgive; moral responsibility; and so on and on and on: these are manifest facts; and, frankly, it strikes me as rather stupid either to propound or to put up with theories that, whether in their presuppositions or in their conclusions, or often both, fail to do justice to such facts. The advocates of such theories, when challenged, usually fall back for defence on the plea that their theories, however seemingly absurd or inhumane, are 'scientific'; which succeeds only in giving science a bad name.

The second premiss is the equally inescapable one that the knowing mind is human; is not outside, and cannot get outside, the human race to look at it externally, objectively. This has long been recognised in objectivist theories as a difficulty; but it has been regarded as unfortunate, as a regrettable weakness, and attempts have been made to reduce its significance as far as possible, to approach as closely as feasible to externalised viewing. I, on the other hand, regard the participation of the knowing mind in the humanity that it seeks to know as an asset, and not merely an inescapable fact; and I would order our intellectual inquiry in accord with it, not in opposition to it nor in flight from it. Among my several reasons, one is simple: it helps us to know.

The empirical observations on which the position rests have had to do, in my own personal case, primarily with the particular field of study with which I have been involved for forty years: the academic study of the Orient and especially of its religious history. The matter is, discernibly, of quite generic validity and reference: and presently we shall be noting certain domestic social-science examples. The significance and force of the new orientation have for me, however, been rendered primarily conspicuous in both the successes and the failures evident in the endeavour of one community to understand another, one civilisation another. The limitations and indeed the fallacies of both the subjective and the objective types of knowledge have here become clear; as well as the enormously rich potential of the new trans-cultural critical self-consciousness.

Accordingly, I will draw my illustrative material first from this realm; but will endeavour to go on to illuminate the general applicability.

In Western understanding of, let us say, India, there has been a clear advance through successive stages: first, ignorance; secondly, impressionistic awareness of random parts of the culture (an outside subjective stage); thirdly, a growingly systematic and accurate yet insensitive and externalist knowledge of facts (an objective stage); and, more recently, and richly promising, the beginnings of serious and even profound humane understanding of the role and meaning of those facts in the lives and the culture of the persons involved. (This last carries strikingly forward, in some cases almost transforms, India's own self-awareness, the erstwhile insider's subjective knowledge.)

I call this last stage personalist. I have already remarked that by 'personal' I do not mean 'individual'. Personality is profoundly social. The earlier stage was of an impersonalist knowledge of facts; it aimed at impersonal knowledge. The newer stage is of a personal knowledge, and understanding, of the meaning of those facts, in the cultural life of Indians. It generates statements about Indian life that Indians and outside observers can jointly recognise as true, and illuminating.

The successive stages of this process might be demonstrated both for the total systems of the religio-cultural complexes which Westerners first objectified by giving them names, such as 'Hinduism' and 'Islam', and also for specific items within each of those complexes. The former would be in some ways the more interesting, but is too sophisticated a matter to go into here. Let us look, rather, not at the over-all patterns but at a particular item within one.

Recently, I had occasion to visit the South Indian city of Madurai, site of a famous and magnificent temple. Again, Western awareness of this temple has gone through the same stages: from ignorance, through impressionistic travellers' tales of its sumptuousness and grandeur, and then through a meticulous and detailed knowledge of the temple as an object of observation (it has, for instance, among other glories a hall of several hundred pillars; a descriptive analysis of its intricate art work might constitute a Western doctoral-thesis topic). I had never been that far south in India before, and I was entranced to observe the temple, in which I spent many hours. It is an interesting question, however, as to what it is at which one looks when visiting such a sacred structure. More engaging than the building itself were persons worshipping within it, and their worship. Or we may say, the important matter was the living complex constituted by the temple and the worshippers within it.

The truth of the temple manifestly lay not in the building itself as an object but in its significance for, and interaction with, these men and women. The temple primarily is what it is perceived by them as being; or, at the least, their perception of it is incontrovertibly part of its truth. Recent Western understanding of the temple has gone forward dramatically as scholars have come to recognise that the role of such a temple in the consciousness and the lives of persons is part of what one must know if one sets out to know the facts. It is out of Hindu religious consciousness that the temple arose in the first place, and in that consciousness its reality continues primarily to lie.

Actually, in this particular case there never was a time when Westerners' apprehension of the building was merely and totally objective; since if it had been so, they would not even have recognised it as a temple. The most rank outsider always participated in Hindu consciousness to at least that extent. The notion of temple, and that of symbol in general, are humane concepts, not objective. No building is objectively a temple. No space is objectively sacred. No object is objectively a symbol, in and of itself: an object becomes a symbol in the consciousness of certain persons.

To have merely objective knowledge of what serves some people or a certain community symbolically is to misunderstand it. This kind of undiscerning knowledge has in historical fact distorted, and at times indeed vitiated, outsiders' observations in this realm.

I do not contend that we must know what a given symbol 'means' in general; rather, what it has in fact meant, to particular persons or groups at particular times. That a given object symbolises one thing for one group of people, something else for another group, and perhaps nothing at all for a third group, is a fact without which human history would have been dramatically different from what it has been and is. Merely objective knowledge not merely fails to illuminate religious conflict, for instance, but actually has often contributed to it. The only knowledge that is accurate of the history of religion, and indeed of culture, and indeed of human history generally, is a knowledge that participates in the consciousness of those involved.

To understand a symbol, I am contending, one must know it objectively and in addition must know what it means, has meant, in the lives and consciousness (including the subconsciousness) of persons. This varies, of course, from community to community, and from age to age. It is never quite precise: like a poem, only much more so, it shimmers with a whole range of meanings, and of innuendo – overt, subtle, hidden, conscious and unconscious, quiescent and activating. Moreover, it is not simply what the symbol itself means to persons, but what life means, what the universe means, in the light of that symbol. My own studies have led me to the view that a symbol in principle never means exactly the same thing to any two persons (nor even necessarily to any one person at different times); although on this both Jung and Eliade, two of the greatest twentieth-century scholars in this realm, have tended to presume otherwise, as we shall later note. We need not go into that issue here, beyond my indicating that as an historian I am inescapably aware of diversity and change. In any case there is no dispute but that the meaning of things in human history lies in their relation to persons, in the interaction of human beings with them, and not in themselves as objects.

An objective knowledge of the moon, provided by natural science, is different from, and for humane studies is less than, a knowledge of the role of the moon in human life and in the history of human culture and of poetry and religion and love; and even in the history of human science, and of technology and space travel. The natural sciences cannot tell us about the moon all that we wish to know, or that is worth knowing or that is true. Let us not be so fatuous as to forget this massive fact.

I would go further, and insist that the role of the moon, or of a temple of the moon in ancient Babylon, or of that temple of Minaksi in Madurai, in the consciousness and the lives of men and women – that is, their role in human history: what they have meant and signified and been and done – is not fully nor accurately knowable by behavioural sciences either, which are externalistic, objective, and explicitly leave out of consideration the self-consciousness of those involved.

To understand man, and to understand history, it is necessary to know not only what man does, the behaviourist's little province, but also what he refrains from doing, what he dreams of doing, what he fears to do; what he does with exultation, hesitation, guilt or boredom. An action is not understood unless one discerns what courage went into it, what routine, what integrity or duplicity, what choice. To read a statement in a Sanskrit or Arabic text one must know what it says but also what it takes for granted. One must listen to what people leave unsaid, be sensitive to their failures, recognise what they do in terms of what they are trying to do. As Dilthey long ago insisted, the behaviour of human beings is to be seen and interpreted as within a context of the consciousness that gives meaning to their lives and to that behaviour.

Fundamentally, one makes a rather stupid historian if one fails to recognise that other people are in fact human beings like ourselves. This statement seems so obvious, and so innocent, and yet the depth of our academic crisis lies in the fact that it is so radical. If one does not see and feel that the people whom one studies are human beings like ourselves – and if as teacher and scholar one does not enable one's students and one's readers to see and to feel it – then one has failed as an historian, has failed to arrive at knowledge. If some wish to call this kind of humane knowledge 'unscientific' I do not much mind; I would rather be on the right track than orthodox. Yet by this kind of conformism one has merely legislated limits to the capacity of science to know – unnecessarily and foolishly. There are things in human consciousness waiting to be known, things of enormous significance for all of us; and some of us are resolved to know them, and have devised methods and procedures and understandings for knowing them and for making them known. It is true that these things are not objects, and cannot be known objectively; but they are real, and can be known accurately, verifiably, humanely. It is the task of the humane sciences to know them and to make them known.

To return to that Madurai temple. I remarked earlier that from the very beginning outside observers went beyond mere objectivity to knowing that it was indeed a temple. Their notion of what a temple is, however, was limited and inadequate; in some cases, distorted. Some Christians, some secularists, had a quite imperceptive or false sense of Hindu religious life, even though they were not unaware that it existed and was important. It is worth noting that even now, despite a great deal of progress in this realm, so that our understanding of temples in general and of this one in particular is vastly richer, deeper, truer, than was theirs, none the less it is still the case today that no one on earth, neither Hindu nor outsider, yet fully knows what a temple is. No one fully understands what it means, in human life and in cosmic life, that that building is 'a temple' for those persons. Our knowledge of 'templeness', if I may coin a term, is much better that it was; yet it is by no means complete.

To appreciate the significance of that temple as a temple, we must get inside the consciousness of those for whom it is a sacred space, must know how it feels and what it means to be a worshipper within it; although we must also know all the objective facts about it; and as well, in order to know the full truth about that temple, we must know its significance in the lives of shopkeepers in its environment, must know its crucial role in the whole city life and the town plan of Madurai (and the significance for the citizens of living in a town integrated around a temple), and must know how it is perceived also by the small iconoclastic Muslim group in the area, for whom temple worship is a sin, and how it is perceived by secularists and by Marxists, whose analysis of its economic role is impertinent in one sense but not in both.

True knowledge of the temple as a human institution, as a reality in the life of several million persons, must incorporate its role in the consciousness of worshippers within it as well as of critical observers on the outside, in so far as each is valid. The insider, if dedicated to full knowledge, full self-consciousness, must and ideally will incorporate into his or her awareness the truth that outsiders see, so far as it be true; and the external observer, if resolute to attain to true knowledge, must incorporate into his or her understanding not only the critical analyses from the outside, in all their rigour, but also the reality that the temple constitutes in the life of the pious devotee, which after all is the primary reality of the temple as a fact in human affairs. There is no theoretical reason why these two persons, and indeed why all human beings who may direct their attention to this temple, should not ideally converge in synthesising all this truth into one conceptual apprehension. This would then constitute what I am calling corporate critical self-consciousness: with all of us recognising in full awareness that some of us worship in this temple and some of us look on. This, and not the outsiders' partial knowledge, is, I am suggesting, the ideal at which to aim for human knowledge of that particular reality.

(Such an ideal does not impose a limitedly humanistic ceiling on the conception of truth; since some, at least, of the critical observers, and some, no doubt, of the pious participants, will bring to the whole a recognition of truth's transcendence. The question is rather of the route along which one moves towards that transcending goal.

When at the beginning of last century the early Christian missionary Bishop Heber, who had almost no understanding of Hindu spirituality, said that Hindu 'idolators' 'bow down to wood and stone', he was objectively right, but, I would argue, scientifically wrong. At least, he was humanely wrong. For he failed to participate in the consciousness of those whom he was observing; or to realise that that consciousness was part of the truth of that at which he was looking. They bowed down not to the wood and stone, but before what these symbolised to them. In his externalist observation, Heber was a forerunner of modern behavioural scientists: like them, although in one sense what he said was true though misleading, in a much more significant sense he just did not know what he was talking about.

Any objectivist, externalist, behaviourist observer who leaves out human consciousness simply does not know what he or she is talking about. Skinner at modern Harvard, and that early missionary in India, have more in common than is sometimes noted.

The truth of anything that pertains to man lies – has lain, historically – not sheerly in that thing, but in man's involvement with it; and in the end, in man's involvement through it, with oneself, with one's neighbour and with God (or: with the universe *in toto*).

To return to the thesis of our preceding chapter: in order to understand the faith of Muslims, one must know the data of what I have called the Islamic tradition, at a particular time and place; must know the facts that to those particular Muslims were religiously significant. The tradition at any given moment is observable, is concrete, is objective. It can, therefore, and must, therefore, be studied objectively. This requires the utmost rigour of scholarly exactitude: meticulous care, scrupulous precision and erudite attention to minutiae. All this is needed in order to reconstruct, in the strictest factual accuracy, what the tradition historically was (has been, is).

This inescapable first step is, however, only the first step: he or she who takes it is an historian of a religious tradition, not yet an historian of religion. For this is *human* history. The tradition came into existence in the first place, and survived, and developed, as an element in the life of human beings; and we have understood it, intellectually, academically, truly, only in so far as we can see human lives in terms of it: can see the significance that the data had for men and women (and children), and the meaning that life had for them because of those data. That significance, that meaning, the role of those data in their lives – not only in their overt behaviour but in their aspirations and their fears, their imagination and their embarrassments, their self-understanding and their perception of the world: these are not an object, and cannot be known objectively.

Yet they can be known, more or less accurately. To apprehend them requires interpretation, imagination, insight, perceptivity, human sympathy, humility, and a whole series of qualities – human qualities. It requires, fundamentally, that the student be himself or herself a human person; and indeed as fully human as may be. Not flashes of imagination, necessarily: it may demand long hours, or years, of patient, careful wrestling with the material. And not 'subjective' interpretation, by any means: requisite are careful discipline, cross-checking, the framing of hypotheses and the testing of them against new data, or against personal inquiry, and a whole apparatus of critical and self-critical procedures. To be an historian is an art; and, like most arts, it requires skill.

To understand any human behaviour, any human feeling, any human hope or vision, is to recognise that if you had been in that situation, you would have had that particular act or quality or value-judgement as one of your options. Not that you would necessarily have acted as that person did: that would deny human freedom, and indeed one has not understood him or her unless one recognises that they *might* not have acted that way either, although in the end they in fact chose to do so. But to act so would strike you as reasonable in those circumstances; as one of the clearly available, and to some degree cogent, possibilities. You know how it felt to be in that situation, and how it felt to act in that way.

The goal of the historian or other student of human affairs is to reconstruct a given situation in the past or at a distance from oneself with such accuracy that we can know what that situation, factually, was; and with such insight that we can know how it felt to be a human being in that situation. To be an historian, or, indeed, a rational student in any humane field, is to stand imaginatively in the shoes of others. This is possible, in principle, because we are persons, and because they are persons. Two of the fundamental qualities of humanity are the capacity to understand one another and to be understood.

Not fully, certainly. Yet not negligibly, certainly.

Human beings are that kind of reality, it so happens, that any given two of them – no matter how close together, no matter how far apart, in space, time, culture, temperament – any two of them can arrive at an understanding that is neither 100 per cent nor zero. There is no person on earth that I can fully understand. There is and has been no person on earth that I cannot understand at all.

Studies across cultural boundaries, and especially across religious boundaries, make the matter vivid. Yet one need not go so far afield. Even intra-cultural work has begun to recognise some of the same problems and to move in the direction of somewhat comparable solutions. In modern sociological thought, for example, regarding the insufficiency of objectivity two problems have been receiving attention: not only the need for empathy, *Einfühlung, verstehen*, in Dilthey's mode, but also and more recently the potentially incriminating interdependence of subject and object, or their actual collision. There is a growing recognition that the traditional subject–object relationship of externalist 'knowing' may itself in certain situations set up a polarity that vitiates rather than guarantees understanding. Pointed examples of this now being cited are the study of the condition of blacks in the United States by white scholars; of the role of women by male scholars; of homosexuality by heterosexual investigators. In these examples, at issue is the point that the intimate dynamic interaction, in the past and still continuing, between the subject group and the object group in each case is in part constitutive of the situation of the object group – to its discomfort; that the subject group (dominant in each pair, and, in the modern jargon, 'oppressive') has had a hand in perversely making the object group what it is. This fact inevitably introduces a distortion into such research, it is being contended; partly on the grounds that true knowledge in each case is resisted because it would involve the knower in a new awareness of his or her own self.

In such presentations, however, it tends still to be presumed that the deviations from the truth are a function of the fact that pure objectivity is, alas, difficult or impossible to attain. It is argued that candour demands that we recognise the limitations imposed on knowledge by these human or social failings. Yet implicit still is the notion that perfect objectivity would be a good thing, if only we could be innocent enough or clever enough to achieve it. I disagree.

I would postulate a law, that what man does is misunderstood if conceived wholly from the outside.

Some will be quick to retort that modern knowledge makes us more aware than ever also of the contrary law: that what a person does is misunderstood if viewed wholly from the inside. Of course!

Subjectivism is no royal road to truth, either. Of much that goes into our actions, our feelings, our moral choices, our thinking, we are ignorant; and, of what we know, much we distort. We deceive ourselves, as well as others. We elude ourselves, not only outsiders. Objectivity, the externalist approach, was developed to get beyond the inadequacies of individual interiority. That it, too, is in its turn proving inadequate, untrue, less than rational, means that we must go, not back to subjectivity, but forward to a larger vision.

Regarding those sociological problems cited: ideally, I suggest, the goal of research on race relations in the United States is the achievement of an intellectual community comprising at least whites and blacks, and ultimately also third parties, with a corporate self-consciousness, critical and rational, of its own racial condition in this area. The proper aim of those making investigations on this topic is not finally to inform a closed group of scholars, and thus to contribute to the growth of science as a body of objective knowledge in principle outside the lives of those involved; but, rather, is to provide information, evidence, arguments that will be in principle accessible and persuasive to, designed to be assimilated by, all those involved (and also onlookers from Canada or China); and thus to contribute to the construction or promotion of that larger community and to its corporate critical self-consciousness.

The final criterion of the validity of the research, I propose, is its verifiable contribution to such self-consciousness.

Similarly in the status-of-women matter, or other such issues: not 'they', not 'we', not 'you', but 'some of us' are thus and so. The verification test of any statement about women in society would be whether both men and women, in so far as they are rational, and a body of investigators, in so far as they are methodologically sophisticated, critical, scientific, could all three endorse it. The goal is the corporate critical self-consciousness of a community of persons – and I mean community in the true sense of the word; but at the least, intellectual – who can say, and feel, and mean: some of us are men, and some of us are women, and the situation of those among us who are women is such and such.

In every aspect of human affairs, we human beings, we persons, may aspire to a corporate critical self-consciousness. In no other way can we truly know.

Similarly, a descriptive political-science analysis of the functioning of, let us say, cabinet government in Canada will approach excellence and truth in so far as it satisfies and enlightens critical observers of the system, as it were on the outside, and also citizens of the country, participants in the political community of which the system forms a part – the analysis rings true, that is, to the governed, and enlarges their understanding – and as well is recognisably accurate and illuminating to members of the cabinet (and their stenographers). In practice, one may make do with less; but not in principle: not in a theory of knowledge.

I pursue here no further the point that in the case of human affairs objectivisation fails to give true knowledge of what it studies, both in practice and in principle. Rather, let us turn now to two other aspects of the problem. One is that in this realm objectivity inherently disrupts community. Again this is so both in principle and in practice. The second is that it drastically fails to do justice not only to the known but to the knower; not only to the object of knowledge but to the subject. Knowledge of man by man must finally recognise, and affirm, the humanity both of what is studied and of the student. Let us rejoice in, and not bemoan, that humanity; in all its depth and richness.

On the first point: community.

Not only does the new ideal of knowing here proposed have, of course, a positive effect towards community; but also, the current one has a serious negative effect. Humane knowledge in my sense postulates community and serves to promote it. Objective knowledge, on the other hand, with polarity at its base, not only emerges out of separateness but corroborates and furthers it. It serves to disrupt.

It postulates and lends itself not only to prediction but also to control. Objective knowledge of man may then imply, and even promote, that ever-growing menace of technical expertise, manipulation. Further, particularly in psychology, there is the deception practised increasingly and shamelessly on persons being studied. Another facet is the gruesome issue of human experimentation. Objective knowledge is inherently oriented towards the alienation of persons from each other.

Even the matter of prediction, as a goal or criterion of objective knowledge which to some has seemed innocent or even good, is troublesome. It derives from the natural sciences, and once again illustrates that objective knowledge is appropriate in our dealings with objects. There are certain ways, too complicated to go into here, and with important caveats anyway, in which statistical prediction about groups of people is within limits a function of certain kinds of knowledge. Otherwise, however, the notion of predicting personal behaviour – and I mean, as ever, the predicting by some persons of the behaviour of other persons – though less horrendous than experimenting with them or manipulating them, is inhumane. For it denies human freedom. It is an intellectual error, since it postulates what is in fact not true, that men and women act mechanically (or quasi-mechanically). Our further point here is that it affronts human dignity, since it therein ignores or dismisses (is inherently incapable of understanding) one of humankind's most precious, and most characteristic, qualities.

Within the academic world, even at the level of pure theory, objectivity leads to fragmentation. For there is what seems at first the curious paradox that the concept of objective knowledge leads, when the study is of man, to knowledge that is in fact subjective. I call this a seeming paradox only, since I still am enough of an old-fashioned rationalist to perceive it as in fact no whit surprising that an intellectual error will presently, when pursued far enough, end in a self-contradiction. Objective or external knowledge gives us knowledge of objects, of what is external; when the concept is misapplied among persons, by giving some an external knowledge of others, it cuts off from community not only those about whom the knowledge is gained, but also those who gain it. The result is a corporate subjectivity on the part of a group that is in principle limited.

Objectivity began as a reaching out towards universalism. What was objectively true was, in principle and by aspiration, to be true for all humankind, explicitly as contrasted with the subjective impressions of private parties. This worked quite well in the natural sciences; that is, for our knowledge of a world that is equally external to us all. It breaks down, however, when what is involved is a knowledge of some person by other persons. The fallacy, though significant, was somewhat less apparent with intra-cultural studies. We have mentioned as exceptions questions of colour and race, and the sexes, where the problem has been recognised. In general, however, within one's own civilisation (including even these instances, to some degree) and whatever the theory, the knowers, the 'experts', have in fact been participants to some more or less saving degree in the human institution or activity that they have studied, or at least have had some more or less surreptitious understanding of it, some more or less effective sympathy with it, and even some sense that their work would be relevant to its members. (Studies of religion have at times been in the West a somewhat stark exception.) In cross-cultural studies, on the other hand, and conspicuously sometimes in studies of others' faith, the objectivity and externality of the knowing meant quite definitely that the knowledge was designed for, and relevant to, non-participants in the phenomenon, the society, the institution, being analysed.

I have actually known an instance where a Western social scientist had gone to the Islamic world, established himself in a locality there, and deliberately done what he had set out to do: namely, to make what he regarded and intended as an objective study of certain aspects of the life of the people there, being interested in their activities as something that, once studied, would serve either to corroborate or to modify theories in his discipline that he had learned back home. The theoretical justification that undergirded this behaviour of his was that his study would be a contribution to (Western) knowledge – thought of in terms of scientific generalisations. Of course, there was also, if one pressed, a personalist involvement, in that the work with which he came back would, if well done in disciplinary terms, perhaps win him a promotion, or at least professional reputation. In other words, he was explicitly making use of the people of that area for purposes extraneous to them.

In this particular case the man in question actually had in addition no personal interest in the society where he chose to work or in its members, his intellectual concern being merely the general theory that might be abstracted from their behaviour, and reported back to the West. I hope that readers will agree with me that this is dire. In other cases, of course, individual investigators either bring or develop, in addition to their so-called scientific interests, a warm personal rapport with the subjects of their research. None the less, the academic work that they are doing is quite clearly and explicitly designed to be read by, and to be of interest to, the closed group of one's 'discipline' back home.

Now it is clear to many people that this is immoral. It is even beginning to be sensed that perhaps universities as an institution in society, in so far as they sponsor activity theoretically of this kind, have become an immoral institution. Those are strong words; and the matter leads some modern radicals to social action, thinking in terms of new structures and sociological changes. My point here is an intellectualist one, rather. Somewhat in passing, my contention is that objective knowledge in the humane realm is an inherently immoral concept. Many practitioners of this brand of knowledge are, of course, better than their theories; many are better men and women personally than are individual scholars with more humane ideas. The goal of an objective scientific knowledge of man, however, is wrong. One element in this inadequacy, shall we say, is its moral wrongness.

A second element in that increasingly apparent inadequacy (but this comment also is more or less just in passing), is that it does not render a knowledge that penetrates to the personal level of those studied. It does not yield personal understanding, or the kind of knowledge on which to found friendship. One may remark also that last century's Christian missionaries, who were objective in another fashion (individually perhaps very friendly, but in their group's theoretical relation to the 'other' religion, and in their writings, objectivist, alienist), were victims essentially of the same we–they fallacy, and their writings (for those 'back home') are subject then to the same two strictures. Mutual understanding among groups is not available on this basis. Yet mutual understanding among groups is part of the truth, in this realm; it provides a criterion, a verification principle.

My third comment, however, which is the one that is not in passing but is the point signalled at this stage of our general argument, is that objective knowledge is idiosyncratic. Just as the Christian missionary wrote for Christians, so the sociologist has tended to write for sociologists. And this, not as a foible, like his jargon; but on principle. I suggest that there is an intellectual flaw here. The thing is amusingly sectarian: one writes only for those who share certain presuppositions (and whose ritual is certain methodologies).

This fallacy is enshrined in the contemporary concept of 'discipline', which postulates a particular body of people who esoterically share a certain body of knowledge. It has come to be the case that, both in practice and in theory, academics of the objectivist, as distinct from the humane, sort read (academically) only within their own discipline, write only for members of their discipline, accept as authoritative criticism the judgement only of their 'peers', by which they mean other members of their group. And so on. This is subjectivity with a vengeance! Group subjectivity, no doubt; but subjectivity for all that. Objective knowledge of man leads to subjective knowledge by man. The importance of this has been little understood, but is major. Its contribution to fragmentation is serious.

Clark Kerr of California formally proclaimed an acquiescence in this multifarious subjectivism when he launched at Harvard the concept of 'multiversity'. That repellent notion is a modern paraphrase of Heraclitus's ιδιαι φρονησεις, which the university was developed in order to transcend. The concept of diverse disciplines is a sophisticated and institutionalised version almost of the collapse of the university idea. It is a failure of rational knowledge, as well as of the community of scholarship. So deeply have most of us become victims of this pattern of thinking, however, that criticism of it is hardly either understood or entertained.

The social and human devastation wrought by this disciplinary development has been tragic (almost in the Greek sense: there is a certain nobility in the failure). Human loyalties have therein tended to be transferred from the college or university where one works to the 'professional society' of one's discipline, of which one is a member (with consequent segregation, if not alienation, within the institution, of scholars from both students and colleagues). A concept of 'career' has been constructed (so that academic rewards are then conceived in terms of outward status rather than increased vision). The training of graduate students has taken precedence over the educating of undergraduates (the former joining the closed circle of the subjectivism). And so it goes. These social and human ramifications, which are woeful, could be lamented in themselves. It is the intellectual fallacy from which they stem, however, that concerns us here primarily: the notion that knowledge of man (of ourselves, after all) is the domain of a multitude of disparate idiosyncrasies.

The recent concept of 'interdisciplinary' is an attempt to construct a ladder by which to climb out of a hole into which genuinely humane studies never fell. One hopes that it is promising. One fears, however, lest at best it but enlarge the group of those who know externally (enlarge it perhaps ideally to the whole social-science community), without transcending the subjectivity principle of a closed group, of outside observers.

The objectivist ideology is, then, fissiparous within, as well as polarised against the outside. We turn next from the fragmentation of community to our final consideration, concerning the role of the knower in humane learning. Just as there is a quality on the side of the persons being studied that escapes purely externalist knowing, so also, and equally disquieting, is there in the concept of such knowing an under-appreciation of man as learner. Objectivity inherently misapprehends what happens or should happen to the student or scholar in the process of inquiry; to the thinker in the process of becoming aware.

Again, the notion of objectivity has grown out of work in the natural sciences, where what one investigates – the external world, objects – is less than man, is in some fashion beneath him and her; where what is known seems legitimately to be subordinated conceptually to the mind that knows. In objective knowledge here, accordingly, there has arisen a stress on method – a concept, drawn from the arena of ends and means, that inherently implies that what is known is dominated. (Recently I heard an academic 'professional' in the field of English Literature say that that field constitutes a body of material to be mastered. One might better think in terms of the student's being mastered by it, surely!)

Learning in the humanities involves being open to that that may be greater than oneself; greater, at least, than one has been until now. The process of knowing is a process of becoming. It is a matter not of using means, but of assimilating ends. Not primarily a matter of using means, certainly; of applying certain methods external to oneself. Methods, so far as they are systematised in formal methodologies, not only are, but are calculated to be, separable from the person who employs them. The point of learning about the natural world is the joy of knowing, or the resultant ability to change that world, or both. The point of learning about man is the joy (and duty) of knowing, which inherently comprises a changing of oneself.

The concept of methodology, and the stress on method in education, imply that one knows ahead of time what one wants, and has only to find out how to get it. This collides with the principle of humane learning, that one discovers in the course of one's study what one is after, what is worth wanting (what one 'wants' in the old-fashioned literal sense, of what is wanting in one's present stage of becoming). In principle it is possible to learn techniques without ceasing to be basically the kind of person that one was before; to come out of the learning process at heart as one went in.

The student revolution is relevant here. If a university teaches only techniques, proffers only methods of ascertaining what one already wishes to know, then of course students should decide what they wish to know, and in effect should employ the experts to satisfy these aspirations. They should *use* the university for their own purposes.

Humane learning, however, is not a methodological system, for gratifying desires, however worthy. It is an exploration of what man as such is, what he and she have been, what they may be (or shall we not rather say, of what we men and women have been, may be, and thereby what we truly, ultimately, are). The persons (or groups) who enter upon it are therefore exposing their actual selves to their potential selves; are participating in that process of self-transcendence in which being human in part consists.

Such learning requires, of course, a certain humility; which in turn, of course, it extravagantly repays. Specifically in the field of comparative religion, it requires a humility and respect *vis-à-vis* men and women of other cultures, a humility that into the nineteenth century neither Christians nor Western secularists regularly had. Sceptic and believer, at loggerheads at home, joined company to feel superior when they looked abroad; the one presuming that the religious faith of all humankind was superstitious error, the other that that of non-Christians was. At the very least, both for a time often lacked that humility that recognises that one can learn about oneself and about one's own world from other civilisations.

There are some indications that, of the two, Christians currently are the more likely to remedy this failure first, and hence to reap first a rich harvest; though I may be wrong in this, and in the end both must learn it. In any case, to learn it involves more than method. One cannot achieve humility by the application of technique; nor achieve insight, nor compassion, nor respect for human dignity and integrity.

Humane knowing is an exercise in the meeting between or among persons, be it across the centuries or across the world. It is, therefore, not technical, not subordinate to methodological rules. In personal relations, whether face-to-face or mediated by man's symbolic forms of expression, the use of technical procedures, unless rigorously subordinated to primarily personal considerations, is not merely inappropriate but potentially disruptive. Man cannot know man except in mutuality; in respect, trust, and equality, if not ultimately love. In this realm of knowing, accordingly, the attitude with which one approaches one's data proves to be at least as significant, as consequential, as the methods with which one handles them. One must be ready not only to receive the other but to give oneself. In humane knowledge, at stake is one's own humanity, as well as another person's or another community's. And at issue is humanity itself.

Urging a transcending of the objectivist orientation has in my particular case grown in part out of an awareness of the pain and resentment on the part of Asians before the aggression of much Western academic scholarship. More recently and nearer home, I have become alert to the growing resentment of students in Western society before modern academic study's aggression against the person. Universities that have succumbed to the recent mis-orientation, as I call it, are subject to that otherwise enigmatic wonder, of appearing repellent to the sensitive. Let us not underestimate the deep significance of the alienation from the university of many of our most intelligent, sensitive, youth.

So massive, in the eyes of the young, has the inadequacy become of objectivity of knowledge in its relation to man, and so disastrous the distortion of personal and community life, that there seems significant danger of a revolt, not only against the universities, already apparent, but also against science and against reason. Suddenly it is the humanist in whose hands the fate of science lies. It is the advocates of humane transcendence who must come to the rescue of rationality.

(Part of the problem here is that so many have proclaimed so loudly, and so long, that the only alternative to objectivity is subjectivity, that many have come to believe this sorry fallacy; and to opt, therefore, for the subjective – via drugs, even, though also in numerous other ways.)

The matter is felt outside the university too, in Western society at large. As modern culture has become increasingly permeated with what passes for a scientific outlook on knowledge and on the world and also on human matters, the increasing success in dealing with things has been accompanied with an increasing malaise of personal and social life: the depersonalisation of social procedures, the disintegration of community, the alienation of the person from one's neighbour, from oneself, and from the world.

Impersonalism in human affairs is bad science, is irrational; and the intellectual alternative to both objectivity, which is false, and subjectivity, which is radically inadequate, is a rational personalism in community.

This, then, is my thesis: that the new mode of humane knowledge is in terms of a disciplined corporate self-consciousness, critical, comprehensive, global. To study man is to study oneself – even when one person studies another (or one society, another) separated by much space, or time, or both. The corner that we are in the process of turning is one the turning of which enables us to see and to feel this; and presently, let us hope, to act in terms of it. We shall act in terms of it because inherent in this kind of knowledge is the principle that to know something new is to become a new kind of person.

In principle, then, for all humankind to know each other (which is beginning to happen, if only we can contrive it adequately) is for all humankind to become one community. And *vice versa*: only as we move towards community can we come to know.

This applies to the world the principle on which humane study has always been based within one's own culture. What great men and women have produced makes available to us who are lesser a vision by which we overcome in part our lessness. There are facets of our common humanity that lie dormant in most of us until awakened by our coming into touch with others' attainments.

To study a great poem, or a great work of art, or a great idea, is to become more fully human.

And not only what is great can serve us thus. I still hold that there is merit in studying chiefly what people and civilisations have chiefly prized. Yet one can enhance one's vision, one's understanding of oneself, of man, of the universe, can enhance one's humanity, by coming into genuine intellectual apprehension of all persons, whatever; great or small. Difference is educative, as well as greatness. The rest of us read what psychiatrists say about their patients. Since those patients are human, as are we, this means: about us.

Our solidarity precedes our particularity; and is part of our self-transcendence. The truth of all of us is part of the truth of each of us.

The comparative study of religion, of course, marvellously combines difference and greatness. In studying the history of religion we stretch our imagination and our souls by coming to know what is most radically different from that with which we are familiar, at the same time as coming to know what most people have perceived as surpassingly great. (It introduces us in passing also, of course, in a new and enlightening way, to the stark negativities, and subtle relativities, of human religious life, one's own community's and others'.) We shall turn then in our next chapter to the specifically religious dimension of this whole issue.

All humane knowledge, all awareness of man by man, is ideally a form of self-consciousness. The instance *par excellence* is the knowledge of comparative religion.

5 Self-consciousness as the Mode of Humane Knowledge

(ii) The Field of Religion

The argument of our last chapter held that humane knowing – the knowledge wherein one human being knows another human being – is ideally a 'we' or 'us' kind of knowing, generative of partnership, of mutual understanding. The implications of this are major for the development of new intellectual patterns of academic life, but we shall not here pursue them. They are major also for the next phase of intellectual patterns of religious life, and to this matter we now turn. Our consideration picks up especially the effect of knowing on the knower. This is most telling in the religious field. Modern awareness, in making possible a truer and more intimate apprehension by the outsider of communities that once seemed alien – that is, of the world of those around one; of *the* world around one – also and therein leads the learner into truer apprehensions of one's own world – that is, of *the* world: the world in which one lives, which is in process of becoming recognisably the one world in which of course we all live, and to the truth of which we are pledged to try to come. Inter-religious understanding is a form of intra-religious understanding. Or one may say, simply: of religious understanding.

These latter are themselves, no doubt, problematic. I do not wish to seem to overestimate (nor to misconstrue) the role of ideas in religious life. The religious response is a response of the whole person. The life of faith involves will, emotion, intellect, to use those divisions – and indeed any others that one might proffer: practice, community participation, and much else. To be a Christian is to participate in the full integrity of one's personality in the more than intellectual relationship that Christians have with God, Christ, the

Church, one's neighbour, one's cosmic destiny. Comparably for Muslims or Hindus. Yet religious groups are divided more by ideas than by piety. Though it oversimplify, perhaps, yet for the moment it is legitimate to attend to the ideational aspect in religious diversity, supposedly the most detachable and independently viable facet of each religious position. Faith is not belief, as I have elsewhere been at pains to affirm; none the less (or: therein) one is committed to intellectual integrity. This includes the integrating of what one says theologically and what one knows and thinks and understands generally, as well as the integrating of what one knows and what one is.

In this chapter, in any case, we shall focus on questions of conceptualisation, as it bears on the current transformation in one's understanding of others and of oneself.

Of the many facets of this to which one might attend, I choose in particular two. Cursorily, we could say that one pertains to the whole, and the other to a part, as it were, of the conceptuality of a given religious position that one sets out intellectually to understand: the notion of framework of ideas, or world-view, or over-all ideological pattern, on the one hand; and the notion of symbol, on the other. Great strides have been being made in recent decades towards an appreciation of how each of these functions in human life (in our lives, I shall presently be saying). The implications for oneself require pondering. The endeavour to elucidate them even for one's apprehension of others succeeds perhaps at least in elucidating that these issues too serve to bind us all together, in new ways.

To understand Buddhists, I have insisted, we must look not at something called Buddhism but at the world; so far as possible, through Buddhist eyes. For this, we must among other matters learn to use the total system of Buddhist doctrine or world-view as Buddhists use it: as a pattern for ordering the data of observation – not as among the data to be ordered. A conceptual framework can be understood historically and accurately in so far as it is appreciated as it has functioned, as a framework within which the universe is framed: the universe and man; life; oneself; one's hopes and failures, frustrations and joys; one's marriage; one's child's lameness; all that one sees and knows. It has to be grasped as it has been: not part of what a person knows, but the vision by and within which he or she knows (knows, or guesses, or is aware of not knowing). It does not *mean* something; it confers meaning.

Islam is not one of the items in the pattern of a devout Muslim's life, but is itself the pattern into which the various items in his life cohere – into meaningfulness. If he loses faith, maybe nothing in his world will change: the various items in his life may remain as they were – except that they no longer cohere into a pattern for him, are no longer integrated and rendered significant. The observable data that some outsiders have called 'Islam', and that I call the Islamic tradition, function for him as the expression and nurture of his faith, the forms around which the meaning of his life is crystallised, and is activated, in such a way that the rest of his life – what the outsider thinks of as secular data – are also enlivened into meaning, and purpose, and coherence.

Such an ideational pattern is significant primarily not in terms of the several ideas that make it up, considered individually in isolation; and especially not in terms of discrete propositions within the system; and most of all not in terms of how each of these, or even all of them together, may look when set within some quite other over-all pattern, such as the Christian, or the Western academic, or any other outsider's. They are significant, rather, in terms of their total coherence, and of their function of providing a framework within which the factual data and concrete events and spiritual propensities of the person's or the society's life are interpreted.

Many modern Westerners, as we have seen, have as such an ideational framework one that includes a dichotomy between the religious and the secular, as part of its pattern. For such people, religion is an item, is one section of life, alongside various others. One hears talk, then, of 'the religious factor', along with the economic, the political, or whatever. Conceptual outlooks of this kind are exceedingly deep, often, and therefore firm; and such people may have extreme difficulty in understanding, say, traditional Asian patterns that are Islamic, or Hindu, or whatever, not in the sense of having an Islamic or a Hindu 'religious factor' within a larger social complex like the West's, but in the sense of having an Islamic or Hindu over-arching pattern within which the secular fits, as a subordinate part.

It is difficult to come to appreciate such a different orientation. Yet it can be done. Moderns are learning to use their imaginations in sufficiently disciplined and vigorous ways to appreciate with fair accuracy a different pattern from their own; and to understand how specific details of concrete life then appear within that.

Once this is done, it can then happen that the outsider move on not only to apprehend the theoretical system, but also (with the help of an understanding too of symbols, to which specifically we come later, and of faith and other matters) to apprehend some of the drama that takes place within the system, the religious dynamics in the personal lives of those who participate. The outside observer who learns to understand the religious history of Christians, or of Jews or Buddhists, in a significant fashion comes to know not only the external facts of that history but also the involvement of persons in those facts – or, shall we say, through them: the transformation of personal lives. That Christians have seen Christ, or that Muslims have seen (heard) the Qur'an, as the Word of God; that Buddhists have 'taken refuge' in the Three Jewels: these and their like are facts not to be understood apart from their transforming power, from the ability of certain human beings in terms of such facts to live in the world in ways profoundly altered – or shall we say, profoundly human (or, simply: human).

This is all very well; and yet, one may respond, such outside understanding may remain quite superficial. True. It may be urged that there is a vital difference between understanding a Buddhist and being a Buddhist; between our understanding of, let us say, twelfth-century theology (whether Islamic or Christian) and our being twelfth-century persons; between understanding both sides of an Islamic and Hindu quarrel, and being both a Muslim and a Hindu simultaneously. There is a school that denied any such difference between understanding and being, holding that only a Christian could understand Christianity, or only a Muslim, Islam. This has been a serious position, deserving respect; but recent advances have moved us beyond it. This is illustrated in the point that if Muslims do understand Islam, then what about that Christian student to whom Muslims say, 'Yes, (at last) you have understood us!'? We may put the situation this way: we are demonstrably beginning – if only beginning, tentatively and partially – to understand the religious diversity of our world. Understanding is growing. It is one of the exciting phenomena of the modern intellectual scene.

Another problem that arises is that of the relation between such understanding and truth. That issue is mighty: truth and diversity of world-view is a topic at least for another volume. Here we shall but touch on it, by giving heed to the preliminary question, more manageable, of the relation between one's understanding of others' world-views and one's own view of truth. Before addressing that, however, we turn in the meantime to our other notion, that of symbol.

As is well known, this has become a crucially important concept in the comparative study of religion. There are a great many things to be said on the matter; a great many things have been said. I shall proffer only a few observations, on 'symbol' as a concept as it bears on certain aspects of our particular concerns – which it saliently does, we shall see. We begin with a word of caution.

The notion of 'symbol' is quite helpful in interpreting other groups' religious life – strikingly more so than were earlier more impersonalist notions, such as of those heathen bowing down to wood and stone. That the symbol notion may still not be quite adequate, however, is at least hinted by its not altogether serving in one's own case. Christians may regard a cross as a symbol, but find the concept 'symbol' inadequate for what Christ has meant to them. This is so, even though they recognise that an outsider has made significant progress by moving from saying that 'Christians have treated a human being Jesus as if he were divine' to saying that 'a human figure serves Christians as a symbol of the divine'. This last is a vast improvement. It is still, however, not an accurate statement of the traditional Christian position; and is therefore not yet a fully accurate descriptive interpretation, for academic history-of-religion purposes. One must suspect it, therefore, for others' cases. We shall return to this problem presently.

One must affirm, however, and must gratefully recognise, that the symbol concept has on the whole proven extraordinarily helpful. Furthermore, it can serve not only for enhancing the understanding of others' positions but also, we shall presently find, for elucidating our second problem, of self-interpretation. Both these matters are in part because it is an inherently humane, rather than an objectivist, concept. For nothing can be a symbol in and of itself. It is a symbol only in relation to some person or persons. No object is objectively a symbol. This fact is of the utmost consequence, and highly illuminating. We have to do here with a type of conceptual device that allows us, as a rare event in modern times, to think rationally about the world without automatically having depersonalised our intellectualisations.

It is a simple fact of observation that one cannot understand man, and one cannot understand human history, unless one recognise that certain things have functioned symbolically. This is involved in the truth pressed in our last chapter, that one cannot understand man, and cannot understand human history, if one understand things only as things. The objective ('scientific') awareness describes things not as they are in themselves, but as they stand in objectivist relation to man. This, as we saw, does not exhaust the truth of things, however useful it may be for certain purposes. Things exist not only perhaps in themselves (and knowledge of them in themselves may forever elude man, the philosopher Kant and the scientist Conant and others would suggest); and exist not only in objectivist relation to man (the relation that science has brilliantly explored): they exist – have existed – also in other, less impersonalist, relation to man. In this last relation things have been, at times brilliantly, explored by poets; also by moralists, by religious thinkers, and to some degree by everyman. (Certainly by every man or woman who has been in love, and shares something with his or her lover. And the ecology crisis is perhaps leading us to recognise that the natural world is shared by all of us in mutuality – so that to apprehend it without this nature–man mutuality is to misapprehend it.) Of the many non-objectivist relations between the natural world and the human, the symbolic is one. Not to perceive the symbolic quality of objects *vis-à-vis* human beings as an historical fact, and their symbolic potential as a persistent characteristic, is to miss part of the truth.

The interpretation of that truth even when perceived has, however, varied. Given the subjective–objective polarity with which modern minds have generally worked, the symbolic also has tended to be conceived at times in terms of the one or of the other. The matter is intricate, but I should be inclined to stress rather the interaction between things and persons (groups); and to resist what seems perhaps a tendency, even among some who recognise the symbolic as decisive in human life, towards as it were objectivising also symbols. I am never sure that I understand at all adequately what is perhaps rather loosely called 'Phenomenology of Religion'. I get the impression that some, at least, among those who call themselves phenomenologists are inclined to hold that symbols somehow carry their meaning in themselves. They might be seen almost as positing a Platonic idealism of symbolic forms. My own observations as an historian suggest rather that, as I have stated, no object is objectively a symbol: that things are symbols only in relation to certain persons, and not in relation to others.

It is this fact that makes the history of religion dynamic, complex and interesting. The aim of studying, accordingly, it is not by way of the historically changing to arrive at a vision of unchanging prototypes. I certainly do not wish to deny a transcendent reality behind all symbols, apparent to men and women through them. The historical evidence suggests, however, so far as I can see, that the empirical symbol does not itself participate in that transcendence. To speak as if it did is but an elliptic (and potentially misleading) way of describing what happens. More accurate would be to observe that there are some persons (but not others) to whom a given symbol appears as participating in transcendence.

There are many ways of perceiving the world; and, as the history of religion makes clear, there are many ways, differing in place and time, of perceiving transcendence immanent within it. If, however, one is to understand iconoclasm, as a major chapter in that history, let alone much internecine strife, one must bear in mind that the role of symbols is always particularised. *P* may be a symbol to one man or woman, and not to another. *Q* may symbolise something more forcefully, more limpidly, in one age than in another. *R* may be a symbol of something to one person, or class, or community; and of something quite else, even something contrary and perhaps fiercely colliding, to another.

Were this not so, the religious history of mankind would be starkly different from what it has been, and what it is today.

A crucifix may for certain Roman Catholics represent love; for certain Protestants, superstition; for certain Jews, oppression.

The primary locus of religiousness is persons, not things. And the study of religious history is secondarily the study of things, of phenomena, not in themselves but in their relation to persons – to particular persons and groups; so that the relation is always historical, specific, contingent. Psychologists find certain symbolic forms to be more widespread than one might have guessed. Notwithstanding this, the evidence of the religious history of our race would seem overwhelmingly to suggest that nothing within the empirical universe is inherently a symbol. Alongside this, it overwhelmingly indicates the spectacular consequences of the fact that, for certain persons, and groups, and times, and with varying degrees of effectiveness, certain things have indeed been symbols of something other than themselves (than their objective selves).

Many have observed that it is a characteristic of man that things become symbolic for him and her. I think that we must amplify this to read: it is a characteristic of man that things become symbolic for him and her and not for their neighbour.

It is important, further, to add that it is a characteristic of *things* that they become symbolic for man. Some might be tempted even to say, therefore: not to understand religion is not to understand the natural world. This much, at least, may be remarked in passing: that recent historical evidence would seem to suggest that an impoverishment of man's symbolic life is a serious, perhaps catastrophic, aberration; that an attempt to perceive all objects objectively, none symbolically, is devastating. (Not only devastating personally – both socially and individually – but even, it seems, devastating eventually also of things, ecologically and otherwise). May it be that truth is more accurately expressed for man in poetry than in prose? Although I myself am an intellectual, utterly committed to the rational articulation of truth, to the possibility and value of conceptual knowing, yet I can appreciate an argument that he or she would be a poor intellectual who could not conceive theoretically the possibility of the greater truth of poetry, and feel its force. (After all, it is part of the task of the historian of religion to understand, for instance, Chuang Tzu.) If one's dedication is to truth, and not primarily to inherited patterns for it, one's vision is enlarged.

The question of truth and how to conceive it brings us to the effect on oneself of new humane knowing. We shall consider presently the effect on one's religious position; but first in a more general way the matter of the learner's intellectual self-awareness – first and briefly as regards conceptual frameworks generally and then in the specific matter of symbols.

We have previously commented that we set aside, at least for some other occasion, the monumental problem of how to envision truth in relation to a multiplicity of conceptual frameworks. Here we remark only on the dawning awareness that one's own perceptions and conceptions constitute or are constituted by one pattern among others. It is a fallacy to suppose that ideologies are something that only other people have! We shall return presently to the modern attaining, in significant degree, of this self-consciousness for Christian, Islamic, Buddhist and other religious outlooks; here we note rather the counterpart for the Western secular. It has been moving slowly, and only with great resistance, to a recognition of itself also as particular, historical and limited. As we have noted, its adherents were able for a time to absolutise natural science – as, for instance, for Muslims the Qur'an once served as absolute – as a way of averting the self-conscious relativising of their own presuppositions. Yet the new self-understanding is in process of coming.

The issue of pluralism is coming to be a central problem for the rational intellectual as well as for the religious thinker. How to be a relativist without being a nihilist is one way of putting the matter. More enrichingly: how to enlarge one's vision of truth without losing loyalty to one's own, however finite, hold upon it (by it).

Self-consciousness with regard to 'symbol', to which we turn, may serve not as a diversion from this problem but as one useful entry into it. Besides, it rewards attention in itself.

It was an immense step forward, we have already stressed, when one came to understand the data of other persons' religious life not objectively but humanely, as symbols, not as objects of nature or of observation, merely, but as symbols of transcendence; even understanding, if only incipiently, what they symbolise for them. Of the consequences of this attainment, one is this: that once one has understood what a symbol signifies to another person, or community, then to some degree it now signifies that to oneself. Not immediately, as it does to them, and perhaps not actively, engagingly; yet at second remove. In some sense the meaning of the symbol to them has become the meaning of that symbol to you – indirectly, no doubt; mutedly, perhaps; remotely, maybe; yet still. . . . You may become a changed person in consequence.

If the meaning is one that previously you have known through some quite different symbol of your own (of your own community, or culture, or religious system, or secular vision), that is one thing. Your now seeing that it can be, and is, communicated to others through differing media – that truth can be articulated in more than one mode – is a fact that can be enlightening, or provocative. If on the other hand the meaning is one that previously has never come within your range, then the change in you may be of some more radical significance. Your horizon is enlarged, in that you now perceive the world in a new way. Or at the least, you perceive that it can be perceived in a new way, which may come to the same thing. And if the meaning at issue is the meaning of human life, then your discovery of the meaning of that symbol signifies at least that your awareness of man has been enlarged. (This is no mean accomplishment.) And it could even signify that your awareness of the meaning of *your* life is enlarged. Because you are studying what men and women have seen in life and in the universe, and because you are a man or a woman, then you are in some fashion engaged – at the very least, intellectually – in the symbolisation of others.

Of course, there have been some religious persons who have held *a priori*, and firmly, that all relevant truth about man and the universe is to be found within their own particular heritage; let us say, the Christian or the Islamic. They aver that nothing from other sources can supplement this, and that anything that differs is necessarily then either not true or not significant. This is a position that deserves respect. An historian of religion intolerant of exclusivism would cut a sorry figure in understanding his or her material! None the less, no one individual fully understands the meaning of his or her own tradition; especially if all transcendent meaning is indeed there. Accordingly, it can happen that in coming to understand the meaning that an alien symbol has had for an alien community, you may discover therein a meaning – of life, of the universe, of man's destiny, or whatever – that was in your own heritage all along but that previously you personally had not seen.

This sort of thing has in fact happened frequently in our studies.

There is simply no way in which a student of the history of other people's symbols can be precluded from learning through those others' symbols something that they have to teach – or, more accurately, that they have served other persons or groups as teaching or expressing.

If we designate the meaning that a symbol has had historically, for certain persons or communities or ages, as its meaning at a primary level, then we may perhaps designate as its meaning at a secondary level the meaning that it comes to have for the modern student who arrives at an understanding of it. Moreover, rather than the meaning that it 'has', we should speak perhaps of the meaning, at either level, that it mediates, or communicates. For the point of its being a symbol is that it is not 'its own' meaning that it signifies, but something other and greater than itself. A religious symbol, which is what we here are talking about, shimmers with the (a?) meaning of the whole universe in relation to man.

We noted earlier the potential difference between understanding a religious position and accepting it. This is the difference between the two levels here of a symbol's meaning? That difference in level is in principle not fixed. If by the act of understanding one has not joined the community of those for whom the symbol is cogent – and we may remember that it is largely the sharing of symbols that constitutes a human community – none the less one has interlinked oneself with it in some fashion, however peripheral.

Both this, and the broader matter of world-view, come into play in a contemporary historical fact. However incipiently, the boundaries segregating off religious communities radically and finally from each other are beginning, just a little, to weaken or to dissolve, so that being a Hindu and being a Buddhist, or being a Christian and not being a Christian, are not so starkly alternatives as once they seemed.

We have come then to the implication of the new awareness for a religious pattern as such, and we turn now to that. One must remember that the religious movements of the world are, of course, undergoing swift development of various sorts in modern times anyway; this is quite apart from the contribution of global consciousness and self-consciousness among their thinkers to the direction and form of that development. Each has throughout history been in constant process, as we urged in our opening chapters; the novelty is that today that process is unprecedentedly rapid, on the one hand, and, on the other, is complicated or guided by the new knowledge both of past development and of each other. Once again we shall here give attention to world-view and to symbol, as now self-consciously conceptualised in religious life.

As we noted in our last chapter, Western understanding of India has advanced from ignorance, through insensitive externalist knowledge of facts, to, more recently, at least the beginnings of serious and even profound humane understanding. In both the Islamic and the Hindu cases there, the classical and mediaeval outlooks were total human orientations, nurtured and expressed through complex symbolic structures, in terms of which life, death and the empirical world were humanly ordered. There was at this stage no concept 'Hinduism' for Hindus, and the Arabic word 'Islam' for Muslims used to designate an act of personal devotion, not the ramifying intellectual and other social and institutional results of that act – there being no need or room for the reified terms, since the comprehensive systems that these names came subsequently to designate were at this stage not part of the observed data, of which participants were conscious, but were part of the presuppositional pattern, through which they were conscious.

Next, when observers from the West arrived on the scene, and noted unfamiliar and indeed bizarre facts and ideas, at which they looked objectively from outside, they began, once they had moved beyond piecemeal gleaning of disparate items, to construct ideationally as new concepts certain systematised patterns of the religious data, conceptual and other, to which patterns they gave names such as 'Mohammedanism', 'Vishnuism', 'Hinduism'. But whereas for the Muslims and Hindus involved these patterns had functioned as conceptual frameworks or primary ordering agents, for the outside observer they were (if not arrogantly subordinated to their own Christian or secularist convictions) co-ordinated with all the other things that they observed, as they looked around the world. They were examined then as passive (and mundane) objects. A process of reification had begun. This introduced at best a novelty, and often a distortion. By outsiders the data were to a considerable degree misunderstood; but among participants also there began to arise a new way of perceiving themselves and their religious position, in the light of what was happening around them: perceiving that position if not as a closed system, anyway as a system, even a mundane system, one among others; for the first time as an object, at least of the conceptualising activity of the mind.

Partly under the explication of Muslims and Hindus themselves, partly as Western rational inquiry proceeded more penetratingly, the objectivised view has been giving way more recently to a recognition by the outsider of the religious schemes as they actually functioned in the past in the lives of insiders, as interpretative world-view. For those insiders, on the other hand, the task has arisen of endeavouring to clarify for themselves the relations among the outlook as a way of perceiving, as traditionally inherited; the outlook as a conceptualised entity, as modernly generated, in the new imposed self-consciousness; and alternative outlooks (whether secular or religious) that their fellows on earth have reasons for preferring.

The process has, of course, been more intricately complex than this synopsis suggests. I have examined the reification process in general, in world religious history[1], and have looked into the Hindu[2] and in some detail studied the Islamic[3] moves towards self-conscious reification, in other publications. Let us here compare for a moment the instance where the matter has proceeded much the farthest: namely, the Christian. In the Asian cases the onslaught of objectivisation, though substantial, has thus far remained somewhat secondary, whereas in Western Christendom it has been indigenous, sustained and profound.

Like the others, the classical Christian outlook also, of course, envisaged the world through religious – in this case, Christian – categories. God; creation; the Fall; the need and possibility of salvation; the timelessness of transcendent truth and goodness, over against the ephemerality of less important things; the cosmic significance of man (of both oneself and one's neighbour) – these and their like functioned conceptually as the foundations of one's life, personal and social, the ground on which rested whatever else one thought, or felt, or hoped, or feared, or knew. They were presuppositions, constituting the framework within which one looked out upon the world. One did not 'believe' them in the modern sense, of judging them, over against competing human ideas, to be valid, for one saw them not as ideas in men's minds, but as realities of the universe; not as particular theses, but as general truths. On this basis, of course, persons built their lives, and society its civilisations.

The more recent stage in this case, however, has been that the religious orientation has been reduced (and I stress that word) from an active faith to a passive belief; from the *form* of consciousness to an *object* of consciousness.

Thus, *vis-à-vis* the Orient Western awareness has of late been elevated from the objective to the personal, superseding distortion with understanding; while in relation to his or her own heritage, the Westerner's awareness has, rather, degenerated from the existential to the objective. The discernible shift of the creed, over a sequence of centuries, from a pledging of personal loyalty conceived within a taken-for-granted framework, to an intellectual subscribing to a problematic one, has been documented[4]. What used to be the conceptual pattern, through which one looked, has become 'a religion', at which one looks. What used to be the context of transcendence, within which one responded, has become an empirical item among the several objects of one's inquisitive scrutiny, which some people 'believe' – while increasingly many do not: for what at that level are, quite apparently, almost good reasons.

Have we arrived then at the position aphorised by Gibbon, that every religion is to the believer equally true and to the philosopher equally false? When I say that to look at a religious orientation from the outside and to reify it externalistically is to distort it – that to be understood, it has to be seen as serving the insider as premiss – am I saying that each is objectively false, though subjectively true? I am not saying that; although I am almost saying that that is the corner into which those paint themselves who adopt the subjective–objective polarity, and who utilise the objectivist and distorted concept 'a religion'. It is the fallacy of misplaced concreteness, to think of religions – in the plural – at all (or 'a religion', in the concrete singular). It is a further fallacy of misplaced logic, to suppose that they can be (that such things could be) true or false. It is a fallacy of anachronist theology to imagine that people used to 'believe' their religious conceptualisations, or to deem it important that one believe. This entire way of approaching the problem must be superseded if we are to make any progress at all in our present crisis.

The question of their truth or falsity must be set forth in more historical form. In their traditional mode, these orientations cannot be dubbed true or false, in the sense of simplistic logic. They can be seen as less or more true in the sense of enabling those who looked at life and the universe through their patterns to perceive smaller or larger, less important or more important, areas of reality, to formulate and to ponder less or more significant issues, to act less or more truly, less or more truly to be. Once they have moved from being forms of consciousness to being objects of consciousness, however, as is today the case, a quite new mode of thinking in this realm becomes imperative.

My proposal is that critical self-consciousness can move towards truth by, and only by, moving towards becoming corporate. The otherwise intractable intellectual problems posed by the distortions generated by our disparateness and our bifurcations are herein overcome. The solution will appear drastic to some, and is no doubt radical; yet it is both required, and made possible, by our present knowledge, both of others and of ourselves.

Before we pursue what this direction of thought implies at the general systemic level, let us return for a moment to that specific concept 'symbol', and its role in religious self-consciousness.

We have noted that this concept has proven decidedly fruitful for understanding others' religious life, less so for one's own. For an outsider to come to recognise and to understand the Qur'an not as a book simply but as a symbol – with all that that means and has meant historically, spiritually, psychologically, artistically, commercially, legally, humanly; and not as a seventh-century document only but as an eighth-and twelfth- and twentieth-century dynamic force: this is to go far towards understanding Muslim history and faith. For non-Muslims who have thus understood, the Qur'an in particular and indeed scripture in general can become then a symbol at the second level of meaning. Yet, as this way of looking at the world comes also into the self-conscious awareness of the Muslim community, what happens? Come it will, our modern world being what it is and human consciousness being what it is. Muslims used to make sense of life by reading the Qur'an as the Word of God. Can they make as much sense of it reading it as a symbol of that Word?

Further, as we saw, for Christians Christ has appeared not as a symbol of the Divine but as the Divine Himself.

The question about God is a little more complicated. As a word, even as a concept, the term 'God' is clearly a symbol; but to say that God Himself is a symbol is less lucid and less powerful. (It is better, however, to speak of God as a symbol than as a problem!) Some there be who are content to say and to feel that God or the concept 'God' is a symbol of transcendence; but they are a minority, for whom the latter term happens to be attractive and charged with overtones. Moreover, there are some, but again doubtless a minority, though perhaps presently there will be more, who are able and content to live with the conviction that all our religious heritage is symbolic, and to counter the question 'symbolic of what?' with the cheerful observation that if one could say (or even know) what a symbol symbolises, the symbol would then be unnecessary (and life and the world would be reduced).

The analysis at which we previously arrived would seem to need further developing. What is a symbol for the committed participant at the first level, of faith response, can become a symbol for the perceptive student at the second level, of intellectual understanding. We must perhaps now add a new position, which might go something like this: that what is seen by the perceptive but non-participant observer as a symbol for participants, is in some cases by those participants themselves seen at what the observer might call a zero level – higher than the first level, and, indeed, not recognised by the devout as a 'symbol' at all. It is important for the outside observer to note that if Christians do not recognise Christ as a first-level symbol (but see Him as something more than that), then that observer misunderstands, or inadequately understands, those Christians if he or she proceeds as if they did, or conceptualises the history of religion in those terms. We can understand Sankara perhaps if we say that Siva was a symbol for him, but not Ramanuja if we say that Vishnu was; and not even Sankara if we say that Brahman was.

I can imagine the subtlety of a modern Athanasius expended on explicating the relation between zero-level and first-level symbols, as a present-day version of that between the divine and the human natures in Christ – or that of a modern Nagarjuna on the relation of *dharma* as symbol and *dharma* as ultimate reality for the Buddhist. To live in a world of mystery variously symbolised in various ways, and for certain groups of us truly symbolised in such-and-such a way, is a possible vision for the next stage in the religious history of the world; but let us admit that it would constitute a new stage. The conceptualisations to go with the new insights have yet to be hammered out; and how effective they will prove has yet to be tested. We do not yet know how men and women can live most truly with the new self-conscious knowledge; whether this particular form for it will serve. Can a Muslim be a devout and fully committed Muslim knowing that all that he or she knows is symbolic? Would that kind of belief nurture a faith that would save? *Mutatis mutandis* for the Christian. (For the alert Hindu, the answer is already 'yes'.)

Certainly it is possible, and has become probably requisite, to ask whether the concept 'symbol', for all its excellence, is really adequate to the task that today we are tempted to put upon it. Some find the related but more dynamic concept 'myth' more serviceable; others, partly because of its strongly pejorative history, less. In any case, the two are supplementary. Theologians in their various worlds are at work on these conceptual issues; it is an area in which both they and intellectuals in the comparative-religion field have made some progress, but not yet enough in forging conceptual forms and constructing theoretical statements to do justice even to what we already know.

Perhaps all that we need is a new interpretation of 'symbol'. Perhaps what will serve us is a new interpretation of 'revelation'. (Particularly for Christians, I shall suggest in later chapters, this latter may prove decisive.) Or progress may come, rather, from development in concepts of faith and involvement. These three areas correspond, one might feel, to whether one gives attention primarily to the religious object, or to the Divine that it mediates, or to the person who responds. A good Trinitarian, one might suppose, will recognise that all three are equally important: all three are facets of one process in which man in his and her religious life is caught up.

Let me say, rather: in which we men and women in our religious life are caught up. For, whatever conceptual pattern we may construct in order to deal intellectually with this dimension of human affairs, the critical, and novel, requirement is that it be for us all. I stress both the 'us' and the 'all'. We are today reaching in human knowledge, in human history, and in religious evolution, a stage where consciousness must be a universal self-consciousness: corporate; critical; both analytic and synthesising.

We are back, then, to the question of one's comprehensive religious outlook, and may move forward now with both it in general and the symbolic conceptualisation in particular as they are transmuted by incorporation into the wider self-consciousness of our modern world. The striving is towards validity within that: validity of intellectual interpretation, and a rational formulation for faith today.

In the matter of validity, it will be recalled that from the natural sciences we adopted the verificationist principle that a position is not valid unless another observer will get the same results; and universalised this for the humane sciences. Humane knowledge is much more complicated than is objective, of course; but here a verificationist principle is this: that no observer's statement about a group of persons is valid that cannot be appropriated by those persons. In the history-of-religion instance, this applies to faith, if not to tradition (which latter can be known objectively).

No statement about Islamic faith is true that Muslims cannot accept. No personalist statement about Hindu religious life is legitimate in which Hindus cannot recognise themselves. No interpretation of Buddhist doctrine is valid unless Buddhists can respond, 'Yes! That is what we hold'.

It is also the case, however, that these statements are made by outsiders, presumably honest; so that first of all they must satisfy the non-participant, and satisfy all the most exacting requirements of rational inquiry and academic rigour. They must be more than objectively true; not less. Thus, no statement about Islamic faith is true that non-Muslims cannot accept. No statement about Hindu religious life is legitimate in which the Hindus' non-Hindu neighbours cannot recognise them. No statement about Buddhist doctrine is valid unless non-Buddhists can respond, 'Yes – now we understand what those Buddhists hold'.

Christians will readily recognise the force of the first principle for their own case: a purported descriptive statement of Christian faith, they themselves can judge as accurate or mistaken. None the less, some Westerners might feel uneasy at the thesis set forth, on such grounds as that a proposition surely does not require (and could not secure) unanimous endorsement, or that the operational problem is teasing as to who is a 'representative' Buddhist or Muslim or whatever. One could restrict the assertions by speaking of 'intelligent Muslims' or 'knowledgeable Hindus' and so on in our formulations; but the basic problem is rather that these hesitations depend upon reificationist assumptions that I of course leave far behind. All statements of the form 'Muslims affirm *X*' (and, even more: 'Islam teaches *X*') or 'Buddhists practise *Y*' or 'Hindus feel *Z*' are, and should be known as, at best shorthand for in principle quite testable assertions that 'most Muslims have affirmed (or currently affirm, or interpret Islam as affirming) *X*', or 'a significant number of Buddhists in Japan in such-and-such a century practised *Y*', or 'among those whom the modern world calls Hindus, there is evidence that a certain (specifiable) group feel *Z*'. All general statements about religious matters should be recognised as generalised abstractions about the personal (including social) life of historical men and women. So long as one's mind operates in terms of this foundational truth, the difficulties mentioned hardly arise.

An academic statement about a religious community must be simultaneously intelligible to that community and to the academic community with its non-participant observers. In comparative religion, the intellectual task is to construct statements that will be simultaneously intelligible within two religious communities as well as in the academic world.

Humane knowledge is not easy; yet neither is it impossible. Progress is being made in these matters, and, as might be expected, it is exciting and consequential. The principles involved can be and have been academically institutionalised. The Institute of Islamic Studies at McGill University, for instance, where I had the privilege of working for some years, had as operative principle that half the teaching staff, half the research associates, half the students, should be Muslim, half non-Muslim. Seminars were always joint. In every classroom, and at every coffee-break, therefore, every remark about Islamics was made in the presence of both Muslims and non-Muslims; and in the relentless pursuit of new knowledge that characterises a university both Muslims and outsiders chose to collaborate. Similarly, in a multilateral if as yet less closely structured fashion, the Center for the Study of World Religions at Harvard aims explicitly and self-consciously at rigorously academic collaborative knowledge.

These are small and admittedly special instances. The process involved in fact operates, if less deliberately, yet widely and forcefully, across the modern world. For academic knowledge is public knowledge. Muslims read orientalists' books on Islamics.

Hindus read anthropologists' studies of caste. Buddhists read Western studies of Buddhist history. Christians read Freudian and Marxist and secular philosophers' critiques of religion.

The fact is eloquent that Muslim scholars and students choose to attend the McGill Institute, opting to study their own religious matters in the company of analytic observers from the outside, and in collaboration with them; and Hindus, Buddhists, Jews and, again, Muslims, the Harvard Center. Christian theological colleges and seminaries, similarly, are increasingly seeking out university affiliation. The religious intellectual in modern times, as in classical, is not isolationist with regard to knowledge or to truth (despite an historical interlude recently, when theologies turned for a while introvert). Consciousness grows and widens.

When Muslims have in the past read Western studies of Islamics, they usually have not liked them, to put it mildly. They have resented the arrogance, inherent in those days in most Christian, most secularist and all behaviourist orientations. They have been repelled by the distortions, introduced by externalist viewing. They have been made uncomfortable, by having what were premisses turned into objects of scrutiny. None the less, there is at least a grain of truth – and sometimes, much more than a grain – in many of those alien observations. Objectivist knowledge of man is always inadequate, and for the specifically human aspects, as distinct from the object aspects, is regularly distorted; yet it is not the case that 'there is nothing in it'. And more recently, the sympathetic, humane studies of perceptive outside scholars working not from above but alongside are avidly welcomed. Intelligent, self-critical, disciplined Muslims are nowadays becoming very aware of the new perspective opened up by outsiders' views of their tradition (and incipiently, even of their faith).

In principle, to be a rational Muslim is to assimilate all knowledge about Islamics from whatever source. Indeed, some rational Muslims are themselves taking part in constructing the world-wide new awareness of the Islamic sector of our universal humanity. In that kind of statement about Islamics to which we referred above, one that is simultaneously cogent for the Muslim and for the outsider, Muslims are of course especially interested. They are interested both as consumers and as producers, and for the sake of communication. Thus, too, self-consciousness grows.

We may observe this the more poignantly in the Christian case. It is the Western world that has in recent centuries generated the objectivist, critical approach. Western Christians have lived in a society where the externalistic intellectual reduction of religion has been active and familiar. Modern Christians know very well what their outlook looks like to those on the outside who disparage it. In fact, as we noted earlier, the problem for many modern Christians is that they themselves have come to think of what they call their religion, or Christianity, in objectivist terms, as one item in the pattern of their lives, or one element in their societies; and are in danger of having lost the ability to see it any other way: the ability to look at the world through it, rather than to look at it in the world. (As Tillich and others have complained, they think of God as an object, one alongside others; and ask, whether He exists.)

A sophisticated Christian, however, is one who both is a person of faith and, simultaneously, is fully aware of what the world, including the form of his faith, is like objectively: viewed from the outside. In the modern world the intellectualisation of a serious Christian form of faith that is not obscurantist is highly self-conscious. (Is Barth perhaps the last great theologian of whom this is not true?)

The intellectual study of religion, then, in general, and, more recently, comparative religion in particular, after their first objectivist stage, have enabled us Christians, for example, not merely to see 'Islam' and 'Hinduism' as reified systems but, secondly, to see the world from Islamic and Hindu viewpoints; and, thirdly, have enabled us to see our own system as others see it, externally – and even to see the fact that, when viewed so, it can appear human, corrupt and absurd. Barth, who did not rise to a synthesis, did see the dichotomy; and affirmed that all 'religion' is to be condemned – including our own (*die Aufhebung der Religion*) – while Christian faith, which he valiantly rescued from that objectivity, he saw and proclaimed, is salvific.

His interpretation of Christian faith was still largely subjectivistic (despite his vigorous disclaimers); and he quite failed to see the faith of others, behind *their* objectified 'religions'. He did not even know that they had faith.

The fourth step has yet to be fully articulated, but it is clear that we are already engaged in taking it, all of us. It is towards a state of group self-consciousness (ideally global) where we know what we are doing in being religious; and others know; and both can rationally approve (or, at the very least, rationally understand). The Christian in comparative-religion study learns, as we have already remarked, not only to see the Islamic tradition as it appears to outside critical analysis and also as it appears to Muslims, but also to see the Christian Church, Christian doctrine and Christ Himself as they appear to Muslims too – and to Hindus, atheists, Marxists, Jews, and eclectic perplexed inquirers. An intelligent modern Christian, and an intelligent modern Muslim, in principle (and even to some degree now in fact) both know what both forms of faith look like to an outsider, and feel like to a participant. Intellectually they converge.

Several years ago I had occasion to characterise the study of comparative religion as moving from talk of an 'it' to talk of a 'they'; which became a 'we' talking of a 'they'; and presently a 'we' talking of 'you'; then 'we' talking 'with' you; and finally – the goal – a 'we all' talking together about 'us'[5]. The study of comparative religion is the process, now begun, where we human beings learn, through critical analysis, empirical inquiry, and collaborative discourse, to conceptualise a world in which some of us are Christians, some of us are Muslims, some of us are Hindus, some of us are Jews, some of us are sceptics; and where all of us are, and recognise each other as being, rational men and women.

We averred above that any statement about personal faith should in principle be intellectually persuasive both to him or her or those whose faith it is and to the perceptive outside observer. Some traditionalists would maybe shudder to think of going along with me, a Christian, in perhaps speculating (the idea is rather novel, is it not?) that no statement about Christian faith is valid to which in principle a non-Christian could not agree? Theologians have not usually adopted such a principle, I guess. Even in our concluding sections we shall not fully sound the depths of this suggestion; but it may be borne in mind. I deem it more promising than one might at first suppose. At least intelligibility, if not acceptability, is a possible and fruitful criterion.

At issue here is the momentous distinction between faith and belief, which I have felt it important to elaborate elsewhere[6]. I personally tend to feel that there is probably no statement about my faith that I would wish to make that I could not on principle hope to explain to an intelligent, modern, devout, informed, Muslim or Hindu friend – and explain so that he would understand, and yes, in the end, would accept. Especially, I suppose, if he were something of a mystic, as well as a rationalist. Nor should I expect him in turn to 'believe' anything, if he were intelligent, that I should not find both intelligible and intelligent. (What reason would he have for believing anything that I would not?)

If this dream seem inept to anyone, is it not either because that person is disdainful of all religion, or of all religion other than his or her own, holding that it is inherently irrational to be Hindu or Muslim, or perhaps Christian; or because he or she is disdainful of reason; or is unaware of modern developments in the religious history of the world, with its interactions among diverse communities, and between each and modern knowledge?

The self-consciousness, I would contend, is coming, willy nilly; in this field, demonstrably, and seemingly in all fields, as a current profound transition in human development. True knowledge, in human affairs, is that knowledge that all intelligent men and women, participants and observers, can share, and can jointly verify, by observation and by participation. True humane knowledge is disciplined and corporate self-consciousness.

In addition to the rationalist there is a practical verification for such knowledge, continuous with yet beyond that for the natural sciences. Like it, it lies in the realm of application, yet in another mode. Scientific knowledge of the objective world is external, and to apply it is to manipulate, from the outside and above. To manipulate man, however, is evil (as well as the theory on which it rests being faulty). The pragmatic verification of knowledge about man lies in our applying it from alongside as observers, in the form of understanding; from the inside as participants, in the form of wisdom; and between the two as fellows, in the form of mutual intelligibility – which eventuates in community.

Knowledge of Islamics means that kind of awareness of Islamic developments, of the processes through which Muslims have been and are going, that enables outside observers to understand accurately, Muslims to participate intelligently, and both to communicate.

One of the most determinative characteristics of any human being is whom he or she means in saying 'we'. Neither the academic intellectual, nor the person of faith, can any longer be content to mean less than 'we human beings', across the globe, across the centuries: we persons on earth, in all our vast diversity of historical development, cultural particularism, and in our case religious commitment. It requires erudition, critical acumen, imaginative sympathy and penetrating understanding; it takes time, effort and dedication; but it is now possible, and therefore now requisite, to learn to say, and to mean, that we human beings on earth are diverse but not incongruous.

Our solidarity precedes our particularity, and is part of our self-transcendence. The truth of all of us is part of the truth of each of us. It is self-consciously we who differ.

Therefore, we differ, yet we are not disparate. Indeed, yet we ultimately converge. True knowledge of man is self-knowledge, but now on a global scale, and on an historical. Therefore I say that the mode of humane knowledge is corporate, disciplined self-consciousness. This is true in all fields, and the awareness of it grows, and must be implemented, in many ramifications. It is true not least in the religious field, and the growing awareness of it is exciting; ramifyingly for all life, including the life of the mind, but specifically also for religious life.

Not they, not you, but some of *us* are Buddhist, some Muslim, some Jewish, some sceptic, some confused. Some of us are Christian. We are learning to say this, and to know what we are saying, and to mean it.

I close, then, with this transition to our concluding chapters. A Christian theology of comparative religion is, therefore, not a view from within one tradition or community out upon the others. To conceive it so has been the chief error until now, and is inherently bound to fail, whether the other tradition or community perceived as object be considered critically or charitably. Rather, that theology, if it is to be true, becomes a Christian view (and I stress the adjective) from within all. It postulates that we see ourselves as participants in one community, the human: that the Christians see the Christian group and other groups as fellow participants in that one community.

I personally have done something, perhaps, to popularise the phrase, 'The faith of other men'; and I continue earnestly to advocate an apprehension of the faith of all who share this planet: faith at the deepest, most personal, the truest level. I have come to see, however, that to succeed in apprehending such faith, even intellectually, is to discover that a new formulation becomes required. The first step is to recognise the faith of other men. Once that step has been truly taken, the next step is the recognition that there are no *other* men.

Part III

The History of Religion: Theological

6 A 'Christian' Theology of Comparative Religion?

The phrase 'theology of religions' or '. . . of the religions' has sprung up of late in Christian circles, as a parallel formation to 'theology of missions', '. . . of culture', '. . . of the secular', and the like. It marks the important advance whereby Christian theologians have begun to recognise and to wrestle with the problem posed in Christian thought by the Church's new awareness of the faith of other men. Two potential difficulties, however, come to mind that may be involved with his way of conceiving the issue. They pertain to the subject and to the object of the inquiry, respectively.

The first may be pointed up in a question, which can strike with some force, as to whether by 'theology' here is intended 'Christian theology'. That issue is clearly major, yet teasingly ambiguous. There are thorns, whichever way one seize this. Some would say, 'Of course, yes', and feel restive at the watering down or even betrayal that they would fear otherwise. A Christian whose loyalty is serious is hardly likely to be impressed by, or even much concerned with, a theology that is *not* Christian, that does not even claim or aspire to be so. Yet the contrary response also demands to be taken seriously, coming from those whose 'no' would stem from a deep disquiet at what could seem a subterfuge or contradiction. For one thing, it would be interesting that such a point could be tacit. In this of all fields, they might say, is one to take for granted that a theology of diverse religions will indeed be a Christian theology? This might constitute an interesting conclusion. Some would find it a not obvious premiss.

Of course, it could be argued that, since the thinker is Christian, and so, perhaps, is his or her potential or presumed audience or readership, therefore naturally in this particular context theology may be simply assumed to be Christian theology – whatever might be the situation in a larger, or different, perspective. (Besides, the problem being addressed is in a sense a peculiarly Christian problem. Or should we say, a Christian's problem?) If one found in a bookshop in Christendom a volume, by a Christian author, devoted to a consideration of, let us say, the sacraments, or saw a notice announcing a series of these Cadbury Lectures on that topic, in a Western university, again by a speaker known as a Christian, one might casually presume that 'theology of the sacraments' would indeed signify Christian theology of Christian sacraments. Yet such a presumption, and certainly its casualness, would be precisely because, or in so far as, at that level the issue of comparative religion had not yet been seriously faced. Traditional insouciance is here still in evidence. Even in such cases it will not last, one may guess. A time will surely come when also in thinking about 'internal' matters Christian thinkers will have recognised that their positions are consciously and explicitly (and proudly) *Christian* positions. Between theology in general and Christian theology in particular the distinction will no longer be obscure. Christian doctrine about the Bible will come to be propounded, necessarily and explicitly, as a particular instance of scripture as a generic concept, and of the role of scripture in human life.

A study of Christian sacraments elucidating their meaning for Christian life in contrast or comparison with the sacramental aspects of, say, Hindu life – enabling Christians to see their sacraments in the total human context – may become standard only at some time in the future. Regarding comparative religion, on the other hand, either the question is not raised at all or else that time for global perspective has already come.

A Christian theology of other religious positions could hardly be adequate that did not take those other positions seriously. And involved in taking them seriously is a haunting recognition that a Christian position becomes then one among others. This is so at the level of one's most intelligent, most sincere, most vivid confrontation with God.

Thus, if one speaks of a Christian theology of religions, is there also an Islamic theology of religions (my own sensitivity to this pluralism is perhaps the more acute in that I happen to teach a course in Islamic Theology); and, if one interpret 'theology' a whit broadly so as to include counterparts, then also a Hindu, a Buddhist, and so on? It is within such an array that any explicitly Christian interpretation asks to be set. A genuinely comparativist, or global, or human perspective sees a Christian theology of the religions as one in a series.

The force of this, and finally its devastating consequences, are serious.

A notion, then, of 'the theology of religions' may harbour with apparent innocence the implication 'a Christian theology of religions'; but once this is made explicit its innocence disappears. Equally, however, if the resultant theology is to be *not* Christian, its innocence has disappeared also.

For does not the problem of religious diversity lie indeed here? A Christian theology of the matter is in danger of being seen in one of two ways: either as relativistic, one option among several, all equally open, equally cogent; or else as dogmatic, accepted because it is Christian, in which case it may seem a mere rationalisation rather than a solution of its problem. A Christian theology of religions, then, in this particular sense, might serve the apologist but not the inquirer: one who seeks to win a debate, or to maintain a prior commitment, but not one who really wants to know. Of intelligent, informed, sincere, it cannot be all three.

Nor is this by chance. At this sort of result one arrives not incidentally but perforce, given this sort of starting point. Radhakrishnan's interpretation of Christianity, some Christians may feel, will become valid only when Christians adopt a Hindu attitude to religion and to Christ. An Islamic theology of the religions, if its commitment, criterion and goal are within the Islamic system, cannot in the nature of the case come to a true appreciation of, let us say, Christian or Hindu faith; for it inescapably subordinates the Christian and Hindu to the priorly Islamic. And, by subordinating, *ipso facto* it misunderstands. (That this is so, any Christian and any Hindu will readily perceive.)

Islamic theology may, within its own terms, be substantially true; Islamic faith may be cosmically valid; yet even so, any interpretation of Christian or Hindu faith by Muslims within strictly Islamic terms is still a misinterpretation. It is an inauthentic representation of that with which we Christians and Hindus are involved – simply because our faith is in fact not in Islamic terms, and indeed refuses to be. An historian might conceivably hold (and if himself a Muslim, might well until recently have held) that such Muslims may have had a correct interpretation of the universe, in its ultimate truth, yet as historian must recognise (whether he be Muslim or not) that they have not had a correct apprehension of Christian or Hindu faith, in its concrete actuality. (And there is a problem, again, of the relation between ultimate truth and historical reality. The world that theologians in the past interpreted did not, in their awareness, include the history that today we their successors have come to know.)

Man's religious faith being what it is, any would-be understanding of it from outside itself that subordinates it to alien categories conceptually distorts it. At the theoretical level Islamic theology may seem to be right and Christian theology and Christian faith wrong, but a Muslim who holds this should simply hold it, as a legitimate (if by now somewhat traditional) Islamic position; and should recognise it for what it is, an Islamic position built on Islamic grounds, and should not think that he holds it in relation to Christian faith (and therefore, to world history). What is today called Islamic theology would seem as such to have been a perfectly legitimate intellectual and religious pursuit – as a brilliant history over many centuries amply demonstrates – in its own right: a conceptual explication of or framework for Islamic faith, an interpretation of the world as then known perceived from the then form of that faith. An Islamic theology of Christian faith, on the other hand, verges on being a contradiction in terms. Similarly, Christian theology, many would be quick to aver, is (has been) legitimate in its own right; yet a Christian theology of the religions is an inherently inadequate concept, I am suggesting.

At least, this is so in so far as a Christian (or Islamic, or Hindu) theology of the religions involves an objective genitive, as we used to say in secondary-school Latin classes: a theology that has the religions as its object. This brings us to the second of my two caveats. Not only the subject in 'a theology of religions' is problematic, as to what type of theology this be, Christian or other. There is a query also as to the object: what it is proposing to theologise about. Of what, exactly, is it to proffer an interpretation? What comes within its purview?

There may be a Christian theology of work, of marriage, of art, of science, of political liberation, of almost anything, because faith integrates, so that theology, its intellectual expression, embraces all that one perceives. But there cannot be a Christian theology of the other religions, because religion embraces more than an outsider perceives. Theology theologises about things, garnering them into coherence, because faith, which it verbalises, is central, total, supreme; but for this very reason faith cannot be theologised about by an outsider. It is itself an organising principle, by which the person is open to the infinite and is enabled to see all that is finite in relation to that infinite. Therefore one community's faith is on principle precluded from being the object of another community's theology. Faith can be theologised only from the inside.

Of course, some might expect that I would demur to the phrasing 'of religions', since I have written a book to argue that that particular plural is conceptually invalid, even radically untenable; and not only have averred that those Christians are right who hold that Christian faith is not one of the religions of the world, but also have argued that 'neither is the faith of any other people'[1]. I am quite serious about this, and have become confident that the issue is fundamentally both valid and important. The verbal point, however, is of course in itself in some sense relatively minor, even though the substantive point that the wording conceptualises seems the more consequential and strong the more one tests it.

At play here is the issue that we developed earlier: of the fallacy of objectivity in thinking about human affairs. To treat man and his and her doings as if he or she were an object, even at the conceptual level, is to misrepresent – and, to a degree, to destroy. Nowhere does this principle apply so vividly as in religious matters, I have argued; and nowhere so germanely as in theological. All knowledge of man is (ideally) self-knowledge. Even more incontrovertibly, all theology is self-theology.

Herein, then, a Christian – or Islamic, or Hindu, or liberal-humanist – theology of the religions is an irrational concept, if it conceives them as 'other'.

Some readers will feel that I have gone altogether too far in this direction, have shown far too little sensitivity to the commitment of those Christians whose being Christian is, and is rightly, their central loyalty. On the contrary, I do have sympathy for their position, and indeed may point out that the same argument that I have just used in fact supports also it. For on these very same grounds one may contend – and I must contend – that theology of the religions is an irrational concept also, if it be a theology that is not Christian, or is not Islamic, or whatever – as a Christian or a Muslim or the like will quickly and legitimately see. The concept is untenable if it be a theology excogitated from outside every religious community; by, for instance, a universalist humanist in the irreligious sense. The liberal-humanist movement is no more capable of propounding a valid theology of Christian and Islamic faith (or, to use its own vocabulary, a philosophy of religion), than is a Christian or Muslim theologian of each other's. Christian faith is an awareness of a truth that transcends the empirical, which fact supplies the reason that no outsider can comprehend that faith in that outsider's vision; and supplies also the reason why the Christian cannot legitimately be asked to surrender part of his or her truth – to gratify an unappreciatively (undiscerningly) empirically based theory. A theology (or philosophy) that is less than Christian – or less than Islamic, or less than Hindu – will be not very helpful; nor even very interesting.

Once again, my way of getting out of this seeming theological impasse is to turn to history. Out of the dilemma as static theory, I shall propose that we can be salvaged by taking more seriously the dynamics of historical process. After our introduction, above, readers will hardly be surprised if I suggest that we can and should move forward into a new context and a new consciousness, which are becoming available on earth as a new day is in process of dawning in the intellectual and the religious history of humankind. Historical processes have begun in our day by which we can be carried beyond the limited involvements of our earlier circumscriptions, and beyond the logical paradoxes that they now involve, into something new and grander. If we become intelligently aware of these, and take creative advantage of their potentialities, we may well move ahead into a larger truth – which an enthusiast might be tempted to dub certainly not less than Christian, or Islamic, or whatever, and no longer even only Christian or Islamic or whatever, but a truth in some sense more than Christian, or at least more than what recently has been called that; more than Islamic, in the particularised sense of the term; transcending the adjectival truth of any partial group.

Yet, before we move ahead, and in order that we may be enabled to do so, the reader is invited rather to move back. However exciting our new developments, we do well to recall that history did not begin only this century. The problem in which we have found ourselves and out of which, I suggest, we are able now to move, is one also into which we moved historically, and indeed rather recently. The universalism that is beginning to become available to us, if we are wise, will be a recovery of a universalism that, it turns out, we lost as it were only the other day. The religious pluralism that challenges us is an issue that has arisen in the course of the historical development of each of our communities. It is a phase in each of our religious processes; and it has presented itself as intractable or disruptive only because our first efforts to cope with it were, perhaps not surprisingly, uncouth and inadequate.

In particular, so far as the theological problem is concerned, the conceptualisations that we recently have developed to handle the issues that seemed to confront us were inept, and have let us down. Indeed, not only have they proven incapable of solving the particular challenge that this matter presented; but they have also in fact distorted, it turns out, the several traditions themselves that recently engendered them. Moving ahead to a new vision capable now of interpreting our pluralism will restore the integrity of our older visions – an integrity threatened, we can now see, by succumbing to a false fragmentation.

When I say that the form of the pluralism problem as recently conceived was set by the conceptual categories used in confronting it, and say that those categories have turned out not appropriate, I am making no wild judgement. The assessment is not a mere private opinion. Admittedly, it is difficult for a culture to be critical of the categories through which it thinks; but for its intellectuals impossible not to be, once self-consciousness is made available, as it is by an historical awareness. The categories in this realm were themselves developed as unwitting innovations by the emergence of the very problem that, not surprisingly, they then showed themselves not up to solving. Traditional concepts were unselfconsciously modified under the impact of the new situation in a distorting way; and moderns then endeavoured for a time to cope with that new situation crippled by intellectualisations that were in fact part of the problem.

An example of what I here mean is vividly available in the concept 'faith'. We shall in our later chapters be looking at faith as a universal quality of human life; but here we look at it as a particular concept. The history of the notion will illustrate our general problem. Let us begin with the Christian instance. Everyone knows that for the New Testament, 'faith' is a saliently vital matter. In the Mediterranean world the idea is virtually introduced by the early Church (there were contemporaneous Jewish developments also), and certainly is developed by it centrally, creatively, dramatically. It plays a brilliant and powerful role in the writings of the New Testament; and, clearly, in the life and growth of the early Church.

Yet nowhere in the New Testament does the concept 'Christian faith' appear.

Faith is an orientation of the personality, to oneself, to one's neighbour, to the universe; a total response; a way of seeing the world and of handling it; a capacity to live at a more than mundane level; to see, to feel, to act in terms of, a transcendent dimension. The early Christians proclaimed that in Christ faith had become available to man, so that a new life thereby became possible: a new loyalty, a new courage, a new openness, a new ability to love and to trust and to hope, a new capacity to die; today we should add, to find life meaningful, to overcome alienation, to be bound in community with one's neighbour, and in integrity with oneself.

The historian must observe that in this the early Christians were right. In the Church men and women did find faith, and by it their lives were indeed transformed. And, not without certain ups and downs, this has been true, more or less, ever since. A Luther found faith so utterly significant a matter that he proclaimed that by it, and by it alone, man is saved. As an historian of human cultural life across the globe, I find myself wondering whether perhaps he was not right. The record makes it not absurd to suggest that faith, especially when one contrasts it with nihilism and despair, is about as important as Luther held. (None the less, the historian as he or she surveys the human scene can hardly but have sympathy also for the Catholic preference for faith informed by love.) However that may be, St Paul and the writer to the Hebrews were not alone in stressing it, nor was Luther: an Augustine, a Peter Lombard, an Aquinas, a George Fox and many another have thought and written about faith.

Explicitly about Christian faith, on the other hand, few, traditionally, have written. The first substantial theological book on it, so far as I know, comes in the nineteenth century. It was by Schleiermacher; and was mistranslated as on 'the' Christian faith only in the twentieth[2]. The German article, as found in *der christliche Glaube*, differs from the English: I myself have come to feel that the English phrase 'the Christian faith' is not serviceable; and even 'Christian faith', which I have used for a time, may give way to 'faith in its Christian form' or something of the sort, one may speculate. We shall return to this; I mention it now only to note that Schleiermacher, anyway, agreed. Despite his translators, his book is in fact about Christian piety 'and *other forms* of faith'[3]. It was later in the nineteenth century that a plural, speaking of the various 'faiths', came into general usage: so that one hears of the Christian faith, the Jewish, the Islamic, and the other faiths. (German writers still protest against this.)

This way of perceiving human religious life, though it quickly became established, was novel; and (to say the least) inaccurate. The pluralistic reification operative here was in addition to (but, indeed, was of course correlated with) that still more disastrous distortion whereby faith came to be imagined in terms of 'belief' – a process to which I have devoted a recent book and into which therefore I shall not go here. Even at the faith level, however, the systematised particularism was damaging.

Faith is a foundational category for all religious life, and, indeed, for all human life, as I have argued elsewhere at length[4]; as well as having been a conceptual category for Christian thinking. We shall be returning to this matter, therefore: meanwhile, let us note a quick analogy to this recent concretising development of '(the) faith', in the gradual reifying of the concepts also of 'religion' and 'theology'. So far as 'religion' is concerned, I have already traced the evolution of thinking fairly fully in my study, *The Meaning and End* . . . . The first book on *Christiana religio* was written in the late fifteenth century; and the phrase there meant 'Christ-oriented piety'. It was not until the nineteenth century that Calvin's great essay on 'Grounding in Christian Piety' was mistranslated as 'Institutes of the Christian Religion'. The notion (foreign, certainly, to Calvin) was by then becoming prevalent of a series of entities called religions, with Christians thinking of themselves as having one of them. Over by far the majority, however, of its twenty centuries thus far, Christians have participated in the Church and its on-going life, and in its succession of doctrinal formulations and institutional practices, and through these have found faith and renewal of life and have found God, have been found by Him, without any notion that what they were doing was in relation to one of various religions of the world. What I have called the on-going historical process in which they were participating generated for them this particular ideational pattern of 'the religions' (or in considerable part they adopted it, rather, to a considerable extent unwittingly, from their deist–humanist neighbours) rather recently. This is one more instance of their first and not very successful attempt to deal intellectually with the new situation of religious pluralism that the Church was encountering.

A similar course can be discerned in the Western development of the conceptualising of theology. A St Paul, an Augustine, a Wesley wrote and thought about theology; not about 'Christian theology'. This latter phrase would have seemed to them bizarre, and limited; would have seemed to concede too much. St Thomas Aquinas produced a *Summa Theologiae*[5]. We looking back may call that work a Christian theology; but we do so because we are aware, as he was not, that at about the same time a Shinran, in Japan, and a Ramunuja, in India, were theologising in divergent ways. It is not quite clear, however, that from our vantage point we do well to identify or to explain away his limitations by characterising his works as Christian theology, as though that adjective both justified and even sanctified those limitations, rather than seeing his system as, let us say, thirteenth-century theology. This latter is the epithet that in fact accounts for his omitting all reference to Buddhist Pure Land and Hindu Sri Vaisn̄ava faith. Were he alive today, we may be quite sure that he would take note of them!

St Thomas Aquinas, after all, with his powerfully integrating mind, brought into one conceptual system everything that came within the range of his vision. He was attacked at the time for being too independent, for being an intellectual not nearly subservient enough to traditional Church positions. He mightily brought to bear on his understanding of God, and of man's relation to God which is faith, and surely felt that he had to bring to bear on that momentous task, all the resources available to him. These resources included, of course, those proffered to him by the Church, its sacraments and its teachings and its devotional life. They included also the insights and teachings of whatever non-Christian civilisations he was aware of: specifically, of course, Greece; and monumentally, Aristotle. He was criticised for *that*, too: there were Christians at the time for whom it was not at all obvious that a right understanding of religious truth is attainable through a synthesis of Christian and 'pagan' thought, whereas to him it was obvious that one excludes from this great undertaking nothing that one knows. Less self-consciously, as we reminded ourselves earlier, he was responsive to Islamic culture, and especially Ibn Rushd ('Averroes'). He has been criticised for that, too.

Yet one might almost hear him answering that there is, indeed, something not merely petty, but, from the religious or faith point of view, skirting blasphemy, and, from the intellectual point of view, skirting irresponsibility, in approaching an issue of this seriousness with anything less than the fullest range of data, method and preparation.

Once we have come to recognise that the Christian form of faith has been one form, that Christian beliefs have been one set of beliefs, and that the thirteenth century is but one century in Christian history, we have no option but to reflect on faith generically, and about beliefs comparatively. As in the case of a Thomas (or of a Shinran, or a Ramanuja) we may come or may wish to come to a Christian (or Buddhist, or Hindu) view of faith, and of God. Yet, like Thomas's, it will be a view, however particular, of faith generically, and of God absolutely.

I may press that concept 'faith', since historically it has been central for theology (at least theology in its Christian form; also its Islamic, as we shall presently note). It will be central also to the theology of the future, I shall be arguing: the theology of comparative religion that we seek. Accordingly, it may serve nicely to illumine our general problem, and the question in what sense the new theology will be Christian, or Islamic, or whatever.

In classical Christian thought, then, faith, as the relation of man to God, the human response to the divine, the divine gift to man, has been conceived in absolute terms, not particularist. Until Schleiermacher, the faith of Christians was thought of simply as faith; not as one kind of faith, one out of many alternatives. This is true not only of Aquinas, but of every Christian thinker until 1800. The weight of this tradition is massive; we should not be surprised to find that it has persisted until today. In recent history other more particularist views arose, in response to the impinging new religious pluralism of the world's modern life; yet these did not fully oust from the Church this traditional outlook. (No doubt, some uncouth and complicated intermixtures did emerge.) The new development of conceiving 'Christianity' as one religion among many, was as we have said a notion derived in significant part from deist – humanist thought, where it served the 'Natural Religion' people, who envisaged the Christian and Jewish 'religions' as aberrations from a generic ideal. It was in large part appropriated by the Church rather than generated by it. Yet alongside it the older sense of faith persisted among Christians who rejected the new. Thus, a number of serious thinkers have asseverated that other groups around the globe are involved in religions but what Christians are concerned with is faith. (This was to misunderstand others, as the price for maintaining a significant insight for oneself.) Karl Barth, who culminated this trend, wrote to show into what problems of shallowness that other line of thought had mis-led the Church. (His own depth was accompanied by a narrowness that led the Church into other problems, perhaps at least equally devastating.) There are, however, other examples of a less aggressive sort. It is not only the New Testament in which we read of faith but not of Christian faith. In the 1971 edition of the *Encyclopaedia Britannica*, also, there is no article 'Christian faith' (and even no such entry in the voluminous index); while its article FAITH deals in fact only with the Christian instance. It speaks of faith as defined in Christian thought (its opening sentence) and of faith as a Christian virtue. But nowhere does it mention 'Christian faith', as if it were one among others. Of faith as known or experienced by other communities, it does not think to speak. It neither denies nor interprets; it ignores. [The same is virtually the situation with the entry FAITH in the new *Britannica III*, 1974.]

Another example is the several-hundred page article on Faith in the large *Dictionnaire de théologie catholique*, of 1920. By today's standards, the intellectual horizon of this article is woefully limited (virtually, for instance, to the Western world; as well as in other ways). And its vigorous polemic is engaged in controversies today strikingly dated. None the less, germane to our purpose is that this major contribution, of a major thinker, on a major occasion, interprets faith in altogether absolutist terms. To its author, faith is a particular relation to God: made available through Christ, and found normally in the Church. He writes therefore not of Christian faith; and, despite his lusty disagreements with various opponents, Protestant and Catholic, he writes not of right and wrong faith, or of true and heretical faith; simply of faith. He has no conception even of distorted, or inadequate, or mistaken, or unsalvific, faith. For him, faith is not the sort of thing of which there is more than one kind; and not the sort of thing that can be false. The only alternative is non-faith, or infidelity.

In the twentieth century, this reads oddly; although a similar position in a thirteenth-century writer, or a fifth-century or first-, is understandable. In the past, Christian theologians have on the whole considered faith only as it is met with in Christian instances. Similarly, Muslim theologians have in the past considered it only as met with in Islamic. And so it has gone. This is in no negligible part because those were the only forms that they knew.

Let us turn to consider the Islamic instance, for a moment. As usual, these issues can be more surely grasped if one can see them at work in at least two cases. Now Muslims, in both their classical and their mediaeval articulations of theological thought, also give central emphasis to a concept faith, *iman*, which they too have seen as the cosmic and decisive quality in human life. For them, too, salvation is by faith: the Day of Judgement in its catalepsis of the whole sweep of human history will divide mankind into two great groups: those with faith and those without. For the former, Paradise is prepared; and for the latter, Hell. In the entire range of Islamic theology, however, a concept of 'Islamic' faith is nowhere to be found, to my knowledge, and, indeed, in Arabic the phrase would be turbid to a degree.

In Arabic the definite article, as in German and French, is used for both the specific and the generic, both being distinct from the indefinite; so that *al-iman*, like *der Glaube* and *la foi*, could mean either 'faith' or 'the faith', or both. Yet there is no question but that faith, for Muslim thinkers, is a given, cosmically, and is not of various kinds. The theologians discussed back and forth whether a human being may have more or less faith, or whether it is, rather, decisively and simply a yes-or-no matter; but in any case, in kind as distinct from quantity faith has for Muslims been conceived as absolute and universal, undifferentiated.

As in the Jewish case, so in the Islamic, there is a strongly moralistic orientation to the whole religious enterprise. God is conceived as revealing primarily imperatives, and men's and women's response is an activist acceptance of their moral obligations. One of the definitions of faith commonly given by Muslims, on which I personally have done recently some quite entrancing inquiry, is that faith is one's existential *engagement* with what one knows to be true or good, obligatory. It is the committing of oneself to act in terms of what one recognises as cosmically valid. There were interesting discussions as to whether the commitment so to act requires also the acting in order to be faith.

I have found in the Arabic texts several passages where the characterisations of what faith is could be introduced word-for-word into Christian discussions without revision, and with considerable profit. Of course, in defining faith as a recognising of the generically true as true also for oneself, an active interiorising and personalising of what one knows theoretically to be valid, the Muslims took for granted that certain things are in fact true, good, valid, and are known to be so – matters on which outside their community there is in fact no agreement. Their world-view, however, was the framework within which they operated; and their notion of faith is formulated theologically within that schema, not in assessment of it. The same has tended to be the case also for most other religious communities' positions. Muslim theology (*kalam*) is a statement within, not about, their total position.

Taftazani, one of the most widely read of the later theological commentators, on whom I have done some work, is interestingly a whit embarrassed at times, it seems, in that his definitions of faith would seem on the face of it to apply perhaps also to devout non-Muslims; and he takes various steps to explain how this apparently logical inference can be circumvented. Even though he in fact recognises faith only in the form with which he is himself familiar, the one that we call the Islamic form, yet in principle for him, as for all Muslim thinkers, faith is absolute and potentially universal.

The situation is similar with Islamic theology as a whole. Paralleling the situation in Christendom, what we today call 'Islamic' theology was to Muslims themselves without adjectives. It never occurred to them to limit it conceptually. They were talking about God, not about some community's opinions about God.

Let me return, then, to our point that throughout most of history until very recently, Christian theologians have reflected on and theorised about faith only in those forms in which it has been implicated with Christian patterns. Muslim theologians have considered it only as implicated with Islamic ones. This was largely because they knew no other. They vaguely or remotely knew other patterns, without attending to them; but they did not know the faith that those patterns mediated. Largely, then, they knew no other form of faith.

More positively, although I would myself give this less weight, when they did think about the matter they actively supposed that other men and women, other religious communities, did not have faith. In this they were wrong, we now know. Yet it has troubled us unduly. Theologians of another age were wrong about many things, we now recognise; yet surely we can take that in our stride. All that we ask is that should have been right, or at least illuminating, about their own sector of the whole – about their own group's faith.

They did not know about other people's faith; may we not accept their ignorance as ignorance? There were many things that they did not know, about geology and the circulation of the blood and the shape of oceans and about human history. Add to this list, forms of faith other than their own. They did not know that such faith existed, let alone their not understanding and appreciating it, or not being able to interpret it theologically, or to integrate it into a grand pattern that would do justice to those other forms of faith and also to their own. That is our task, not theirs. We should neither chide them for having failed to accomplish it, nor be deterred by them from tackling it ourselves.

So much for the past. With an historical view, we can thus see both that our intellectual problem is relatively new, and therefore it is not surprising that it is as yet unsolved, and also that the preparation that we bring to the task is not so discouraging as it may at first have seemed. Classical formulations, although limited in scope, were in our matter more congenial in spirit, we can now see – were deeper, more open; were more, if one may say so, faith-ful – than were recent Christian positions. These we called above the Church's 'first and not very successful attempt to deal intellectually with the new . . . pluralism'. Its second attempt at a conceptual framework for coming to grips with this task it is called upon to make now. To it, current thinking must contribute constructively; and, given its vastly greater understanding of the data, both abroad and at home, can do so with confidence. At least, Christians will now be forming their interpretative categories more advisedly, more aware of what they are doing.

Obviously we have much to learn from the past two centuries; yet a certain amount also to unlearn. While our new attainment will have to be new, yet theologically it need not be bogged down in the impasses of the recent early gropings towards a solution. It may rather, and probably much more helpfully, be continuous with the universalist and absolutist aspiration of the earlier, more classical, phase of the process. The line that led from Schleiermacher to Troeltsch, and as well the line, opposing this, that led to Barth and Kraemer, can be transcended now, if not indeed dismantled, as we begin as it were again with new categories.

Indeed, we may draw some encouragement that the theology of comparative religion that we seek may legitimately be thus continuous with the highest formulations of classical Christian theology in the past; and not only so, but also and therein continuous with those of Islamic, and indeed Hindu, Buddhist, Jewish.

It is perhaps worth mentioning too that what we seek must be continuous also with the academic–humanist tradition. This too has aspired to universality and absolutism; although in fact, especially in its interpretations in the religious field, it too for a time achieved rather just one more point of view among others. Western academic studies of religious life, both oriental and Christian, tended for a time to be reductionist and dogmatic. They were often so far out of sympathy with what they were studying as to dismiss all transcendent involvement, either by prior resolute disparagement, with a commitment to the conviction that it is not there, or else by the more casual disparagement of studying only outward observables with a virtually deliberate ignoring of their meaning: a study of traditions without faith.

There was thus a time in the developing process of Western intellectual life when, as we have previously noted, the virtually official academic stand on religion constituted in effect a given ideology, at best naturalist not merely by conclusion but by starting point, which was explicitly an alternative to 'the various religions of the world'. Enlightenment rationalism was constituted in significant part by a negative critique of 'religion'. (Every major ideological movement, religious and not, has begun with a rejecting of the others.)

This stage is passing. The opening of new departments of religion in university faculties of Arts & Sciences around the world evinces a new openness. This represents something deeply significant and potentially creative: a new mode of inquiry rather than of attack; a new enterprise to study religion rather than either to teach it or to debunk it; a new humane seeking to understand, rather than either to defend or to explain away.

From this comes the most exciting of the new ventures in the study of religion in our day, the incipient endeavour to understand faith as a universal human quality. The last hundred years have seen the universities doing an impressive task of uncovering, reporting, analysing, the data of the variegated religious traditions of the world. If during the next hundred years we can make a comparably effective study of faith in its many forms, the results will be momentous.

It is in this context, too, that the present work emerges. It is a university that set up these lectures, that invited a public to attend and that did me the honour of inviting me to speak. And I came as from Harvard, in terms of my fundamental role, that of participant in a university enterprise. I am an intellectual, and envisage my task as first and foremost that of an intellectual; rejoicing to participate in the current evolution of the academic process in which the mind reaches out to wrestle with the intellectual problems of man's participation in the processes of faith; or, to use more participatory language, by which we, human beings who are intellectuals, wrestle with the questions of the history-long and world-wide participation of us human beings in the processes of faith.

Yet I speak also and at the same time as a Christian – in the sense defined above, as one who participates in faith in the process of the Church's on-going development; and as a theologian, actively in its intellectual history. Theology is an intellectual activity. Yet a Christian's theology should be informed not only by a wrestling with the truth but also by hope and by love. Some secular intellectuals, nearer to modern scepticism than to classical humanism – nearer to Bacon's notion that knowledge is power than to Socrates's that it is virtue; nearer to the multiversity than to the university – may perchance have found my argument in the past two chapters, in its purported rationalism, too optimistic, too readily inclined to assume that to know is to love and that true knowing requires loving, or at the least that true knowing of man requires a fundamental respect for the other and a reverence for his reverence; too old-fashioned in its holistic vision. Religious intellectuals, on the other hand – whether Christian, Jewish, Muslim, Hindu, Sikh, Buddhist or whatever – will presumably find that rational argument more cogent. So long as one is dedicated to a search for truth, and holds that Truth is, in theists' phrasing, God – or that, in any intellectual's faith perspective, it deserves and demands and rewards an integrated response of the whole person – then one finds persuasive, as the non-transcendentalist might not, the rational appeal to comprehensiveness, and the postulating of convergence of the true and the good.

Let us return, then, to the problem with which we began: a theology of the religions. An enhanced historical consciousness of the past can modify the question so as to help us to outflank its conundra. An historical consciousness of the present and of a potential future will help us answer it. We turn to that.

I must perhaps reiterate that I am not proposing to set forth here a theology of comparative religion. Alas, all of us are a long way yet from it. My aim rather is to delineate what sort of thing such a theology will be: what it is that we are seeking and what it means to seek it. That, I am venturesome enough to suggest, we have reached a position of being able at last to say. Furthermore, we are, I believe, moving into a position of being able to forge some of the new concepts that may serve to construct such a theology when it is produced.

Thus, we can not only recognise, but do something about the

recognition, that the theology required is a theology of religions, if at all, not in the sense of an objective genitive – a theology about religions; a Christian theology of other religions; or an academic theology of all of them. The exciting new phase in religious history, into which we are just on the threshold of entering, is the emergence of which we spoke in our historical section above: of a global and verified self-consciousness of religious diversity.

Given this, the theology to which we may aspire becomes a theology not 'of religions', if by that we mean something 'over there', something that other people do or have. Yet neither is it a theology of one religion, even as subjective genitive, even one's own; that too has become inadequate. All theology is self-theology, and yet it must exclude no one. History has brought us to a point where we can see, so far as 'a theology of religions' is concerned, not only that it is now requisite but also that it is now possible to have it in a sense more closely approaching that of a subjective genitive: a theology for which 'the religions' are the subject, not the object; a theology that emerges out of 'all the religions of the world', or I would say, all the religious communities of the world, or better still (incipiently) all the religious sub-communities of the world human community.

We have had in the past what has been loosely called a Christian or an Islamic theology, but on more careful analysis turns out to have been a theology of faith in its Christian forms, and one of faith in its Islamic forms. We are able nowadays, and indeed compelled, to speculate about, and to aspire towards, a theology of faith in its many forms. Even its Islamic forms, modern consciousness is aware, have been more various, more historically particular, than theologians used to realise. Similarly its Christian forms. And of course, Hindu forms have proudly been more variegated than the West used to know or to guess, and more historically evolving than India used to know or to care.

One hardly knows whether, in place of the unacceptable phrase 'of religions', something of our new involvement is communicated by my wording 'a theology of comparative religion'. Perhaps not. The phrase 'comparative religion' has become for a time prejudicial among many in the United States; although it has an honourable history in Britain, as in Canada. (The analogy is close with Comparative Anatomy, Comparative Literature, and the like.) Part of what one wishes to convey is the sense of including oneself, at the same time as embracing pluralism, at the same time as using a singular. What I have in mind might best be formulated, perhaps, as 'a theology of the religious history of humankind'.

This might, to the insensitive, still allow room for externalising? Similarly, 'theology in global perspective', otherwise attractive, might be perceived as non-self-engaging? Our task is to attain a theology of the religious history of *us* human beings on earth. Or, to articulate more clearly the basic issue, we should perhaps say: of the faith history of us human beings. Theology is critical intellectualisation of (and for) faith, and of the world as known in faith; and what we seek is a theology that will interpret the history of our race in a way that will give intellectual expression to our faith, the faith of all of us, and to our modern perception of the world.

We can thus also answer now the query about the adjective. In giving conceptual articulation to our faith, the faith of all of us, it must not dilute Christian faith – the faith of some of us – but transcend it. A theology of comparative religion must be Islamic, but it must not be an Islamic theology. Similarly, it must be Hindu, it must be Buddhist; yet – as any Muslim or Christian can see – it. must not be a Hindu or a Buddhist theology. Without being a Christian theology it would be invalid if it were not Christian, plus. It would be invalid also if it were not Islamic plus; Jewish plus; and so on. An analogy here from the ecumenical Church would be fairly straightforward. There is clearly a difference between an ecumenical (Christian) theology, and a specifically Presbyterian theology of ecumenicism; even though the former would not be valid if it were not in some sense Presbyterian, yet not merely Presbyterian.

St Thomas Aquinas, we may recall, produced not a 'Christian' theology, not an interpretation of 'Christian' faith, but a Christian view of theology, a Christian interpretation of faith. It was a thirteenth-century Christian view and interpretation, at that. Yet it was of human faith – or: divine faith.

I have argued that, on principle, there cannot be a theology of faith from the outside. Neither, however, can theology ideally be simply the personal statement of a single individual. Rather, it is a formulation of the faith of a community. It is produced, no doubt, by a person, but from and for a community. The theology of comparative religion, accordingly, must be the product of thinkers who see, who feel and, indeed, who know men and women of all religious groups and all centuries, as members of one community, one in which they themselves also participate. And this situation is just beginning – but *very* incipiently – to emerge.

Perhaps we should say, to emerge again; and the community to be visible to intellectuals, potential theologians. The mystics have seen, and felt, and indeed known, that community all along. Moreover, as a matter of sober fact, in the past it is primarily the mystics who have produced religious statements that can at all legitimately or even approximately be called a theology of religions. Twentieth-century history, however, is making this vision available to others of us as well. Modern knowledge, modern transportation, modern interinvolvements, all mean that the community to which, as religious persons, each of us is beginning to belong is now the community of humankind. We human beings have been religious in a great variety of ways. The variety of faith has been prodigious, we now know, even within one boundaried segment of our total community, such as the Christian Church. The task, therefore, is indeed exacting of any thinker who attempts to formulate a theology interpreting, intellectualising, our multiform faith. Clearly it is not yet possible to formulate such a theology adequately: the theology of comparative religion has not yet been written. This, however, I submit, is its task.

In practical terms, it has always been unrealistic for a Christian thinker to suppose that he or she could write a theology that would be acceptable to all Christians. None the less, in principle that has been valid as an ideal. Similarly, ideally the theology of comparative religion, when constructed, should be acceptable to, even cogent for, all humankind. (We may dream, may we not?) That is a long way off; it may be an eschatological rather than an historical goal? Yet we may not, must not, surrender it as an ideal. We aspire to a theology of the faith of man. More etymologically: we aspire to a statement of God and His diverse involvements with humankind.

Is there not a touch of blasphemy, now, in deciding to speak about God less comprehensively?

One way of putting what I am contending would be this: henceforth the data for theology must be the data of the history of religion. The material on the basis of which a theological interpretation shall be proffered, of the world, man, the truth, and of salvation – of God and of His dealings with His world – is to be the material that the study of the history of religion provides. Yet here once more come into play the difficulties of recent misconceptualisation. The phrase 'history of religion' has of late been used by Christians (and even by other Westerners) to designate the history only of religious communities other than their own. This drastic conceptual distortion has been institutionalised not only in theological colleges and seminaries but to a great extent also in Religion departments in academia – quite irrationally and nevertheless powerfully. It patterns the structure and permeates the mode of scholarly literature, organisation, and thought. One consequence is that a proposal to make the history of religion the basis for theologising will be heard by many as if this were suggesting a switch, rather than an enlargement, of one's outlook. Emotionally if not intellectually, many Christians will resist it, because they will feel or think that they are being asked to give up something; indeed, something precious; indeed, the most precious thing that they know, their Christian heritage and what it means to them. This would be ridiculous were it not bleakly sad. Not to see that Christian history, faith, truth are an integral and monumental part of the history of religion – the world history of human religious life – is both preposterous and poignant.

There is another dimension of the misconceptualising involved; and this error has obstructed those who call themselves historians of religion professionally, as well as theologians, from perceiving our new situation. It is the prejudice that we mentioned earlier about 'history': the positing of a concept of history that explicitly excludes the transcendent reference. Yet if there be anything that the study of human religious history across the ages and across the planet makes clear, it is that human history has regularly had a transcendent reference; that most human beings at most times and most places have lived historically in relation to the more than mundane. History is not a closed system; for in it stands man, open to the infinite. The study of religious history has been a study of the observable results of that fact, the data of the traditions. Yet it is an inadequate study of history if it omit or ignore the massive fact itself, the faith that the traditions have everywhere nurtured and expressed. The history of religion is the history of man's (Christian and other) continuing involvement, within history, in transcendence.

Those who feel, for instance, that theology's task is to explicate, say, revelation rather than history, perpetrate a quite false dichotomy. We shall return to the concept 'revelation' in later chapters; for the moment I affirm but this, that all revelation that has ever taken place has taken place in history. The Christian theologian who is invited to make the history of religion his or her data base is being asked not to neglect Christian revelation (nor the

Muslim theologian, Islamic) but to interpret it within the context in which in fact it has occurred – that of world history; and also to ponder the newly available information about other revelation. Indeed, he and she are being invited to use the conceptual category 'revelation' only, if at all, in a way that is intellectually appropriate to our new and enlarged awareness of what has in fact been going on.

The task of theology is to make rationally intelligible the meaning of human life in faith, and of the world in which that faith is lived.

I have disclaimed propounding here and now such a theology. Yet I am haunted by the challenge to contribute something towards it. That consideration will allow us to close this chapter, with a resolution of the question that constitutes its title: in what sense is the theology that we seek 'Christian'? Let us not be carried away by my enthusiasm for universalism. However disappointed various Christians among my readers may be at my not being nearly Christian enough, one may be quite sure that any Jews or Muslims or Buddhists or Hindus who may read this will readily have recognised my approach as a *particular* interpretation, redolent with what they will perceive as Christian orientations, innuendo, preconceptions, and the like.

Indeed, the whole problem, as I hinted at the beginning, has a specifically Christian formulation. 'Theology' has been first a Greek metaphysical and then a Christian concept, historically. The Islamic counterpart, *kalam*, has not been quite the same thing, and I realised that I was paraphrasing and taking liberties in setting aside the differentiations. In the Hindu world there has been no distinct field of intellectual endeavour quite corresponding to theology; nor (for different reasons, and until quite recently) in the Jewish. For the Buddhist, of course, the phrase would constitute a merry malapropism.

Moreover, the notion of 'faith', on which I build, and to which we shall in our next chapters attend still more seriously, has centrally been after all a Christian–Jewish–Islamic concept, until recently. I myself have been working towards forging a new conceptualisation for faith that will be appropriate for other traditions as well; I am well aware that considerable refinement in our understanding is required before the concept can serve adequately the new tasks that it is being called upon today to fulfil. (That same refinement, however, is requisite before it can today and tomorrow serve even internally in the Christian, or even the Islamic, case.) None the less, the fact that this term comes primarily from a Christian background, and that we have no word, either in Western languages or in oriental, for the new concept that is being born, constitutes a problem – and illustrates our challenges.

Can we not say, then, that the theology towards which we strive shall be global; and that in the meantime what I can proffer is a Christian contribution to it? Inadequately Christian, certainly: yet, inescapably so. Or perhaps we should simply say: a Christian's contribution to it. As I shall stress in our final chapter, our task is, finally, a collaborative one. My aspiration is to participate Christianly in the total life of mankind – the intellectual life, and the religious, as well as (as we already all do) the economic and political. And I invite others to do so Jewishly, Islamically, Buddhistically, or whatever – including, humanistically.

It will not be easy to build on earth a world community. It will not be possible, unless each of us brings to it the resources of his or her mind, and his or her faith.

7 Muslim? Hindu? Jewish? Buddhist?

A Theology of Comparative Religion with Special Reference to Communities other than the Christian

The preceding chapter posed a question as to whether, and in what sense, the theology of comparative religion that we envisage could or should be Christian. Our answer was that it could and should be Christian as much as it could and should be Islamic, Hindu, Jewish, and the rest: that it should be historically continuous with the ongoing evolution of each community's thought until now, the appropriate next step in the development of all. The world theology will not displace but subsume its erstwhile sectional parts. The degree of its verification or failure will be measured, one might almost say, by its ability not to destroy but to fulfil.

Yet, however generic in principle, the presentation thus far has been in fact from a Christian's hand. The argument, however cogent in intention as to inherent intellectual validity, may in fact appear addressed to a Western audience. One must ponder these matters more directly in relation to the world's other major forms of faith. It would be both just and helpful if we could see how the problem might present itself to the orientations of other groups.

To do this in any adequate fashion would be a formidable assignment, far beyond the scope of this present introductory work. Unless I were persuaded that it could in principle be done (and that in fact it will be done, in due course), obviously I would not now propound it even as a suggestion. (Nor, indeed, would I publish this book.) None the less, I leave it as hardly more than a suggestion, here almost unelaborated. On the other hand, a brief introductory essaying of this question here may serve to exemplify an approach, to illustrate diversity (perhaps that is hardly needed?), and to set the context for our then more particularist statement.

For any such attempt, an array of four instances furnished by Islamic, Buddhist, Hindu and Jewish would seem to provide a significant range of positions. Superficially, and in schematic form, one might outline this range perhaps as follows. *Vis-à-vis* a theology of comparative religion as conceived in Christian terms or in continuity with Christian concerns, the Islamic problem might be seen as formally quite similar – and for that reason in some ways perhaps the most intractable. The issue would be that of, as it were, translating the position delineated into Islamic terms. At the opposite pole, the Buddhist would be similar substantially but starkly divergent formally. For the very notion of theology is in this case quite inappropriate, not merely in the talk about 'God' but also in the attitude to talk, as such: the ascription of a normative idealised role to a conceptual system formulating one's version of ultimates. The Hindu case would be of a different sort: one might aphorise here that, at the conceptual level Hindus have already and indeed long since come up with theoretical interpretations of religious diversity that are comprehensive, perceptive and metaphysically supportive, whereas it is at the sociological level that their problem lies. The question here is to translate 'the essential unity of all religions', to use a Hindu phrase[1], into an historical unity here on earth as well. The cohesion of Hindu society has been attained not through shared ideas, but through the non-universalisable caste system. The Jewish position, finally, could be seen as exemplifying quite another type of orientation. Over against the Christian and Muslim, this community does not in principle envision all humankind's being Jewish, so that traditionally there is not a question of one religious theory to which Jews may loyally subscribe, on the one hand, and that will cover all human instances of faith, on the other. For the Jew, however inscrutably, it is God's will that one rather small community be religiously Jewish, other persons being answerable to God for their conduct, individual and social, within the framework of being something else.

I have oversimplified, of course. Let us look at each of these a little more closely. Above, I spoke of my aspiring to participate Christianly in the one spiritual community of all humankind, and in the constructing of a theory for it – a community of communities, and a theory of pluralism; and I invited others to do so as Hindus, Buddhists, or whatever. I have wondered whether I might allow ourselves to speculate on how things might look if this invitation were taken up. My inevitable ineptitude and inadequacy in attempting this have to be taken into account. Yet I have decided to risk it, on the grounds that the damage done by that inadequacy will conceivably be outweighed by the usefulness of illustrating, even if not too accurately, the kind of thing involved, or at least its scope, and the multiform context within which our task is set. Let me try, with due apologies to those concerned. I shall not attempt to develop an independent position in each case, however sketchily; rather, to proffer a comment on my own position that has been set forth, or on the invitation. Of course, from the beginning it must be clear that this part of the endeavour is suggestive only. By assigning one chapter to all four, compressing each into a few paragraphs, over against two chapters for a Christian focus, above and below, I am deliberately making clear that I am not trying to develop a series of points, but to make, simply, one.

If I were a Muslim, I should imagine myself responding in somewhat the following way. In the first place, I should have to remark that my very willingness to participate in the discussion already raises an issue, of no mean import: one of basic attitude and of present context. You yourself, I would say, have stressed the historical dimension of human thinking and being, and have argued that it is the present moment in world religious development that provides the particular occasion for 'the next step' that you propound. You are right that history is important – theologically important; and no doubt you do well to appeal to present-day requirements and future possibilities in your call for a new global theology. History is important also, however, and this you tend to overlook, as the immediate past. One must reckon with the circumstances that have led us to our present situation, and in some degree constitute it (and us), as well as with those that may lead us out of it. In the realm of inter-community encounter, those circumstances are these: that in an era when our fortunes here on earth were ebbing, when the mundane ('historical') position of Islamic life was, after its earlier glory and brilliance, going through a rather weak phase, while Christendom's was blustering into new and expansive power, you attacked us. You, as Western civilisation, attacked us literally, with guns and economic might and at times ruthless and certainly heavy domination. As Christians, even apart from your complicity in worldly imperialisms, you attacked us theologically. You ridiculed our faith patterns. You sent your missionaries, resolute to defeat our faith and confident that you would conquer us spiritually. You failed. Those were difficult times for us, confronted with your intellectual sophistication, cultural buoyancy, and wealth. Yet morally and spiritually we held our own. You made hardly a single convert, for all your vast effort; although you did succeed in pulling some few from among our group, educated in Western ways, away from all faith. Then, just as we are emerging from this struggle, having managed to turn back at last the onslaught of your missionary vehemence and your secularist denunciations, we find ourselves being approached in a new way, with the voices of sweet liberalism, the blandishments of 'dialogue', and a parade of gentleness. Frankly, we are suspicious.

Most of my community distrusts yours: not because of what you are saying, but because of what your fellows have said, and done. You yourself have stressed that the gulf between religious groups is deep and wide. History is too imperious, the immediate past history of our interrelations is too bitter, for that gulf to be bridged by a simple gesture of goodwill, or a nice new theory.

Having made that major point, however, I may go on in a different key, our supposed Muslim may perhaps be imagined to continue. Most of my community, we may hear him saying, turn from your new overtures in sorry disbelief. A handful among us, however, and I personally happen to be one, we may suppose him to aver, rightly or wrongly do listen, and are willing to risk involvement. We recognise that some in the Church, even in high places, are insincere, hoping to use the new strategies as covert devices for the old proselytising ambitions. Others are perhaps more innocently oriented to undermining firm faith with its present-day watered-down liberalistic substitute, wishy-washy and formless: one part goodwill, two parts momentum from an inherited faith tradition no longer alive, and three parts scepticism. None the less, others in the Church, some few of us have come to perceive, are genuinely struggling to move drastically beyond the earlier conflicts. Of this minority the motives seem perhaps genuine, and among us a minority is tempted to trust, and to collaborate. Moreover, we recognise that in fact our community too is in disarray; that modernity, and not merely Westernisation, suffuses our life; and that the future of our community is integral to and with the future of the human race, in its coming global interdependence. Our *ummah* is no longer a self-subsistent community, independently viable. Besides, we have something to contribute, not only to our own survival but to the world's.

Therefore, I should be inclined to come to grips with this issue in somewhat the following way. I should begin by observing that I understand the problem, and even your Western way of formulating it; although those of us who are Muslims, I would say, have never taken theology so seriously as has the Christian Church, and especially not during recent centuries. None the less, with certain deeply important reservations, we have tended to ask the same kind of question as have you, however different our answers. We give formulated expression to faith more congenially in moral–legal patterns than in abstract intellectual ones; what we call *sharī'ah* and you sometimes call 'law'. Piety, for us, is a practical, not primarily a theoretical, matter. Yet I admit that we can now see that the *sharī'ah* framework has been a phase within our total evolution, and can also see that it fundamentally rests upon a prior theoretical orientation of our faith, down to which we must also once again dig in rethinking anything so basic as not our interrelations among ourselves nor our personal relation to God or His to us but our relations (and God's relations) with our fellow human beings outside our *ummah* community.

Up to a point I would even agree with, and indeed stress, the substance of your 'theology' notion: not in the sense of systematic theology as an important branch of study, which with us it is not, but then you yourself do not think of it as a 'discipline', either. I mean here theology in the straightforward sense of talking or thinking about God; and I would certainly stress that approach, in the sense that the fundamental motif of our whole tradition, as well as the fundamental convergence point for all forms of faith, is God. As you know, a central Islamic thrust is the affirmation (and the exhortation to recognise) that He is one – for all men, everywhere. You never hear us speak in those absurd or blasphemous ways about the God of the Christians, the Jewish God, the God of the Hindus. We certainly never talk of *our* God. We are His. He is not ours! Another central thrust, also of salient import for comparative religion, is our emphasis that He is transcendent. *Allahu akbar*, as we say. This means not 'God is great!', as it sometimes gets rendered, but 'God is greater!' – than anything whatever: certainly than religion, than any one religion or than they all; greater than our law, than our ancestors' or any men's idea of Him, than our or other men's faith.

Another point is that traditionally we have had the concept of every people's having its own prophet. In the past, admittedly we have tended, like most groups, to perceive other communities' religious systems in the terms of our own; and therefore to interpret literally in this connection 'prophet' and ideas of scripture, as in our 'People of the Book' idea. In the future, we may well learn to do this more metaphorically, accepting the analogy that Christ is to Christians as the Qur'an is to us, that the Word of God has appeared to us in verbal form, but to the Christian community in the form of a person, in the figure of Jesus Christ; and so on. More startling to some of my fellow Muslims would be the interpreting in this way of what many of us, like most Christians in the past, have sometimes misperceived as 'idols' – serving Hindus and Buddhists as the form for them of God's revelation. This would not, however, startle *all* my fellow Muslims, by any means; for our Sufis, not least in India, have been saying this now for many centuries. In fact, by drawing on the mystic Sufi component of our tradition thus far, which is still very much alive in our world, we could give our participation in the world community's religious multiformity depth and warmth and force, to say nothing of an altogether unrivalled poetic expression. The philosophic tradition in our classical and mediaeval past, also, which is being restudied by some in our community these days, is one more source for a humanist and universalist conceptualising of faith, less powerful than the Sufi no doubt but still certainly not negligible. One of my fellow Muslims also, a practising psychiatrist but deeply interested in questions of faith, has publicly agreed with you that there may indeed be a significant analogy as suggested between our pious practice of committing the Qur'an to memory and the Christian celebration of the Eucharist – remote though this seemed at first[2].

As you could predict, I am not altogether content with a phrasing that the task in this realm could be posited as the translating into Islamic terms of a theology of comparative religion that, presumably valid for both groups, might first have been formulated in Christian terms or even Western academic terms. One might, however, perhaps turn that around and suggest that the validity of such a theology, if set forth in concepts appropriate to Christians, could be tested by the possibility of its purport being expressible also and in some fashion equivalently in Islamic concepts – concepts continuous with ours historically and intelligible to us, cogent for us. Like Christians, we too have tended to conceptualise our faith in terms that gave the impression, at least – even to many within our own group – of exclusivism: of a once-for-all revelation, historical, particular; and of missionary proclamation, envisaging universalism partly in chronological terms of proselytising, with an eventual world-wide community constituted by, in our case, Musalmans. Like Christians too, however, we have all along in part known, and some of us today can see quite clearly, that God's will for that eventual global community is in some ways subtler than that. We have all along known, and today feel the more clearly, that to discern His will for us today is exacting, transcending, and something that we have, in fear and trembling though not without guidance, to learn.

Finally, if you conceive of me as a Bangladeshi Muslim – after what we went through in 1971; but I imagine that many Iranian and Turkish, also Indian and Indonesian, Muslims will concur – then you will not be surprised to hear me agree that the historical Muslim community, not least in West Pakistan, could indeed be served by a more active and accurate perception of a theology of comparative religion. We Muslims, like you Christians, have to learn to get along with others, and it is a fallacy that God does not really want us to do so.

If we call next on a Buddhist, he will reply first with the observation: What I am to say will, of course, depend on whether you conceive me as a Theravadin or as a member of one or another of the many and richly differing Mahayana groups. In Tokyo and Kyoto in recent years, intellectuals, especially of Pure Land and Zen persuasions, have been actively publishing in the realm of Christian–Buddhist interrelations, especially in the realm of comparison of ideas, if not so much in the wider range of globally comparative theology; and Comparative Religion has been an active study in Japanese universities since the 1890's. Let me therefore situate myself, our imaginary interlocutor might go on, rather in the Theravadin wing, primarily; though I shall try to keep in mind the wider range of our diversified community.

To begin with, yes, you are right in saying that the terms of reference fall oddly on our ears; and yet with the spirit of what you are proposing our hearts are definitely in tune. Of all the great 'religious' movements in human history, if we are to use your terminology, we Buddhists certainly see the point when you

Christians sometimes say that the mood and quality of ours has had the closest affinity with yours, even though formally between the two the divergence is stark. Indeed, we feel that ours is not a religion at all, and I was happy to hear you say that yours is not either; but you do use the adjective 'religious', and that seems to us not merely unfortunate, but definitely obfuscating. We began by rejecting religion, in its several forms in India, rather like some of your Western rationalists and secularists; and in some ways we would wish to compare ourselves rather with the Greek philosophic and Western humanist outlook. I was interested to hear that you would include those among the major religious traditions of the world; we will think about that. We have met a comparable question in the case of the Confucian tradition in China, I admit. In any case, while we are quick to sympathise with the moral dimension of the goal of recognising global community, we are not sure that your attempt to make what you call a theology for it is our cup of tea. As you yourself rightly said, it is not only that we are perplexed, even offended, at the wording involving talk of 'God'. We are sceptical also of the whole tenor of an enterprise involving some theological-type ideational scheme. Our community boasts many intellectuals; but the Buddha saw clearly that metaphysical systems of ideas do not salvage humankind from its woes. The aphorism 'Christians believe in God; Buddhists believe in meditating' illustrates not the actual point at issue here – it is much too quippish – but the kind of difference on which I am trying to touch.

Another way of making my point might be to remark that few Buddhists have had the counterpart problem to that Christian for whom theology has been an obstacle to brotherhood: the Christian who sees the moral inference from his revelation to be towards community with all humanity, regardless of religious affiliations, yet sees the theological inference – even when he says, 'alas' – to be away from it.

In this attitude to the role of ideas we diverge also even from the Western rationalist tradition, which I mentioned just now. Altogether we tend to perceive what we seek not as an alternative to what you would call other systems, whether religious or other, but as of a different order. I suppose that here there may be some sort of parallel to the Barthian 'Others have religion but we have faith' notion! That might be worth exploring. You must admit, though, that we have been a good deal less explosive and more irenic about it – although, admittedly, missionary. Although we have not made so much of that particular concept, I do think that your concern with 'faith', as a generic human quality, may prove a good deal more promising than your talk either of theology on the one hand or of comparative religion on the other.

It is not only that we Theravadins are explicitly atheist. Admittedly that can be seen as ultimately a verbal issue, and some of us have agreed with the thesis that our concept of *dharma* can perhaps fruitfully be compared – and contrasted! – with the Christian concept 'God'. Rather, my point would come out in the fact that even our Mahayanists, who some of you Westerners have thought have succumbed more to what you call the religious mode, have developed their movement throughout the Far East alongside of, and interpenetrating with, the so-called religions of the people there. To the confusion of some outside observers, we Theravadins in Ceylon, Burma, and the like, as well as our Mahayana brothers in China and Japan, as well as in a different fashion our fellows in Tibet, and so everywhere, have not ceased to practise traditional religious ways on becoming Buddhist, nor have our missionaries asked people to do so. I do not wish self-righteously to be blind to a few exceptions here and there; none the less, in general I think that you would agree that inter-religious conflict has not been one of our problems through history.

Once I have made these points, however, let me conclude by saying that nevertheless, as a *Buddhist*, I of course share your concern for human brotherhood throughout the world; and, as an *intellectual* (and the first heading of the Noble Eightfold Path is right ideas), I share your concern for conceptual clarity and for the communication intellectually as well as every other way of insights that will conduce to it; as an *historian* – and a human being – I of course recognise that not only Buddhists have been, or are, inspired to seek these goals; and as a *modern man* I of course recognise that our century is impelling us towards new inter-involvements. We in our community are certainly ready to sit down with men of goodwill and of intellectual striving wherever they be, to participate jointly in the momentous task of our age, of turning our world society into a world community. Indeed, we are not merely ready; we have already begun. And while our conceptualisation of what it will involve may be different from yours, we are sufficiently accustomed to differing at the conceptual level even among ourselves that that does not bother us, and we trust that it will not bother you.

It may even turn out that our ideas, too, will in the process change. Maybe you will end up with something less theological, less comparative-religionish, than you expect; but maybe we shall, with something more so than we expect. Many of us have long held that there have been more than one Buddha – one of our group in China spoke of 84 trillion; maybe we shall find on deeper inquiry that what you call religious leaders are what we call 'Enlightened Ones'. Many of us have long held that Dharma is a transcendent truth, far beyond all our words for it and yet personal, lived, immediate: not personal in your Western sense, for we do not believe in 'persons' in the Western sense, yet humane. Provided that you leave us room for our integrity, count us in on your project.

Next, a Hindu. Again, we have to choose one from among hundreds of sorts of Hindu, or, again, imaginatively construct some kind of amalgam. Can we not hear him speak somewhat as follows? We Hindus understand perfectly your problem even though we have never understood the conspicuous difficulty, even anguish, that you have had with it. For us it all seems relatively simple, since we tend to feel that we have it solved. It is true that historically India has not in its classical and mediaeval phases been quite so free of religious controversy as our modern apologists would make out. It may be that our recent thinkers, elaborating what Western scholars like to call neo-Hinduism, have in fact been more original and creative than either they themselves or others have fully recognised. A Vivekananda, startling his unaccustomed Western audience with his irenic universalism at the Parliament of Religions at Chicago in 1893, a Radhakrishnan, an Aurobindo, may prove to be more significant contributors to the process of which you speak, that of world religious integration, and less merely champions of an inherited Indian vision. This would make them more significantly active and innovative participants in on-going religious processes, to use and to illustrate your conceptual analysis, than we thought. However that may be, I personally can hardly doubt but that the interpretations of diverse religious forms set forth already in mediaeval times by, for instance, a Ramanuja, and many another thinker from the Upanisads on, will be of profound and creative significance in our Hindu contribution to a world theology, or philosophy of religion; and even, soon, to Christian formulations of that theology. The greatest Christian theologians of the past have profited from a Plato and an Aristotle; I cannot see why those of the future may not or will not profit from a Sankara.

So far as our learning from you is concerned, that has already begun – and in earnest. During the last hundred years the profundity can hardly be exaggerated of India's delving into and transforming its intellectual and religious outlook in relation to Western orientations. We have not simply substituted yours for ours, however, and I personally think those Westerners mistaken who imagine that we are merely following behind the West but inevitably moving in the direction set by it: becoming secular, for instance, in the Western sense of that confusing and in some ways threatening word. The religious history of India is very decidedly in process. It is in process of its own internal development, as well as of participating more and more, both actively and receptively, and indeed self-consciously, in the growing inter-religious history of humankind to which you call attention.

Now I admit two things, both of which will perhaps lead to strikingly significant new developments in our process as it continues to proceed. Since we have no fixed pattern to which as such it is our business to be loyal, we can contemplate such newness with equanimity, and even excitement; though once again I insist on our independence and self-responsibility, our critical proceeding. One thing that I admit is that our polymorphic monism, though it has given us an intellectually satisfying interpretation of all religious forms whatever, has never really come to intellectual grips with those who do not themselves sympathise with it – most conspicuously, Islamic and Christian exclusivists. Although we can interpret them, in our own terms, we really have never understood how any intelligent or sensitive person can hold that one religious position, his own, is right and all others wrong, which is what Muslims and Christians seem to us to be saying. We cannot imagine how people can be like that; and cannot imagine how God can be thought of as like that. They are so, however; and He is so thought. And we must put our minds to it. I am not quite sure whether in the end they will abandon these positions, or whether we shall change our theories in order better to accommodate them (our present ones really do not, as I say). I am not sure whether there is a third alternative.

Your appeal to history rings unusual in our ears; traditionally we approach problems analytically and conceptually, rather. You are right, however, that historically these exclusivist – to us, arrogant – movements have played enormous roles on earth, have commanded the allegiance of thousands of millions of men, and inspired them to much greatness – although historically also they seem to us to have wrought from time to time enormous havoc on earth.

This brings us to my second admission: on the question of sociological integration. You are right that developments of the modern world, technological and economic and all that, are bringing us into a quite new type of world togetherness, and generating or requiring quite new social interrelationships. Traditionally our conceptually diverse positions in what you call our 'Hindu' complex have had as cohesive social force sociological structures of considerable firmness that are, in principle, explicitly limited. We have been met, then, with the charge that, while a Christian or a Muslim may think that outsiders will go to Hell for their views when they die, none the less in the meantime the Christian or Muslim is quite willing on earth to sit down and have lunch with them. Now, of course, if I wished, I could come back at this by retorting that actually this is not quite true; that not merely the Crusades and the Pakistan/East-Bengal business but also apartheid in South Africa, and much else, and the whole sorry history of anti-Semitism, have been in sizeable part a function of a we–they metaphysics of the saved–damned dichotomy of traditional Christian and Islamic thought.

I do not wish, however, to turn this into a polemic or even a debate. To do that would be to succumb to the very bipolar stance that I am decrying. What will or should happen to the caste system in modern world integration, I do not know. Americans proclaim that all men are created equal. To us that is not 'self-evident'; not on the equality matter, but we do not believe that men and women are created. Their souls we see as eternal – and equal. The part of men and women that comes into historical mundane existence in a particular context and form, on the other hand, seems to us self-evidently not equal. Certainly there has been mistreatment and abuse with our system, as with all; though some of us are not convinced that what your Western sociologist Dumont calls our *homo hierarchicus* is inherently absurd, or that the future manifestly lies with that kind of total and stark egalitarianism that has no concept of respect for authority, nor for parents, and no sense of moral responsibility of each person for the development of his own character and the performance of his work in society with its rewards. To hold that the irresponsible is equal with the responsible strikes us as frankly irresponsible.

Of both human beings and religious systems, we do see the

ultimate unity as transcendent, rather than historical; there you are right. Perhaps, however, we are coming to an awareness of history as surely as the Western world is of transcendence. Yet for us history is not, as the West still seems to imagine, on a track towards some goal. It is the arena for personal salvation, not the avenue towards corporate. God we see as not active in history in the sense of striving to salvage its course, to make it go in some divine direction; He saves men and women within history, from within history, by enabling them to transcend it.

Nevertheless, as the context for salvation, we must note that it is indeed a changing context. In the new intermingling into which historical movements are leading us, we have much to learn, most vividly in the realm of mundane effectiveness. We have suffered enough from Western arrogance to be suspicious, but in any move genuinely to collaborate in the constructing of an intellectual groundwork for global harmony we are ready and happy to participate. Our inclination would be to stress ideas that will contribute to mutual respect for differences, while undergirding the colourful diversity within mankind, rather than processes that may conduce to integration but pressure or force conformity. Your very hypothesis of a theology to embrace all religious positions smacks of the old Western or Christian notion of a single doctrine for all. We would look rather for a multiplicity of doctrines – and for that matter, of non-doctrinal orientations too – of each of which a component would be a clear recognition that it is partial, and that other men may disagree and still be right. In other words, we should much prefer a spiritual mood in which human beings agree to differ, rather than a striving after some theoretical position about which there would ideally be no need to differ.

The Jew enters our discussion from an altogether unusual situation. I join in an enterprise of this kind, we can almost hear him saying, awkwardly, embarrassingly. We Jews have always been able to recognise religious diversity, with ourselves as one small group in a larger world. We have not itched to impose our position, or any one position, on the rest of the world, even theoretically, the way you Christians, and to a lesser extent you secularists, have done. All that we have asked is that we be allowed to live our religious life in our own way – and that, we have been denied. More than any other group on earth, we have suffered from the implacable...hatred, shall we say?, of others, and especially, of course, of Christians. We have been victims of fanaticism, brutality and horror whenever men have succumbed to the ugly side of human life; but even at the very best of times and in the case of decent and upright Christians we have been victims of theories that accorded us as Jews no legitimate metaphysical status, and therefore no secure earthly one. Of course, therefore, we are interested in any discussion that aspires to move beyond a phase, as you would like to have it, in the world's religious history that denied us room, and in this century denied us life. Yet to ask us to participate in the discussion is perhaps a whit uncouth; no? It is not our problem, but yours. In so far as our hope has not been crushed, our ability to trust not wrenched from us, we do not have to learn to accept others, intellectually; do not have to change our understanding of our truth.

If, however, you ask us to contribute precisely from our position as observers (and victims) of the problem, perhaps we can attempt that. We see our task, under God, as in part that of bearing witness to the moral stature of man (of all men and women) and the divine imperative to cherish it. When you say that religious diversity among human beings poses an intellectual problem, a moral problem, and a theological problem, we see the first two, feeling the second especially; and we recognise that the third is the case for some groups, especially Muslims and above all Christians. (Despite our current problems with the Arabs, throughout the general course of history we have suffered less from Muslims than from Christians, have found the Islamic position less intolerant conceptually as well as socially.) And it is not merely our own suffering that engages us, vivid though that be in our minds and hearts. Looking out over human affairs in broad perspective, we note deeply and poignantly enough the general devastation that wars of religion have recurrently wrought in history, and the fragmentation of human community that religious cleavage has wrought. Yes, we must respond. And you are right, of course, that we have already become deeply engaged in the actual interpenetrating among communities that you stress. While we Jews don't read Buber as much as you do, we do read Tillich and Harvey Cox, earnestly; and the day has long passed that we write only for ourselves. As the word 'assimilation', however, connotes, this very matter constitutes a problem for us, as do more generally its much, much wider ramifications: our involvement in a society only in minute, and diminishing, part our own. The problem, however, is not at the theological level.

I agree with my Hindu colleague's remark that the chief point to look out for is the preservation of differences, the dignity of deviation. To recognise and to guarantee that is the central point. We would base our insistence on it, however, not, like them, on an epistemological theory or any analysis of man's capacity or lack of capacity to conceptualise ultimate truth: their thesis that, in the Vedic phrase, truth is one, men calling it by different names. They have treated us well, historically; and yet we sympathise a whit with Christians and Muslims on this in sensing it as a threat to true distinctiveness: a smothering embrace that we are all Hindus at bottom (–at top, I suppose they would say). No: we Jews base our sense of difference, rather, on what you would call a firm and definite theology, held without apology. Or in our own terms, rather: squarely on God's revealed will, revealed particularly, at a given time and place.

It is not the case, in our view, that all men are called to a common destiny. For His own purposes, God has assigned to us, a small handful of men, a special role of suffering.

This correlates with our moralist orientation, which you Christians have called legalist. It correlates too with our suspicion of theology, with its dubious pretensions. There is a remark of a mediaeval Islamic thinker of which I am very fond, and which I am surprised that our Muslim colleague just now did not cite against you – there are similar Jewish observations, but I quote this one in order to broaden the point. And he was protesting not even against theological pretensions, but against mystical. Over against the Sufi's zeal for knowing God, he pronounced: 'Our task is not to know God, but to serve Him'. The sum and substance of our Jewish faith is our dedication to, our joy in, serving God as He has instructed us. Other people should serve Him as He has instructed them, or as they think best, or should go about their business as they choose; our only global, inter-community principles are two. The first is that both we and others should be left to do so without interference, or at least without being massacred. Secondly, we are instructed so far as the outside world is concerned to bear witness to, and to serve, general human justice, mercy, humaneness. But we do not at all hold that the particular burden laid upon us is incumbent upon others. Neither do we claim to know, or seek to know, why God has chosen us to suffer, or to witness in a special way, to carry peculiar and unbearable responsibilities; while of others He seems to ask much less. His will is inscrutable: our task is to obey it, not to scrutinise it, not to speculate about it in what seems to us your armchair theologising way. The devastating instances around the world of man's inhumanity to man in intercredal strife – in northern Ireland and eastern Bengal, to take two current examples in which we for once are not involved but that yet pain us to observe: these are moral problems, not theological problems. If groups more theologically oriented than are we can learn decency to their neighbours only if they first amend fierce theologies that set neighbour against neighbour, then by all means let us hammer out a theology that will be less catastrophic. If you ask us Jews to take part in the task, however, our contribution is more likely to be one of asking whether you are not perhaps mistaken in taking theology so seriously in the first place, in being so dogmatic not necessarily in the vulgar pejorative meaning of that term but in the literal meaning, in any meaning. Religious life is at heart a matter not of creed but of character and conduct. The world needs not a theology of comparative religion but a morality of it.

And if you will allow me to say so, that sentiment would hardly seem foreign to Jesus of Nazareth.

Finally, a secular rationalist speaks up. I have not been explicitly invited into the discussion, he might say; none the less I beg to be heard, on the grounds at least that I am involved in the problem, even if I may not seem to the other participants to be qualified to take part. I and my fellow sceptics, irreligious men, have to live in a world lacerated by religious strife; and what we have to say may perhaps prove germane, since at least we have thought about the matter a good deal. And while admittedly we do not share your premisses, neither do you share each other's premisses, of course. I was glad to hear you affirm that a theology of comparative religion must include within its purview the Western rationalist-humanist tradition; will you not consider also a case that it must include that movement's modern successors, persons of no ideology or grand philosophic system, but impelled by the sense that we share this space-ship earth and all of us must plan together lest we make an even sorrier mess of it than we already have done or threaten to do?

Seventy-five years ago we should not have wished to join in. For at that point we believed that you religious groups of your diverse brands were all wrong – and, were all disappearing; that progress would sweep you aside, or rather, that you yourselves would shed your religious illusions and join us, in due course. By now, we have become more sobered. For one thing, even the most unengaged among us has come to see that the whole religious complex is indeed complex, much more so than we – or even you – used to think. Yes, admittedly, it is partly our expanded awareness of the history of religion that has led us to see, as it has led you to see, that the thing is much more elaborate and involute than can be either dismissed or defended by the old considerations. We thought the idea of God wrong; we have found that some deeply religious people do not use it – and those who do, can discuss it as an idea. We thought all religious forms symbolic; we have found that many deeply religious people say so too, with great intelligence, and much more insight than we. We thought all religious orientations fundamentally anthropological; we have found that this demolishes some myths, at least superficially, but makes others much more intelligible than they were, and in turn this makes anthropology, one's doctrine of man, turn out to be in effect religious, at least potentially. We used to think the psychological study of religious behaviour important; we still do, but have come to see that a religiously sophisticated study of psychology is at least equally penetrating. And a religiously sophisticated analysis of social structures and even of rationalism turns out to be as illuminating, as cogent, as a sociological or rational analysis of religion.

Our problem is man; but we have come to see that you are probably right that faith is a constitutive component of what it means to be human, however bizarre the forms that it has taken – and however new the forms that it will take. Man is *homo symbolicus*; and may well be *homo religiosus*. His and her religious performance over the centuries, however discouraging to some of us, is not something added to man's essence but an expression of it, in constant process of evolving. I agree with your self-consciousness bit: we used to think, even those of my persuasion, that the new challenge facing humankind of shaping its own future – 'man makes himself', and all that; man directs his and her history – could be picked up only by those who repudiated the religions. We now recognise that this may turn out to be man's most central religious task. Some of my friends might be startled to hear me say that. Yet I guess that some of your more traditional Christian friends, or our Muslim colleague's Muslim ones, and our Buddhist's Buddhist, are not so sure about *your* taking part in this new joint enterprise into which we have ventured, either. I'm not really giving in to your theses yet; but I can see that we share a common, human problem. And in a way it would contradict my own liberalism if I were unwilling to sit down and to discuss our variant approaches.

Besides all this, another development has shifted our view, of late. In addition to our having acquired a new and much better understanding of what religious faith and religious systems are all about, now that we have been able to see them in other forms than the particular one that we could not accept for ourselves, there is a further point. For we have also, and over against this, acquired during, say, my lifetime a quite new humility about our own position. We used to imagine that man, once liberated from superstition, could and would solve all his and her problems with rationality, and with goodwill. It turns out that this was a trifle hasty. Man's rationality and goodwill are no longer premisses for us, but problems; as for you. It is not only that the wickedness that we used to see at work in religious systems has re-appeared on earth, in secular patterns: fanaticism and brutality and narrow dogmatism and oppression of minorities and on and on. A secular society is not necessarily a good society, we have come to recognise; even those among us who saw that a religious society was in many ways bad. A secular society can be bad too; even technology and medicine, affluence, education and all our proudest boasts have turned sour. Alienation and despair, or at least anomie and boredom, loom as potential characteristics of the earthly godless paradise that we have struggled to achieve.

Even the university, the temple as well as the workshop of our secular rationalism, has come to seem to our own children inhumane, repulsive. Something has gone profoundly wrong with Western humanism, it would almost seem; maybe, if you didn't press the *religious*-faith emphasis, we could agree that our problem is perhaps our loss of faith – certainly if by faith you mean wholeness, integrity, loyalty, freedom, rapport. Above all, this is so if faith means meaningfulness: the ability to perceive life (one's own, one's neighbour's, the universe's) as 'meaningful', to use that modern jargon. Those of us who perceive man's central problem as that of finding meaning, and even those of us who, more sceptically, hold that there is no meaning and that man's central problem accordingly is not to find it but to give it, to create meaning out of himself and herself – or to posit it, to generate it – both these groups see man's religious history as rather self-deluded yet significant movements constituting man's chief experiments in the past with the meaning problem. What you are calling a theology of comparative religion, we would rephrase as a general theory of human attempts to find or to give meaning in, or to, human life. The word 'attempt' is, I admit, tendentious: you score against us at that start, because in the case of the great religious movements in history, and for that matter even the tiny ones on remote sea islands, the attempts historically have been successful; though we score against you in the present day, because right now so often they are not. It would be interesting to toy with a formulation of the sort: a general theory of how it is that the universe and human life have appeared meaningful to some people and not to others; and to the former in many, many diverse ways. But that way of going at it concedes too much. Our starting point and focus must be man, and I revert to my earlier wording. My concession to your theological prejudices is to leave in the words "find or give", and not to insist from the first on man's simply giving meaning. Hindus, of course, would pooh-pooh the distinction; and they may be right. Maybe we could settle on a compromise: a general theory of man's varying capacity in history, or incapacity, to live life meaningfully.

In striving towards this, we should have much to learn from you people, certainly. Yet I think it hardly bumptious of me to say that we could contribute something also; and perhaps even that you need us. For one thing, it is not so obvious to us as it seems to be to you that the future in this realm is likely to be continuous with the past. You concede that the processes of religious history from ancient times are entering in our day a radically new phase: newness, profoundly, is coming. Yet stressing continuity and flexibility also from of old, you conceive that those processes, however modified, will continue. I am not so sure. You base your guess in part, no doubt, on your feeling that the secularist world-view is failing, and will fail, to work. You have something of a point there, alas; yet sheer observation unbuttressed by predilections could lead some analysts to say equally that the religious movements are not working in the fully modern context either; and we secularists may learn to cope sooner than do you religious chaps, with what is certainly a set of formidable problems, intellectual and practical, different from any that either of us has faced before now. Let's not quarrel on the point, in any case; we can afford to wait and see, and really we can't afford not to work together and to help each other, at any points that we possibly can, rather than bickering among ourselves in silly endeavours to prove ourselves right and each other wrong – the very thing that you see so clearly among religious groups, but that I should like to extend also to obtain between religious groups and non-religious. I will admit, however, that, in the universities over the last century, secularists have been more anti-religious than you religionists have been anti each other. (Not outside the universities, however!)

I suppose that it was your sense of being beleaguered in this way by hostile critics insensitive to religious positions that underlay your rather belligerent repudiation of non-transcendentalist intellectuals such as certain social scientists; yet frankly I was disappointed in that. As a Christian you ought to be able to respond to attack with reconciliation rather than rejection. Your 'we', enlarged to include Buddhists and Jews and all, ought somehow also to include us too, ought it not?

I think it important that we be in there, because we can contribute a still greatly needed criticism. No doubt it is true that we, observing only outward forms and overt behaviour, and having no way to perceive the inner meaning, have tended to interpret religious life as wooden at best, and often much worse – the way Protestants used to do of Catholics; Christians, of Muslims; and both Christians and Muslims, of Hindus. It is a fact, I guess, that all religious systems have tended to appear grotesque to outsiders, however precious from within. Yet that grotesqueness has to be dealt with. I even sense some danger that, once you are over the hurdle of being able to see the point – you as a Christian – of Muslim and Hindu foibles, you begin to condone them, and even not to see them; just as, as a Christian, you do not see, at least not fully and clearly, the Christian Church's sins. You religious people somehow have access through your religious symbols to something so transcendentally worth the struggle that you become blinded to the appallingly great price that you pay, or make others pay, for your hold on that pearl. Perhaps, in your new camaraderie, you will remind each other of your several communities' failings. But you may be carried away by your new-found friendship; and I have a suspicion that you need us sceptics outside of all, to keep you truly alert to the possibilities of sanctimonious self-deception; and to the absurdities of the human condition even in its most sacred forms.

And, yes, we need you, too; in part for the same reason. There is certainly a self-righteous secularism, as well as the appalling devastation of the nihilist version of our stand. Between you, you are in touch with something in human nature of profound significance; and while we cannot have it in any of the forms or packages in which you wrap it up, neither do we wish that human beings leave it out of account in our self-understanding. It is not religious history that is entering a new phase, so much as human history.

Allow me – that is, me myself as now a real rather than imaginary person; as chairman, if you like, of this imaginary panel presentation – to re-appear, thanking these pseudo-representatives for their pseudo-contributions, and now dismissing them into thin air. And allow me once again to register my apologies for their pseudo-ness: my having fabricated their remarks out of whole cloth without having sat down with actual Muslims, Buddhists and the others after they might have first read my first six Chapters[3].

In any case, the excursus may perhaps have contributed to our over-all task, in terms at least of perspective. It might be seen to illumine both what we are trying to attain, and how far we yet are from attaining it – were it not that community consists not in shared attainments so much as in shared goals; and the intellect may be served by a partial approximation to truth as much as by a contentment with partial truths. Certainly the approximationist vision is dynamic; and to recognise the validity and worth of the journey does not rule out a recognising also of the stage at which, merely, one has meanwhile arrived.

At the end of Chapter 6 I observed that readers from other backgrounds would readily perceive that in fact my exposition is that of a Christian, however generic I might endeavour or delude myself to be. A possible result of this chapter's adventure might perhaps lie in its making the same point a whit more evident also to those of Christian background. The aspiration, noted earlier, to transcend 'Christian' theology, to get back to an earlier and more innocent 'theology' *simpliciter* or to move forward towards it, may be seen more clearly as unduly pretentious (or anachronistic)?

We return, then, to wrestle with the question of how Christian, and how generic, is the position that I envisage. Does it fail in both, rather than correlate? Or is a possible direction of movement towards a correlation indeed suggested? As remarked, Christians may see or feel that I am not nearly Christian enough. Others, however, and maybe also Christians, will see that none the less – limpingly, inadequately, perhaps forgiveably – my views are Christian at least in the sense of being of Christian provenance. Moreover, they are proffered with (*inter alia*) Christian aim. Their target is truth; has any Christian theologian had any other (or Muslim theologian, or Buddhist philosopher . . .)?

Truth, however, is apprehended historically. The particular sense of it delineated here arises intellectually in the Western university and theologically out of the historical process of the Church's development thus far (at the epoch of its emergence into a wider world); and is offered as a contribution to the next phase of those two developments. This is so, even though its degree of truth be a function of its approximation to being recognisably continuous also with other communities' development thus far, and its approximation to being serviceable also to those others' further development. This chapter has perhaps served to suggest that those approximations are neither close nor illegitimate.

The discussion thus far will have prepared us also for the use of the word 'theology' in an altogether informal sense. By it I mean, quite literally, talk about God; or more generically, about the transcendent dimension of human life and of the universe to which the history of religion (the history of man's spirit) bears witness and which it elucidates, and to which Christians have historically given the name 'God'. I do not primarily mean, as all will have gleaned by now, a formal systematic theology in the sense of an established discipline. (That establishment, those inside it know, is currently groping for direction; new light must come to it from outside the 'discipline'.) My aim is to make a small contribution to talking about comparative religion in relation of God, or to talking about God in relation to comparative religion.

Usually, those who talk about God (those who speak theologically) talk about only one religious complex. Usually, those who talk about comparative religion do so without talking about God. In this chapter, I have tried to suggest that there are Muslims, Hindus, Buddhists, Jews and even secularists for whom it is not impertinent to look at and to reflect upon the comparative-religion field not merely in descriptive terms but with reference to its cosmic context, and – self-consciously – in reference to oneself, one's own ultimate concern. In the next chapter I shall venture to talk about it with reference to God, since for a Christian that has been the cosmic context, and for me as a Christian that (alias Truth; alias Love) is my ultimate concern.

8 A Theology of Comparative Religion for those among us who are Christians

There cannot legitimately be a Christian theology of other religions, I have contended, in the sense of a we–they interpretation from within a boundaried and self-sufficient Christian position looking out over the world's other communities of faith as objects or even people upon whom to make pronouncements, however generous. Nor can there be a self-sufficient Islamic, nor academic rationalist, interpretation; nor even, despite the differences, a Hindu or Buddhist or Jewish. On the other hand, a Christian – and we hope also the others, in their various ways – may attempt something grander. (Indeed, he or she or they must, if the matter is to move forward, hazard this; and, the more that do so, the better.) That grander attempt, we have said, is to interpret intellectually all human faith, one's own and others'; comprehensively, and justly. Seeing one's own group and its history thus far as making up one complex strand in the total history of religion until now, a total history that one is endeavouring to understand from within, one may essay a theory that aspires to be part of a movement towards the truth. Seeing one's own group as a component in the total community of humankind, a total community whose corporate critical self-consciousness in this matter has yet to be articulated, again one may endeavour to contribute to its formulation. A Christian, no more than but no less than any other member of that human community, may and must think in these realms.

That the resultant theory be true, and do justice to all who are involved, though a matter in the first instance of the intellectual and other integrity and depth of those who propound or adopt it, is controlled by a testing as to whether it do justice to the facts of human religious history, on the one hand, and, on the other, to the faith, experience, insight of both Christians (or whichever group it be from which it emerges) and the others. Regarding those others we spoke in brief in our last chapter, and in our next we shall return for a more theoretical consideration, pondering the universalisability of our matter and reckoning with its problems. Manifestly, one can hope for no more than progress, however scant, in a valid direction. In the meantime, we here attend to the Christian instance. What are Christians to say?

A further question is: how are they to say it. For one is faced at the outset, of course, apart from issues of substance, with a problem of vocabulary, since various groups use differing terminology even for understanding things of common concern. This issue too we leave until our final chapter. Christian terms (not Christian alone) such as 'faith', 'theology' and the like, and their legitimacy for our wider purposes, we shall there discuss, but here, in Christian context, simply use.

The most important concept of this sort is, of course, 'God'. We have already touched on this, and shall return to it. (That some modern Christians have themselves, under secularist-ideology pressure, become perplexed about this traditional term, also we shall consider in our next chapter.) In the meantime allow me to speak as if addressing myself to, let us say, Christians and Jews and Muslims, and many Hindus; to whom the term has meant much. These groups, I realise, do not agree among themselves on what they mean by 'God'; but two considerations impinge. One is that they all agree that He transcends whatever they personally have the wit or even the grace to mean by the term; the second, that no one of the groups agrees among itself, either. While we await further clarification, let the word 'God' mean to each of my readers whatever it does mean personally to him or her, as a theist; or if not one, then what he or she thinks that it has meant to theists. (It is a requirement of modern intellectuality that one understand those from whom one differs even in the matter of conceptual categories.) If this be accepted, it will enable me to speak about human religious history in relation to God.

Accordingly, we shall adumbrate here an interpretation of human religious history proffered as it were by a Christian to Christians, and to others as an illustration of how Christians might be envisaged as envisaging the wider scene in which they play their part. In this sense the proposal may be dubbed a Christian theology of comparative religion; or in the words of our title, a theology of comparative religion for those among us who are Christians. It represents the sort of step that Christian thinking may begin to take as it moves into the new consciousness.

As before, we suggest that, in order for us to move forward, recent patterns of thought require revising, to become more in line simultaneously both with more traditional Christian modes before the aberrations of the modern disarray, and with the newer awareness that is emerging. I begin with the concept 'religion', as of that whose history we participate in and observe. As at the historical level with which we began, so now at the theological, modern understanding cannot but be classically new.

Thinkers in the West, and perhaps especially Protestants, in interpreting the history of religion, their own and others', have tended to operate with what I may call the 'big-bang' theory of origins. I propose to offer in its stead a view of religious history that would come closer to a theory of continuous creation. Let me try to make clear what I have in mind.

The notion against which I will argue may be seen to derive in interesting part and at a couple of removes from the Protestant Reformation. That development, in its critique of the religious institutions and practices and theories of its day, affirmed the view that the true form of Christian life and thought was to be found at the historical beginnings. 'Back to the original, to the pristine' was a major element in the Reformers' outlook. Their own personal piety, and that of the massive movement that they launched, was oriented to the contemporary relevance of what they preached: the first-century Christ whom they proclaimed, and the long-since-composed Bible that they read and popularised, played a burning role in their lives as immediately present realities. They were no antiquarians. Nevertheless, over against the Roman Catholic Church and its long history, the Reformation repudiated in principle Christian development through time, and located Christian truth rather in its earliest appearance. Although emphatic about what God could do for men and women 'here and now', the Reformers were not much interested in what He had been doing in on-going Christian history over the centuries, but rather in what He had done 'once for all' in Christ. Church History was for them the locus of spiritual truth only in its origin.

This view was subsequently given an important twist by the Deist movement, which among other things reduced the 'here and now' dimension of the outlook. This was carried further in later Enlightenment thought; and a still more truncated version coloured nineteenth-century attitudes to history generally, and especially to historical research. Historians, even secular ones, and not least historians of religion, were deeply affected by the notion that 'the original is the true', and that the task of historiography is to unearth beginnings. In the new awareness in nineteenth-century Europe of what at that time it called others' religions, this backward-looking stance was firm. Western conceptions of 'Buddhism', 'Mohammedanism' and the like, but even Christians' understanding of 'Christianity' also, evinced this bias.

What I am calling 'the big-bang theory' is the notion that a religion begins with one great seismic event, as it were: a cosmic happening within history, in the reverberations and resonances of whose explosive power down the succeeding ages subsequent generations of the faithful live. Buttressed by the bifurcationist stance earlier remarked, this was a way of seeing the religion as a kind of additive to history, something that has been injected into the temporal world from the outside and that remains there as a more or less stable extra, available to men and women in more or less purity depending on how close to its original form they are able to get hold of it. In this view, the original is the true. The task of the historian, then, is to get back to origins; and the task of the theologian is to prove that the charge on that originating pole is so intensely powerful as not to be unable to leap across the increasingly great gap of time and culture that separates us from it.

'The original is the true.' 'The task of the historian is to get back to origins.' How profoundly this orientation has affected all historiography! The clearing away of later 'accretions', the exploding and dismissal of accumulated legends, the analysis of everything into the parts out of which it was made up, the tracing back of those parts each to *its* origin, the search for causes (not for effects): all these constitute the zeal of the historical researcher. It leads to what I have called 'studying history backwards', the so-called historical outlook having become one that looks at anything and perceives it in terms of its antecedents; forgetting that in fact time's arrow points the other way.

History is not the past; history is process. The history of our galaxy is only half over; its future history can in some measure be calculated. Of human history the future sector is unpredictable, though important; only the present one is open to our observation, and only its past is subject (in part) to investigation. Yet the study even of that earlier segment of human history is not in principle a study of the past. It is a study of movement – and that means, of movement forwards. By all means, if we are to consider anything long ago, let us become aware of, let us ferret out, the process by which it came to be. Let us, however, see the lines of force integrating its antecedent parts into wholeness as leading up to it, not leading back away from it. Let us recognise that what we are challenged to understand is not how we today can analyse an historical reality into its constituting factors: rather our task is to discern those constituent factors and to understand how they were once synthesised into something coherent and new. Moreover, once a thing exists, its consequences are at least as important as its background. A truly historical outlook, one might counter, would look at anything and perceive it in terms of its subsequent ramifications, its effects.

The typical Western Protestant response to the discovery of the Buddhist origin of the Barlaam and Josaphat story, was to subtract that story's activity from one's understanding of the history of Christianity, instead of adding it to one's understanding of the Buddha and his role in world history (including Christian history). Remarkably little is changed, in actual fact, in our knowledge of what has gone on in the history of the Church, by that discovery: what is changed, enlarged, is our knowledge of history outside the Church, and of the interpenetrating of the two. Anyone presenting that to a Christian, or even to a Western-secular, audience is likely to meet some resistance to wishing to keep the historical facts in their place, to keep the story conceptually in the lives of the Saints: a feeling like that of the editor whom I cited, that a knowledge of origins somehow dissolves the data, makes them go away – at least from the religion of which they were previously felt to be a part, and to some degree even from our consciousness. To learn that *B* is a later, modified version of *A* diverts our attention from *B* to *A* as though *A* were therefore truer, more important, more historical, somehow; that *B* does not matter anymore.

Both origins and consequences are part of the truth of any historical fact. Put in dynamic terms, anything is what it is as a moment in an on-going process of which it is a part. Neither antecedents nor consequents, however, nor both together, are the full truth of any historical fact, and should not be allowed to displace from our awareness the moment itself, as fully real. The historian's task is to reconstruct, not merely to analyse; and especially not to analyse away.

Especially is this so of man. Every moment of one's life one is what one is in considerable part because of what went before; and every moment of one's life one acts with consequences ramifying into the future, in a way that makes inescapable responsibility one of man's grandest or most harrowing characteristics. Yet neither the past nor the future must blind us to perceiving each person and understanding him or her as he or she is at that hour.

They are no historians at all who see no interconnections among things. Yet they are bad historians who see everything in terms of something else; and doubly bad humane historians, or no humane historians at all.

The notion is false, that to understand anything is simply to understand the background out of which it has come. Given natural causality, this is somewhat more plausible in science; but of human history it has been seriously distorting.

As we stressed in our second chapter, the life, including the religious life, including the faith, of a twelfth-century Buddhist in Japan can be understood in part in terms of what went before, including the life and teachings of the Buddha in north-east India seventeen centuries earlier. None the less, the truth of that person's life, including the truth of his or her religious life, including the truth of his or her faith, lies not in that or any other past but in twelfth-century Japan.

Let us look more closely at one or two specific religious processes, as illustrative of how inadequacies and distortions introduced by the big-bang outlook are overcome in the new interpretation. From a plethora of examples that might be chosen I begin, almost as it were at random, with one that concerns the Sikhs. Outside historiography on this small and striking religious community is typical enough. Western conceptualisations, whether Christian or secular, tended at one time to focus on Guru Nanak, interpreting him as 'the founder of Sikhism' while neglecting the historical role that his figure has played in the religious life of the community since, and the development that that miscalled '-ism' has continuingly evinced. They tended to neglect also (or even formally to exclude) the transcendent, indeed infinite, truth ('God'), beyond history and continuingly contemporaneous, to which he, and any concrete details of the 'system' that survived or were added, were remembered only because they pointed.

A standard research study of his life would set out to separate fact from legend, to uncover *was wahrlich geschehen ist*, to recover 'the truth'. It might begin with the presently accepted accounts current in Sikh circles, or that have been current and accepted in the community, and would examine them critically, no doubt with great skill and the utmost rigour, scrupulosity, and in one sense fairness. What happened under this process, however, is that the research would investigate one alleged story after another in the Sikh community's image of its Guru and find that each is in one way or another a later accretion; and once a story was found to be a later invention, it was dismissed. The result was that one ended up with only a minute picture of any actual life of Nanak.

The implication was that the whole rested on an incredibly slim base.

Now let us be quite clear about what I am saying. Such historiography is valid, but inadequate. I dispute none of the data that such research presents. It is the interpretation of those data that I would question. What it presents are facts. Such work is indeed a contribution to knowledge. Yet it is not history. It was an important prolegomenon to our grasp of the historical truth; but only that – and by itself it induced misconception. I say that it is not history, on two scores: first, it moves backwards in its study, from later myths to earlier, sparser, details; and, secondly, it dismisses the myths as if negligible. History, however, moves forwards, not backwards; we understand it truly only in so far as we perceive its forward movement. Secondly, myths are just as much historical facts as are anything else. If about Guru Nanak, who lived in the latter fifteenth and early sixteenth centuries, a myth arose in the eighteenth, and flourished until the twentieth, then of course our understanding of the fifteenth to seventeenth centuries must see them without it, but this is no more important than that our understanding of the eighteenth to twentieth must see them with it. This is particularly relevant, of course, in the history of religion, and for an understanding of that history. Yet there is still more: rather than dismissing the myth, even for our perception of Nanak in the fifteenth century, the historical fact is, and should be appreciated, that here is a figure about whose life in fact we do not know much in detail, except (a) that he wrote certain marvellous hymns that have inspired his community ever since to a life of vibrant faith, as one may witness still today anywhere in the world where Sikhs congregate to worship; and (b) that he inspired a movement that has grown into the present Sikh community, and his personality made on its members at the time the kind of impression that has lasted thus far for five centuries, has instigated devotion and nurtured response, and has attracted to itself gradually a body of imaginative myths. Not many of us, obviously, are the kind of person around whose memory two or three centuries from now, still being warmly cherished, will cluster ever new legends.

Let us look at a specific example. One of the popular stories is that Nanak visited Makkah: that the leader of the Sikhs visited the heartland of the Muslims. The story contains reference to an alleged mention in Baghdad of his passing through *en route*. Modern research has tracked down an inscription there and demonstrated that it has been misrendered and that the Sikh interpretation probably does not go back before the eighteenth century. So far so good. I agree that probably Nanak never left India. None the less, there is a deal of difference between two ways of handling this knowledge. One is: once one has discovered that date and detected a fabrication, to pronounce it a mere legend, to dismiss it therefore, and to hurry on back to earlier, truer, foundations. The other is the newer way of the historian of religion, for whom there are no *mere* legends: who sees the history of religion at work here, and whose account of exactly the same facts would be a presenting of a movement that crystallised around Nanak and his disciples (it did not really *begin* with him: processes of this kind do not 'begin' at precise moments) and whose growth since then one can gradually trace, as it expands, becomes more structured, is enriched. This particular Baghdad-inscription business can be seen as an instance of its still growing, still enriching itself, in the eighteenth century. And what it attests in the matter of links to Islamic affairs is important (and in some senses, even true).

The Sikh process can be observed as it develops also in the nineteenth century: in many new ways – some up, some down; some this way, some that – Sikh community consciousness going on changing, intricately. And in the twentieth century there are many continuingly new developments too – including the fascinating new awareness now available through modern research that this particular myth about Guru Nanak's visiting Makkah entered Sikh history in the eighteenth century. Before our eyes, then, this is in process of becoming transmuted in the twentieth, some would say from a presumedly historical account of the Guru to a recognisedly legendary one; from an unconscious myth to a conscious one. In what way these new awarenesses will affect the on-going process of Sikh religious life in the future one does not yet know; elements in determining that are the fact that Western historians have participated in the process significantly, though in some ways uncouthly, and the fact that Sikh leaders today include intellectuals who participate along with the rest of us in the world-wide process of reconceptualising our self-interpretation of the history of religion, one's own and other people's. Whatever is going to happen now, and whatever happened in the fifteenth or sixteenth century, I am urging that it is bad historiography to fail to see, and to fail to recognise as important in the history of religion, that from the eighteenth century until the middle of the twentieth the religious faith of Sikhs took the form that in fact it took. Before that time and after that time its form was, will be, other, the context of the religious life of Sikhs being then different.

From now on the tune will again be new. But of the intervening period the music is not changed by demonstrating that the bang at the beginning was not so big as once some may have thought. Sikhism is not a system established five hundred years ago. The early forms of the movement are no more significant, and no more true, than its later; and to treat them as if they were is to distort. The task of the theologian is to interpret not a system at all – no more than it is the task of the historian; nor even a movement, if that distract from the locus of religious reality that cosmically counts, the lives of the persons who have made up the movement and who have interacted with whatever successive patterns there may have been, and with each other, and with God.

Guru Nanak did not produce, found or envisage a new religion; he had never heard of Sikhism, and preached no system. (Indeed, he explicitly decried systematisations.) He proclaimed, and practised, mercy and justice and humble dignity and a passionate piety. The vision that he preached, and lived, was set forth in an inspiring life and in moving poetry; some of those who heard were moved, and a movement coalesced around the poetry and the vision and around memories of the person, and – it would be vacuous to forget – in continuing relation to the on-going truth and spirit that, he averred (was he not right?), are available always to all.

So far as prediction is concerned, let me toss in this suggestion: that the future faith of Sikhs will not be helped if they operate, as they might under Western pressure, on a false diagnosis of the nature of religious faith and of religious history. Sikhs who have read it have on the whole been hurt and offended by earlier Western research on their Guru. Some Westerners have tended to dismiss this as a symptom of their prejudices, the unwillingness of religious people to face facts uncovered by 'objective' scholarship. I submit that what has hurt and offended them are not the new facts, but the ordering of those facts within an understanding of religious faith and history that manifestly does violence to both. The presentation has regularly involved a subordinating of its data to an interpretation of those data that is false; and it therefore cannot be incorporated in self-consciousness by Sikhs. A truer presentation of the same data would enable both outsiders and Sikhs themselves to understand better (more truly) what has happened in Sikh history – better than they did before, and better than this type of research interpretation does – as well as enabling both outsiders and Sikhs themselves better to think about (and to discuss together) future Sikh and human forms of faith.

Theologically, the point is that neither the *truth* nor the *reality* of Sikh forms of faith lies in the fifteenth century – and has not lain there for now 471 years (and 33 days)[1]. Faith is a relation between man and God; in the case of Sikhs, it has been engendered, shaped and vitalised by their participation in an always contemporary context, the evolving past process of which can now trace, and the future process of which we (those of us who are Sikhs, at least; but I retain that 'we') do and must now in part determine. The past has been religiously important to Sikhs at any time in so far as, and only in so far as, it has been interpreted, in each succeeding generation, as a present avenue leading them to contemporary significance and truth, to justice, mercy, love, and fullness of life; in so far as, and only in so far as, it has introduced them to a divine presence. Some Sikhs have lived in that presence more truly than have others, no doubt (God has found His way into the lives of some more effectively than of others); but that is the theological issue, fresh for every morning. To focus on origins is to miss the point of Sikh religious life. (It is to miss the point even of Sikh interest in those origins.)

Let us look at how Western perceptions of religious realities in the Islamic case were inhibited or distorted for a time by the controlling theory. At first, Islamic history appeared to fit well into the preconceived pattern. It turns out that those parts or facets that did not fit in, were ignored. The casual observer has seen the Islamic complex as a scheme where allegedly God injected into the stream of mundane history in the seventh century in Arabia a supernatural something: either the Qur'an as a reputedly revealed book or, more elaborately, a religion called Islam that Muhammad founded, comprising the Qur'an and various other elements, including Muhammad's doings and character, certain doctrines, and the like, the several elements being fastened together into a rather closely knit and even rigid pattern. This was seen as constituting a neat package for export which then was indeed carried far and wide across the lands and across the centuries. Admittedly the task of wrapping it up ready for long-distance shipment and making sure that it would endure intact across the ages, took a certain time (a few generations, a few centuries) and involved incorporating into the package various elements largely borrowed from other cultures, or extraneous bits and pieces that got stuck to it inadvertently; and in use it was found like other religions to accumulate adhesions of various sorts, so that from time to time reformers might be expected to undo the wrapping and to clean off the adhering foreign matter. The core of the whole affair, however, was thought of as that original seventh-century entity. And the validity of the whole affair was thought of as a question as to whether that original entity did or did not come from outside of history as alleged. Muslims were interpreted as believing that God sent down the original Islam to earth from on high, as an act of revelation in the seventh century; others, who did not believe this, saw the whole thing, then, with its subsequent history, as false. A more liberal view saw it as false in its basic theories but withal a human construct not without cultural value and even, generously, not without truth; but 'natural' truth.

It is not only laymen who have seen things thus, however. Western scholarship too, both secular and Christian, has operated on some such view.

Conspicuously in the nineteenth century, but on into this, it is revealing how high a portion of Western scholarly energy on Islamics has been devoted to origins and to the early centuries. Even today at Harvard the History Department has two courses, one covering the early centuries and called 'Islamic History', one on the more recent called 'History of the Near East'.

A lot of energy went also into searching out origins; tracking down ever-earlier sources; in zeal, a critic might say, to *prove* that Islam did *not* begin full-blown coming down from the sky like the meteorite black stone at Makkah but could be shown to have been pieced together from preceding mundane sources. The background of Islam was a focus of academic investigation, long before it seemed respectable in modern universities to examine the foreground; or to study the long process in between during which, and in terms of which, most Muslims lived their lives and formed their faith. The process by which Islam came into being is certainly historically important; yet surely it is less interesting, historically much less important, and certainly religiously enormously less important, than the on-going process to which it gave rise once it had come into being.

Let us take one example: the Qur'an. As a scripture, this has functioned with might and colour in the personal lives and societies of Muslims. It has patterned their prayers, regulated their commerce, guided their governments sometimes less, sometimes more, determined their laws, teased their intellects, inspired their poetry, coloured their dreams, decorated their architecture, fashioned their outlook on the world – in ways that have been fascinatingly constant in some respects, marvellously diverse in others in different times and at different places. The question for the historian of religion is to search out what the Qur'an has meant to Muslims in this age and in that; what to mystics, what to lawyers, what to philosophers, what to rebellious nationalist movements or leaders of class uprisings, what to court interpreters salaried to keep those uprisings defused.

Western studies of the Qur'an, however, have tended to ignore all this, and to concentrate on only one issue: origins. For fourteen centuries now, Muslims of many stripes have written commentaries on the Qur'an. In the past, Western students used to brush all that aside, as probably (or 'obviously') full of 'misinterpretations' – and to get back to the original meaning, that of the seventh century. These Westerners felt that they themselves with their 'lack of prejudice', and with their apparatus of sophisticated modern scholarship, could find out more accurately than those Muslims ever did the truth (the original truth). And of course, they found out many interesting, and many true, things. So far as the history of religion is concerned, however, they missed most of it. The religiously important question, *and* the historically important question, is not what the Qur'an 'means' in itself: rather, what it has meant to Muslims, over each of these fourteen centuries; and what it means to them today. Of late, we have been finding it enormously rewarding to study that sequence of commentaries, listening very carefully to what they have to say.

This is the better question for the historian, I have argued. Yet my real point is that this is the better question for the theologian. We are coming now closer to the heart of our discussion. The question 'Is the Qur'an the word of God?' used to be taken to mean: Did God in the seventh century A.D. in western Arabia obtrude into the mundane processes of human development, *ab extra*, a supernatural something, constituting, or helping to constitute, at that point an additive to history in the form of one more of the religions of the world, which has persisted since then more or less pure; that is, with as much of its pristine genuineness as Muslims could manage?'

We are now recognising that the question 'Is the Qur'an the Word of God' may be taken to mean, more responsibly, 'Has God spoken to Muslims through the Qur'an across the centuries?' In its former version, historically lest apt, Christian theologians felt that they had to answer 'No'; as did Western scholars. With its latter meaning there is no reason why Christians and Hindus should not reply 'Yes' at times, and also Buddhists and even Western humanist scholars if they be allowed to add, 'It depends what you mean by God'.

We have touched on this last question, and, as remarked, shall in our last chapter revert to it. In the meantime let me but comment that in the modern world, while a Christian need not adopt terms such as 'Nirvana' and 'Buddhahood' for his own vocabulary, yet it has become requisite surely that he or she understand (try to, wish to, understand) what these have meant and mean to Buddhists, and should even be able (should endeavour, hope) to follow intelligently a Buddhist argument using them; similarly, our Buddhist or other non-theists need not 'believe in' God, and yet one need hardly apologise, perhaps, for asking that they allow themselves to understand for a moment a theist's discourse. They can hardly aspire to an understanding of comparative religion (of the world in which they live) if they cannot or will not follow a conversation involving Christian and Muslim groups: a Christian's speaking about Islamic religious history and of man within it, in relation to God'.

The thesis that I would defend before my fellow Christians and anyone else who can grasp it is that on any given morning in Baghdad or Jogjakarta or Timbuktu, in this century or in that, the faith of a particular Muslim, member of a particular society, had a specific form constituted by his participation in the Islamic context of his life that was that particular moment of the total process of the Islamic strand in world religious history; and that in that faith in that particular form he was in touch with God, and God with him.

God spoke to him; more or less clearly, more or less effectively, with more or less response – in a voice muffled by the din of distracting worldly beguilements and inner personal deflections, muffled also by the perennial inadequacies of the channels available to Him, muffled by the limited capacity of that man to hear; none the less, He spoke, and He was heard.

I have no urge to idealise that Muslim. No doubt he was a sinner, like me. Yet he had faith, however oddly patterned and however small; perhaps only as a grain of mustard seed. By that faith, I believe and suggest, he was saved. A sinner, yes; but *simul justus et peccator*.

Speaking as an historian, I can defend this interpretation warmly. Speaking as a theologian, I shall defend it presently. As an historian, I can demonstrate, first, that his faith was particular, personal, immediate; was Islamic not in some textbook fashion, in some abstractly general or idealised theoretic form, but specific, concrete: a form that was a function of his personality, education, interest, sensitivity and self-dedication on the one hand, and of his time and place, what I have called the context of his life, on the other. It may well have been the Qur'an through which God spoke to him, but it was almost surely not only the Qur'an. Over most centuries of Islamic history (though not all) it would probably have been through the pattern of the law, with its particular moral imperatives on the one hand, and its over-all sense of order on the other; its comprehensive direction to his life and his society, its conferring of the sense that meaning is in the moral dimension of our life, and that responsibility, corporate and individual, is the heart both of history and of personal destiny.

It may at certain periods have been rather, or also, through the rather heavily fictionalised Lives of the Saints, or the imaginatively embroidered lives of the prophets (Muhammad and the pre-Muhammad Islamic prophets, from Adam, and including Jesus). God (one finds) can speak through fiction as well as through pedestrian prose; He uses myths, an historian observes, and not merely demythologised historiography.

If – as is statistically likely during the centuries that we in the West would call the thirteenth to nineteenth, and especially if he lived in one or other of certain specifiable geographic areas – if he was a member of or at least touched by one or other of the great Sufi orders, his faith would have been of more or less mystic quality, in which case God's task of speaking to him, reaching out to him and embracing him, would have been facilitated (do you acquiesce in that word? – you could say 'complicated' if you liked; but I choose 'facilitated') by that quality in his faith and person. If he lived after about 1250 and spoke Persian, God may have spoken to him (as he has to me) through the poetry of Jalalu-d-din Rumi, or another of the Persian Sufis whose stamp for good or ill has impressed itself with eloquence and power on the context of a major sector of the community.

His faith may, however, probably without his clearly realising it, also have been given shape, and vitality, and force, by art. This would be more obvious, perhaps, for those particular persons who confronted the great works of art, or even the medium level of a cultured city home, with its highly disciplined elegance. It could be true, however, for every man's faith, through the particular works of art in his environment, perhaps modest or even rude little items if he were an uncouth peasant or proletarian: odd artifacts in his home or crude styles in his village or quarter that none the less served to keep him open to the fusion of utility and beauty, unconsciously reminding him that human life is more than a meaningless succession of blind buffeting circumstance; and the minaret of the local mosque pointing perhaps narrowly upwards and insinuating into his soul the sense of higher things, the dim or vivid awareness that, being human, he somehow has access to a splendour that is not altogether obvious here on earth.

His faith would be nurtured and formed also through ritual, his life being by it endued with pattern and coherence as he focused, or shall we say, had focused for him, in ritual acts the intensity of his sense of the divine in activated symbolic forms. Even the prayer beads, which we mentioned in Chapter 1, and which some observers have tended to think of as peripheral to faith, were for some at times perhaps an almost central avenue for it. The matter varied, of course, not only from region to region and century to century, and certainly from person to person, but also for a given person from occasion to occasion and from mood to mood. One can readily imagine a Muslim for whom at times the telling of his beads would be an almost perfunctory routine, performed perhaps not insouciantly yet semi-mechanically as a pious habit or a discipline imposed. One should maybe not under-estimate the potential significance for a man's faith of even that kind of casual act, even as an obligation discharged, a chore that one almost grudgingly gets over with quickly. For even so it does represent at least taking time off from other concerns to maintain one's tie with the system oriented to transcendence, if not with transcendence itself. One should maybe not under-estimate God's ability to use even a man's mechanical habits to sustain His succour of that soul. None the less, all this pales almost into insignificance beside a moment on one particular afternoon when a given Muslim more devoutly is telling his beads and touches, let us say, the twenty-seventh bead and names to himself that particular divine attribute and his soul is suddenly or deeply, or just a whit more deeply than before, suffused with a realisation that mercy, or patience, or whatever it be, is indeed of cosmic import, or that man is in the hands of a just or awesome or powerful or eternal God.

Historically, it has happened that God speaks to men and women by means of rosaries.

I said that as an historian I could establish the point that each person's faith has been particular, personal, has been of a specific historical form. I go on now to urge a further point: that as an historian also I can demonstrate that by that specific historical faith he was saved. Salvation is usually thought of as having a metaphysical or otherworldly dimension, and I shall postpone that aspect of the thesis to defend presently at a theological level. Salvation has also, however, most would agree or would like to agree, an historical dimension: something within this world, something empirical. I at least think it has, and the historian of religion can hardly but be interested in the matter.

I submit the following as an empirical observation, and in some ways almost verifiable: that the particular Muslim about whom we spoke, the man of faith whom I called *simul justus et peccator*, was by that faith saved, in the mundane sense of the word (in the mundane aspects of salvation, if you prefer). On earth, no man is fully saved (salvation in its mundane aspects is always imperfect); but in so far as he *is* saved, he is saved by faith.

Phrased in that form, the statement smacks of being an analytic one (since I come close to meaning by faith, if pressed, that quality of human life that saves). A further matter repeats a point noted earlier: to say that in so far as any human being is saved, he or she is saved by faith, is what has been classically affirmed also by Christian writers. Most Christian theologians, as we saw, have insisted with zeal that salvation is by faith, without speaking of Christian faith. (We may recall the example of that conservative author of the exclusivist article on 'Faith' in the *Dictionnaire de théologie catholique.*) Most Christian thinkers, both Protestant and Catholic, have not known anything about the faith of others. They have often believed (wrongly) that others were without faith; but they have not held that there are different kinds of faith, some of which save and some do not. That Christian faith saves, other faith fails to do so, is – so far as I am aware – the considered doctrine of no significant Christian theologian.

My submission would be this: that faith differs in form, but not in kind. This applies both within communities and from one community to another. My observation, as an historian of religion, would be put thus: in so far as he or she has been saved, the Muslim has been saved by Islamic faith (faith of an Islamic form, through Islamic patterns; faith mediated by an Islamic context); the Buddhist by Buddhist faith, the Jew by Jewish.

Once amplified so, it becomes only more or less true, an empirically based inductive generalisation: significantly valid, and indeed important, although not without specific exceptions here and there that can be historically understood – and, during the present half-century, I have been arguing, room must be left for the emergence of less separated divisions. I do not wish, through historical caution, to weaken the thrust of my thesis, however; and perhaps this can be salvaged by a further refinement, introduced by recognising that whatever exceptions or subtleties have to be acknowledged have their counterpart also in the Christian case, historically. Put as follows, I would stand by the statement fully, as an historical report: just as Christians have been saved by Christian faith, so have Muslims by Islamic, Buddhists by Buddhist.

To stand by it fully theologically as well as historically, I should have to revise this still further to read: just as Christians have been saved by faith of a Christian form, so have Muslims by faith of an Islamic, Andaman Islanders of an Andaman.

By 'saved' here, mundanely, I mean, in a way that unfortunately modern people are in a position to understand: saved from nihilism, from alienation, anomie, despair; from the bleak despondency of meaninglessness. Saved from unfreedom; from being the victim of one's own whims within, or of pressures without; saved from being merely an organism reacting to its environment. I mean that, as an historian, and as an observer of the Islamic world, I note that in fact Muslims derive their courage, their dignity, their capacity to suffer without disintegrating and to succeed without gloating, their sense of belonging to a community, of accepting and being accepted, their ability to trust and to be trusted, to discipline themselves, to formulate ideals, to postpone reward, to work hard towards a distant goal . . . and so on and on – they derive all this from, and nurture it through, a participation in an Islamic context for their lives. They have derived it from reading the Qur'an, from revering the law, from praying in a mosque. A more humanist interpretation would be that, having derived all this from somewhere, perhaps from being human, they invest it in that Islamic grid of symbols, crystallising it around those particular representations – invest it at interest. Some theologians, both Christian and Muslim, would say that this faith is a sheer gift from God, and cannot be induced by anything that men and women do. Fair enough. I shall myself say that in a moment. Yet that faith received in gift bears an Islamic-context form, is nurtured and sustained by participation in Islamic patterns. Muslims themselves do not confuse the mundane patterns with the God Whom, they say, they find, or are found by, as they participate in them. Neither should we. Anyway, I am simply averring that Muslims have been saved from ego-diffusion, to use that modern jargon, and their societies from chaos, by their faith – or, by God through their faith. And their faith has had usually an Islamic form.

Usually; although not always. I have said that there are historical exceptions. Islamic patterns have sometimes encouraged men to stupidities or even brutalities; and sometimes in such cases they have been saved from those by common sense, or by rational thought, or by personal vision. We know the like from Christian history: the most orthodox Christian historian must admit that the mundane forms of the Christian process have always been imperfect and sometimes horrendous. We have had our Crusades and our Inquisitions, our brutalities in the name of the Lord. Christian patterns (in the historical sense of 'Christian' – Church contexts) have inspired some Christians at times to woeful deeds; and at other times would have done, but the Christian was saved from them by Greek enlightenment or a Jewish neighbour. The inspiration to delivery that some Christians have at some times derived from the Church was not faith, a theologian would say: it was the fruit of something other than the Spirit. The problem need not detain us; I wish only to make the point that, like other religious problems, it is altogether global.

The Church, it has been posited, is a divine – human complex in motion. If it is the body of Christ, it is also the bodies of me and other members. I am suggesting that every other religious community on earth is similarly divine and similarly human – and similarly in motion. God saves us in any way He can, I suppose; but, thus far, primarily through our religious systems.

One may accept this world-wide analysis without committing oneself to any specific ratio, in the varying cases, of the divine to the merely human, the mundanely human, the mundane. On whether it be the same in all cases, or, indeed, whether it be the same in any one case, we need not necessarily agree. My own view would be that that ratio varies within any given community from century to century, from person to person, even from hour to hour. Perhaps few would dispute my impression that in the history of the Christian Church, for example, the ratio of the Holy Spirit's activity to that of human devilment has fluctuated wildly over different times and places. Further, to calculate whether the proportion in the past between divine and merely or perversely human has been higher on the average for one community than for another, would require the use of more complex data inputs and more subtle computers than my mind could either operate or conceive.

I simply set forth the thesis that the religious person in Christendom or in Tierra del Fuego has had his or her relationship to God formed primarily by a participation in the on-going historical movement of one or another of the world's religious communities. And I call that relationship 'faith'.

Not that I am quite sure how to correlate its saving mundanely with its saving cosmically, in either the Christian or in other cases. I *am* sure that those of us who have been saved for all eternity by God's grace have been saved also here on earth from some appalling bathos of vacuity within and bleakness without. In fact, I am more sure of that than I am of how to speak about the extra-mundane dimension of salvation, which both Christians and Muslims for a time, and some others, expressed through the metaphor of Heaven but for which just now the Church is having difficulty in finding either prose or poetry. Yet however to picture it, of this I *am* sure: that that cosmic salvation too is the same for an African tribesman and for a Taoist and for a Muslim as it is for me, or for any Christian.

And if a fellow Christian ask me how I know that, how can I be so sure, my answer is really quite simple, although perhaps too naïvely Christian. I know the empirical dimension from my historical studies (and my friendships); and I know the theological dimension because of what I know of God; by what I find revealed to me of

Him in Christ. The God whom Christ reveals is a God of mercy and love, who reaches out after all men and women everywhere in compassion and yearning; who delights in a sinner's repentance, who delights to save. It contradicts, I admit, certain man-made formulations of Christian theologians, to say this; but it contradicts the central revelation of Christ to say anything else. If St Paul or anybody else thought or thinks that only Christians can be saved, St Paul was wrong. It is Christ, and the God who has given me faith through Christ, that save me from believing so blasphemous a doctrine. St Paul was right in seeing, and proclaiming, that faith in Christ, or faith in God through Christ, saves. He had never heard of faith in the Buddha, or of faith in God through Islamic patterns. Those of us who have heard of these and know something of them must affirm with joy and triumph, and a sense of *Christian* delight, that the fact that God saves through those forms of faith too corroborates our Christian vision of God as active in history, redemptive, reaching out to all men to love and to embrace them. If it had turned out that God does not care about other men and women, or was stumped and had thought up no way to save them, *then* that would have proven our Christian understanding of God to be wrong. For a century or so recently, much of the Church seemed to take this line; and a good many members decided that Christian teaching must indeed be wrong, and left.

I reject one strand of Christian thought since 1800, and certain specific but minor formulations from earlier times made before this issue has risen; but I present this picture as continuous both with the central (major) emphases of Christian theology over most of its course, and with modern historical knowledge of the human condition. Faith is a global human quality. And the religious history of the world is the record of God's loving, creative, inspiring dealings with recalcitrant and sinful but not unresponsive men and women. Christians He has saved through Christ's death and resurrection, through membership in the Church, through the sacraments, through the myths and rituals and the art and music and the theology and the vicissitudinal history of the Christian Church. Buddhists He has saved through the teachings of the Buddha; through the imaginative memory of His person; through the scriptures, and the temples, and perhaps especially those superbly powerful and serene statues of the Buddha-image; and through the addenda to the ever-growing Buddhist process that innovative men and women have introduced in various parts of the world. Jews He has saved through that Torah that Christians have made a point of misunderstanding, and through the changing complex of Judaic minutiae, and through a Testament that for them (and for Him, in His relation to them) is not Old. Hindus He has saved, inspired, encouraged, made creative, through the poetry of the Gita and also through forms and doctrines and structures that many Christians find odd, but that God has found effective. God is more imaginative than we Christians used to think. And man more responsive. God has participated more richly in human affairs, man has participated more diversely in God, than we once knew.

All human history is *Heilsgeschichte*. Not Israel's only, either the old or the new; but the history of every religious community, every human community.

This has always been true; although we are the first generation of Christians to see this seriously and corporately, and to be able to respond to the vision. We are the first generation of Christians to discern God's active and splendid and on-going mission to humankind in the Buddhist movement, in the Hindu, in the Amerind, as well as in the Jewish and the Christian.

Such, then, is my thesis on faith. I said above that I came close to meaning by it: that which saves, universally. But I do not quite arrive at that tautology. My concept of faith as a generic human quality is partly inductive, empirically derived from a study of man's religious history throughout the world, and partly is derived from and continuous with the concept in the history of Christian doctrine. Both these points I have set forth carefully, in a recent fairly elaborate volume[2]. The concept does not pretend to be exactly the same as any other one Christian thinker's, of course, just as divers Christian thinkers' conceptions differ among themselves; but it is continuous with them – just different enough to cope with modern knowledge.

What, then, about revelation? My proposed conception here need not delay us long, since it aspires to be similarly inductive, universal and Christian, but furthermore is continuous with everything that I have set forth in my presentation until now regarding history, humane intellectuality, theology, and especially faith. I reject the big-bang theory of revelation also; or any additive theory. Despite the structure of our theological colleges, it is not the case that the first is the most important Christian century. On the one hand, I reject a first-century theory of revelation, as intellectually untenable today along with modern knowledge; and, on the other hand, at the historical level I could, if we had time, proffer a developmental analysis, suggesting that during the past couple of centuries, in particular, Western thought on these matters tended to lose hold of those important facets of the earlier Christian tradition that stressed the continuing contemporaneity of revelation; and gradually got pushed into a corner from which God's and even Christ's revelation seemed personally and historically remote; and supposed at best the same for men and women outside Christendom. Muslim thinkers have been pushed in the same direction, but more recently and less far, I believe; Hindus almost not at all.

First, I proffer revelation not as an objective concept, in our earlier chapter's terms, but as a humane one. Revelation is always a revelation to somebody. Just as one cannot speak of revelation unless something is revealed, so, I suggest, it does not mean anything to say that God has revealed Himself unless He has revealed Himself to some person[3]. And persons, of course, are always particular, and historical.

Secondly, I hold that what God reveals is always Himself. This is not a logical point, alternative views being perhaps reasonably plausible in static theory, but a theological one, based partly on my own Christian background, no doubt; partly on comparativist observation; partly on awareness of historical dynamics; partly on a resolute rationalism. It would take too long to explore the ramifications of this position, at either the theological or the historical level, let alone both; I set it forth rather arbitrarily, then, realising that it is a particular way of formulating a point of subtle and wide purport, one that could be set forth in a multitude of other ways as well, and argued at length. Our earlier view that no symbol carries its meaning in itself, each serving rather as a mediator between particular persons and a reality that transcends both it and them, is the same thesis. God reveals to man not propositions about Himself or institutional structures or specific dance patterns, let us say, but Himself; to contend this is to say that such propositions or structures or patterns as some have deemed revealed may more generically be interpreted as revelatory. Transcendence has rightly been (has let itself be, has rendered itself) perceived as immanent, history richly attests; yet never ceases to transcend, none the less. At least, so the theologian may aver.

I must add, however, an important point that has been insisted upon by Muslim theologians: namely, that since His will 'is not other than He', a revelation of His will is not an exception to this general thesis (provided it be to a specific human person, in an historical context). This notion goes along with my intimation that to do justice, to act morally, is one of the ways (and a highly important one) of being in communion with God, or participating in the life of God; or if we prefer another perspective, one of the ways in which God (or in the Christian phrase, Christ) liveth in us.

(As an aside, which we cannot develop here, I have all along been restless with the ready discrimination between mystical and prophetic religions, as if they were two historically quite separate classes.)

To return to revelation. I would not conceptualise a question of God's revelation to, let us say, al-Ghazzali, a devout and brilliant eleventh-century Muslim intellectual, in terms of whether God had deposited in human history a revelation of Himself in the form of a book four and a half centuries earlier in Arabia, or in the form of a person ten and a half centuries earlier in Palestine, and ask whether such a revelation was available to or accepted by al-Ghazzali. I would ask, rather, whether in the eleventh century in Tus and Baghdad and near Damascus God revealed Himself to this person, and through what forms and context. I would not say that the Qur'an is or is not a revelation from God; but that it was or was not – that it did or did not serve as a channel for God's self-revealing – at various stages in his life to al-Ghazzali.

Put that way, I personally do not quite see how any convinced theist who has read Ghazzali's magnificent writings could doubt that it did so serve him; though if familiar with the man's biography one could hardly fail to judge that it was a more effective divine revelation for him during his childhood and in the latter years of his life than it was during his early thirties when he was teaching at the Nizamiyah College in Baghdad.

Similarly in the Christian case. I do not say that God was revealed in Jesus Christ, just like that, absolutely, impersonally; and I suggest that it is not a good thing to say. I do say that God has been revealed to me in Jesus Christ, and has been to many millions of people throughout history – to some more vividly, more fully, more authentically, more often, more continuously than to others; to some less alloyed with inauthentic elements that they mistakenly thought were divine. I neither know why, nor have to determine how, some persons have (or: are given?) greater capacity to receive (to discern?) God's revelation than are others, whether in Christ or anywhere else.

Christian theology has sometimes said that there is a divine revelation in nature, and in history, but has gone on to say that God is (or: was) revealed fully in Christ. (Some have gone on to say, was revealed fully only in Christ.) I suggest that in the future theology may profitably learn to speak a different language. God is not revealed fully in Jesus Christ to me, nor indeed to anyone that I have met; or that my historical studies have uncovered.

And rather than asking, which is greater – one person's *x* per cent reception of a small revelation, or (in another century and another part of the world) another person's *y* per cent of a greater or even a full one, where y/x is small (the point of the mathematics being to show the absurdity of this way of thinking) – I would suggest this formulation: that all revelation is potentially fuller than it is actually. This preserves the point that the other formulation was trying to make – and universalises it. The point is not fullness but transcendence.

I would accordingly suggest that theology abandon the use of concepts that give rise to statements such as 'God is fully revealed', or 'God was revealed in Christ'. The good news is not that God did something centuries ago in Palestine, however big that bang; but that He can and may do something, and something salvific, however small our capacity, for you and me today. The locus of revelation is always the present, and always the person. The channel of revelation in the Christian case, Christ, is a figure in history. But history, I have insisted, moves forward, and is the process by which He comes to us; is not something to be studied backwards, as the process by which we try to recapture Him.

Muslims do not live in transcendence because something happened in seventh-century Arabia; they live in it because it is there. They represent it to themselves and to each other in the way that they do because they participate on earth in a movement seen as surging from there; and feel enormously grateful to that movement and also to its remembered, and idealised, initiatory launching, it having supplied them with concepts with which to think about the transcendence that they know but that otherwise surpasses apprehension, to nurture their sensibilities and response to it against the ever-distracting pressure of less worthy matters, and to relate its infinite mystery to the concrete and decidedly finite details of their particular life. The events of that earlier period are kept alive (and idealised) in their consciousness as an interpretation of their on-going and always contemporary experience.

Similarly, an historian of religion – one that takes the history of man's religion with true seriousness – might go so far as to suggest that Christian motifs of the Incarnation and the Resurrection should be interpreted historically. I said above that religiously the first is not the most important Christian century. Every generation is equidistant from eternity, as Ranke put it. It is subsequent Christian centuries that have made the first appear important. Historians have tended at times not to notice the present tense in Christians' exultant cries at Christmas and at Easter, no matter what the century. 'Hodie natus est', they have exclaimed; and exuberantly sung, 'Jesus Christ is risen *today*'. Should one not speculate that they perhaps meant what they said? Some historians of religion have tended to opine that Christmas and Easter as celebrated in Europe and elsewhere are symbolic representations of events that took place long ago, in the first century A.D. in Palestine. Might they not rather interpret the observed facts the other way round? Should one not say that on each Easter morning, in this century and in that – and to a less intense degree, each Sunday morning; and in a suffusing way, constantly – something transforming and liberating and exalting, less or much, or simply but importantly sustaining, occurred in the lives of those Christians, of which the tales of first-century events served successive ages as the symbolic representation? That God came into the world in human form on 'the first Christmas' was for many centuries a magnificent way in which most of the West articulated symbolically the fact (it is an historian speaking) that every year, every day, transcendence entered its life anew. Or to put it reciprocally: this was Europe's way of saying that its life participated in transcendence. To over-simplify: a transforming power was continuingly received, an ability to love, to forgive and to know forgiveness, to discern and to live in loyalty to the intangibles, to recognise justice and mercy and compassion as ultimate, suffering as potentially redemptive and a proximate price of righteousness, oneself as cosmically significant and one's neighbour equally, and so on. These things actually happened, generation after generation, in the lives of millions of people. Inadequately, certainly; imperfectly, no doubt; ineptly, often – yet, haltingly, and in varying fashion, God in the shape of Christ did indeed enter the world of man, in the lives of Christians in the course of many centuries, until now.

Whether one interpret the situation in this or in some other way, the important fact – important both for Christians, and for outside observers contemplating the Christian sector of the world's religious life – is the presence of God from day to day in the life of the community. To this all else is ancillary.

A theology conceived in a mode such as I propound is, for a Christian, radical, one might as well admit, at least in the sense that several of its ideas differ saliently from those that have been in prevalent use for the past one or two hundred years. Whether in spirit, as distinct from formulation; and whether from classical as distinct from modern Christian patterns, it differs quite so much, I leave my readers to judge; just as I leave to my Hindu and Muslim friends and to other groups to judge whether indeed I have come forward with anything that offers them a basis at least for discussion, and us all a hope for collaboration. And I leave to my fellow intellectuals to judge whether some such thesis is a rational interpretation of the known data.

Some churchmen, no doubt, will say, 'That is all very well, but what about Christ? You have not made him central in your total vision; a Christian therefore cannot go along.' My answer to that is . . . but perhaps it is bumptious to answer? I have no desire to claim to be more Christian than I am; nor even more legitimate. This much, however, is perhaps worth saying: that my proposal is unabashedly theocentric, and among its many faults, this at least is a virtue. Christian thought has in recent centuries, and especially this century, one may urge, lost sight too drastically of God, and of the Holy Spirit. One may remember the quip that the World Council of Churches has become unitarian, of the Son. If other religious communities, or even the study of them, can help the Christian Church to recover its theocentricity, good. I wonder whether I need shrink from saying: if Christians insist that Christ is the centre of their lives, it is time that we rediscovered that God is the centre of the universe. For me, God is not dead; and the miracle of the Son is that He has shown the glory of the Father – and has enabled me to see and to receive it, and to live in it, through grace.

I repeat, I have no wish to claim that my thesis is more Christian than it inherently be. Every thinker must be sincere. Every theologian formulates the truth as he sees it; and every Christian is as Christian, I suppose, as God gives him the grace, in his honesty, to be. So far as my submission is concerned, it is permissible to remark that it is Christian within the definition proposed earlier for that term: it is formulated by one who historically comes by way of faithful participation in the Christian process, and it is proffered to that community in its on-going endeavour (of theology) to conceptualise in rational terms the reality that it has known and knows. Moreover, it is perhaps not presumptuous to suggest that it is perhaps continuous with some quite major emphases in our traditional vision.

Salvation by faith, for instance: I really have come to believe that! (To my surprise, I might add.) Further, there is represented a conviction, and indeed a discerning, that God is as Christ reveals Him to be, actively and redemptively at work, always and everywhere taking the initiative to seek and to save men and women in the historical context of their lives. Also, I should like to think that I have been true to the central and deep Christian commission of concern for and outreach toward the neighbour, and of reconciliation and the building of community.

There are certain continuities, too, which we shall not develop, with doctrines of sacrament (a better notion than symbol, maybe, for interpreting the religious history of our race); and some will detect a certain leaning, perhaps (curious for a Presbyterian), to a doctrine of the Real Presence.

Continuity also, perhaps again surprisingly, obtains with the traditional Christian concern for the Church's mission in the world, or phrased more accurately, God's mission in the world through the Church–even though the coalescence here of continuity and radical newness be striking. Nineteenth-century 'missions' are drastically superseded; yet not by isolationism or insouciance, un-Christianly. We recognised above historically, in our opening chapters, that in our religiously plural world (the only world there is or has been) the Church in fact has always been involved; and we now add, theologically, always ought to be involved. The former recognition is that of modern knowledge. The latter has yet to find its modern expression, but the type of extraversion that I advocate, with its moral foundations, can be seen as in continuity with central Christian emphases. This is so, however new the concomitant recognition of God's mission to all the world through Buddhist, Islamic, modern Jewish and other movements. On this question I have written elsewhere, however[4]; and therefore do not develop it here.

Other traditional points, similarly, could be pursued but will not be. As I have said, I leave to others to judge whether the innovations propounded constitute too radical a break with current Christian positions to be countenanced as Christian, or whether rather their self-conscious modernity be accepted as apt. They aim at being true; whether they succeed in being Christian is not mine to press.

Thus I bring to an end my endeavours to respond to the challenge of bringing one Christian's contribution to the task of constructing for Christians in our world community a theology of comparative religion. Foolish endeavour? Doubtless. And yet one had to try.

It will have been obvious to the experts among my readers that I am neither a skillful nor an erudite theologian; obvious to the Western humanists among them that I am still what I always professed to be before I somehow agreed to take on the challenge of these lectures: namely, an historian of the Orient, not a philosopher of the West; obvious to the Asians among them that the West has still a long way to go before its understanding of Asian ways is deep; obvious to the saints among them that what I can offer is a not nearly Christian enough Christian's contribution.

None the less, I somehow thought it worth trying. We human beings around the globe all are too torn by our separations, and we Christians are too pained by our own part in the world's estranging misunderstandings and too impelled by faith and hope and a vision of love, for one to remain silent when an invitation came to tackle an impossible yet compelling assignment.

9 Interim Conclusion

It would be entrancing for the others among us to hear an interpretation of the whole of our human religious history, and not merely Buddhist, in its relation to ultimate truth and reality – of the universe and of man – conceptualised in terms such as *dharma*: an interpretation proffered primarily to Buddhists but in principle to be available also to the rest of us. The interpreter might feel tremulous lest he or she fail to do justice either to the others of us being represented or to fellow Buddhists who have previously seen in their own tradition something that lifts it quite above the category 'religion' employed to characterise the rest of us. Yet it would be a pity if such hesitations should inhibit the attempt; and in fact it will increasingly be made. Hindus, Sufis and others have long had their theories, however anhistorical; and the Chinese have traditionally interpreted pluralism quite cheerily and sagely – their own, even if not in the past including the rest of us outside.

New in Christendom is the acceptance of pluralism; and new everywhere is the mutual availability of the several groups' endeavours towards interpreting it, towards conceptualising the whole – our whole. The history of man's religious life, which for some centuries was divided into self-conscious parts, is beginning to include also a developing history of diverse instances of self-consciousness of the whole; instances open to each other.

We are learning each other's languages, both literally and figuratively. (The line between these two modes, as we observed in considering the symbolic, is in principle both tenuous and unstable.) The preceding chapter, therefore, however suggestive or inadequate it might seem – and this would be the case also for Buddhist or Muslim or other counterpart attempts – represents a stage through and beyond which the intellect, in its inherent aspiration to universally valid truth, must move. Similarly must faith, in its parallel aspiration. Not that faith will cease to be specific; we have insisted throughout that it is always personal, particular, historical, and may be seen as indeed a relation of the concrete person to universal truth – reality; the finite finitely apprehending the infinite, or *vice versa*. It is mediated mundanely. Besides, it is always in part communal; though today the community is being enlarged, self-consciously and otherwise. Nevertheless that relation of the specific to the generic, although itself specific, is conceptualised generically; or so intellectuals – theologians – hope and strive. The move, accordingly, is in our day through and beyond the several theologies of comparative religion or their counterparts that might be essayed towards something still more universal (and therein more accurate also to interpreting the specific).

Our aim in this 'interim conclusion' to our present study is not to articulate that universal truth – fond dream! – but to adumbrate a whit more generically the direction in which it may be sought, and along which indications thus far have seemed cumulatively to point. We shall consider the issues to be dealt with under three main headings: vocabulary, truth and history.

In the matter of language, some will remark that in the last chapter, and to some degree elsewhere, I was not able, but I should prefer to say that I did not try, much to escape the conceptual categories of Christian, or at most monotheist, thought; though I would expand them. The fact is that we do not have available to us, and must work towards forging, concepts that will serve us generically (for accurate interpretation, let alone self-interpretation). Even when concepts are attained, the words through which to communicate them in this language or in that may prove inadequate, less for some persons or groups than for others. The processes of intellectual history are in part those of old words' attaining new meanings for small or large sectors of various communities. What persons perceive in their environment, external or internal, is largely but need not be wholly a function of the words and phrases in terms of which they or their group think; and it is their responsibility, certainly if intellectuals, to see to it that their meanings for those words correspond as closely as may be to what they are in a position to see and to know. The history of religion (other people's and our own) has made us aware of things for which it is now our task to construct adequate conceptual categories and terms.

Let us consider four or five terms that merit attention.

A generic concept 'faith', for which I have chosen to use that English word (a term traditionally Christian, also Jewish, Islamic, but with wide-ranging counterparts in India, China and Japan), I have recently devoted a substantial volume to developing careful grounds for generating[1]. I am hopeful that others will find its subsuming of the several specifics persuasive and helpful; in any case, I need not pursue it further here. The notion that 'believing', rather, is what religious people basically do, has also of course required attention[2].

The traditional Christian term 'salvation' is certainly not generic; and while some Christians will continue to use it (in which case they will have to use it also *extra ecclesiam*), others internally have come to find it problematic; not to say, especially among youth in the West, vacuous. The concept behind the word, and to some degree the reality behind the concept, have been lost; part of what was traditionally signified must be recaptured, a new word to express it probably being requisite. 'Liberation' has caught the fancy of some, with but little of its traditional Hindu connotation; and *shalom* is beginning to move beyond Jewish borders. 'Identity' is currently having a surprising vogue; some of us find it less rich and compelling than others seem to do. Those of us who know what we wish to say in this realm have a distance yet to go before we have found or constructed a way of saying it intelligibly.

With the term 'theology', certainly, which I have ventured to preserve even in my title, many will feel decidely ill at ease. This includes not only Buddhists and Western humanists, for whom emotions and ideas on the subject inherited from before the cosmopolitan era still in many instances may reign. To select or to create a more generic term may well be a priority task, and it is possible that I have guessed wrongly in hoping that those for whom it has not been congenial in the past might yet tolerate its interim use. The obvious alternative might seem to be 'philosophy', especially since the philosophy of religion has constituted in the Western world a venerable tradition. My reasons for not preferring it are serious, whether or not persuasive. I am myself an intellectual in the Greek tradition, it is my claim; it is not disparaging to say, and it is important to recognise, that in world perspective that noble tradition is just as particular as is the Christian or the Hindu or another. The very troublesomeness of the concept 'theology' is perhaps an advantage, since it renders our problem evident, over against an illusion that one has already attained universalism by calling oneself a philosopher. The latter might also encourage a tendency surreptitiously to envisage the problem of religion and its diversity from the outside: a cul-de-sac, in my view. (This is doubly so since the meaning of 'philosophy' has been cheapened of late by those who have traded its classical love of a transcendent yet humane wisdom for a positivist practicising of a mundane craft? Christian theology, and to some degree Muslim and Jewish, has long turned outside the bounds of its own tradition to enter into conversation with the philosophers; I am urging that this must be supplemented by conversation with fellow religionists around the globe, and doubly so in so far as the former may represent in our day a turning towards the secular in the recent restricted sense of heeding only two of man's body, mind and spirit.) None the less it is imperative that our new enterprise not in its turn leave the Western philosophic tradition on the outside. If we adopted 'philosophy', Christians and Muslims might feel that the deepest ranges of their faith were being neglected; if 'theology', humanists and Buddhists the most elemental of theirs. Yet terms concocted *de novo* provide no easy solution either – again, part of the central point being to subsume the past, not to supersede it. Is it mere pusillanimity of spirit that makes one hesitate to stomach something like 'transcendentology'?

Terminology, all this illustrates, is inherently part of our problem. The new vision must be not only seen but also intelligibly expressed.

Less obliquely, this issue arises – rages – over the concept 'God'. On this, feelings run high indeed. The term itself is a symbol: for some, infinitely positive; for others, negative, less or more harshly; for some few, quizzical. Historically, as we observed in our opening chapters, the theistic has been one of the tremendous movements on the earth in some of its major sectors. Some of us have participated in it quietly or grandly; others of us – particularly in eastern Asia, but less generally also elsewhere – have not; and recently in the West, fewer have than before. Intellectuals sensitive to the transcendent dimension within and around humankind have to decide whether or not to opt for this particular way to think the matter and to talk it.

Of the theistic mode one may recall especially that aspect that traditionally stressed God's transcending all human conceptualisation of Him (it is a subtle and momentous quality of the human mind that it can formulate highly significant self-transcending concepts). Or one may stress what traditionally the idea has positively shown forth and now bequeathed us. On either or especially both of these grounds, some among us are at ease with that mode, even profoundly grateful to it, and yet are aware that many of our fellows are unmoved or are moved negatively by the term 'God'. I myself have in this study and elsewhere joined that relatively modern group who find the term 'transcendence' congenial and rich; yet, with it as with 'God', I do not know what others will hear in it when I use it. Just as the same person may speak French when he or she is in one part of Canada and English when in another, so one may find oneself using 'transcendence' language in certain company and theist in a different milieu. But that may be like being on friendly terms with both parties to a quarrelling or divorcing couple.

One concept of the term 'God' that has drawn much attention lately is the non-transcendent question of gender. In English, the use of 'He' or 'She' as corresponding pronoun has brought home to many the limitations of the concept. (Yet the problem would not arise if one spoke Persian or Chinese. There is no *a priori* reason to suppose that English is the language best suited to a theology of religious diversity, although historical contingencies point to it in not only my case; and it becomes the task of some of us to help English move in the direction of greater sophistication.) Similarly, the exceedingly important distinction between conceptualising ultimate reality and truth as 'He' or conceptualising either or both of them as 'It', an issue to which Hindu thinking has made and will make decisively helpful contributions, is a distinction that cannot be (should one say, need not be?) thought in Hebrew, Arabic and other Semitic languages, nor, among the Indo-European group, in, for instance, Urdu or French. This excursus would be little germane, except that it can illustrate clearly one part of our problem. Just as a woefully inadequate solution to the She–He issue and to the inability of English to transcend it would be to arrange that all women refer to God as feminine, men as masculine, so on a more global scale it is hardly satisfactory, intellectually or sociologically, to settle for theists' referring to the transcendent as 'God', non-theists' not. We are going to have to learn to understand each other's languages; and also to come to mean by our own terms also what we validly learn from each other. Only after that has happened will the vocabulary problem become soluble.

In the interim, and as a contribution to the process that will lead us beyond it, might one perhaps put forward as a possible basis for discussion between theists and non-theists the suggestion that by the term 'God' one mean a truth–reality that explicitly transcends conception but in so far as conceivable is that to which man's religious history has at its best been a response, human and in some senses inadequate? (In 'religious' history I include, of course, the Western classical tradition, metaphysical–humanist–idealist, where transcendence has appeared primarily as Truth; also as Beauty and Justice, the Good. I include also, of course, quite firmly, Buddhist history and other where transcendence has been conceptualised not as 'God'. Christians will recognise that in this operationalist characterisation I have of course taken a cue from those Christians who, when queried, answer by affirming, 'By "God" we mean Him Whom Jesus Christ has revealed', and have expanded it; or those Muslims who say, 'By "God" we mean Him Who speaks to us through the Qur'an.')

There are plenty of merely mundane and many repugnantly perverse elements clearly visible in the religious history of humankind (one's own and others'); these elements may without too much trouble be sorted out. They cloud, but need not eclipse, the divine. To discriminate them (whether in one's own or in all traditions) is (in one's own has long been) the responsibility of faith.

My suggestion is vulnerable in itself and as it stands may well be inadequate for most purposes other than the discussion envisaged. One could write an entire book on the many refinements that are requisite and the difficulties that arise; here I content myself with remarking that those refinements and difficulties do not in principle differ through the whole history of religion from what they are today in the case of any one tradition. If any is to be taken seriously, all are.

(Or, if 'all' seem too inclusive, especially perhaps to those who may not share the Neo-Platonist tendencies in my perception of data that underlies in my formulation the almost casual phrase 'at its best', one could for the sake of argument restrict it, to any religious tradition that has won the loyalty and admiration of at least, say, a hundred million people, including outstanding saints and intellectual geniuses; has endured for at least, say, a thousand years; and has provided the basis on which at least one great civilisation has been constructed. Yet I think of a few groups whom the arithmetic of this otherwise clarifying restriction would fail to include, but for whom I cannot help but have profound respect. We shall return in a moment to the epistemological question of truth criteria. Meanwhile, should one include as part of the discussion also whether 'search' should replace or supplement 'response' in our formulation – or something like 'that reality that they responded to by searching for'? I myself would give up 'response' none too readily, since it is my empirical impression that religion through history has been a response of human beings to the world in which they and we live and to the fact of being human in that world; but I am willing to discuss this with anyone whose view interprets the data differently.)

My purpose, in any case, is not fondly to define the concept 'God', but to help to make more corporate and more historical the self-consciousness of those who, if they would not define, would explicate or illuminate or ponder it, or would attempt to understand others' rich use of it – in the course of our endeavour in this 'concluding' chapter to bridge the gap between specific and generic. Our topic here is the role of vocabulary in that process.

I have urged, then, that our conceptualising, and our understanding of each other's concepts, be anchored in history, even for history-transcending and self-transcending concepts such as 'God'. I can do this because and only because human history and especially the history of religion, in our non-bifurcationist discernment, has been the locus of man's intercourse with transcendence, of his and her participation in it and its in them. Terms such as 'transcendence', 'theology', 'God', or some counterparts to them, are important to keep or to develop, lest sight or feel be lost of what some would call the objective pole in religious experience. My emphasis on history might seem too anthropocentric, were our history not such as to belie any anthropocentrism that would distract from the vividness or ubiquity of human awareness of a reality greater than man. My emphasis on corporate self-consciousness might seem to lend itself to a charge of collective subjectivism, despite my disclaimers, were there not dramatically included within it that historically persistent consciousness of a surpassingly great Other. Hence the insistence that the understanding that we seek, call it 'theology' or not, is not simply of the history of religion, but of that to which the history of religion has at its best been a response. (These two amount to the same thing, if the former be taken authentically, listened to seriously.) That response has been human and in many senses inadequate, but not ultimately inadequate since sinners and derelicts and the undistinguished, as Shinran and Luther and others have noted, are saved – or more generically, since human history, human life as lived in history, is and has been not inane.

Our new task is to interpret intellectually the cosmic significance of human life generically, not just for one's own group specifically (let alone, not to fail to know or to interpret that significance).

Intellectual interpretations aspire to being true. We turn next to that question; and more generically, to the issue of truth in religion. I distinguish sharply between faith and the intellectual interpretation of faith (or, between faith and the intellectual interpretation of the World, carried out in faith). I distinguish especially for others (and most especially for other eras and world-views); but aspire to correlate them anew for us. This problem will detain us here but briefly, however. The matter is a mighty one, about which many volumes have been and have yet to be written. Here we touch on it only as it pertains to our present inquiry, as to what the truth that one seeks is to be true about; what range of faith it shall interpret; on the basis of what range of data it shall interpret man and the world. Besides, I have elsewhere recently published on related issues.

A superficial reading of my present argument for comprehensiveness might tempt some to imagine that I am contending that all religion is true, or equally true; or all religious statements. That would be indeed silly. I, of course, hold that not even one 'religion' is *equally* true, abstractly in all its instances through history; rather, it becomes less or more true in the case of particular persons as it informs their lives and their groups and shapes and nurtures their faith. So far as religious statements are concerned, their diversity and their role in social and in individual life has been studied in some of the publications mentioned. (Besides, one must note that the period is now coming to an end when one imagined that a religion consisted primarily in a set of propositional tenets, each either true or false. Though that period was short-lived, the position was strong enough to have done much damage.) What I do urge is that the problem of religious truth is in principle not different, but in practice much improved, if one take the whole of religion rather than a sector of it as the question's field.

To be a Christian (or Muslim) in the most fiercely exclusivist sense, denigrating outsiders, does not mean not to discriminate among insiders: to accept everything that every Christian (Muslim) has done, or felt, or said, as right for oneself, to regard every sect as inerrant and exemplary, every century's theology as authoritative. One may affirm that the whole truth regarding man's salvation is found in and only in Christian (or only in Islamic) revelation; one still has to use one's judgement to discern it. One still has to develop criteria for distinguishing more true from less true, better from worse (should one add: true from false, good from evil?), among the plethora of interpretations and orientations with which Christian history has been and is today variegated (Islamic history appears not quite so profusely diverse; yet only the uninformed can fail to appreciate variety). In principle, a shifting from the specific to the generic, while broadening the range of history that one takes seriously, modifies the form but does not transmute the substance of intellectual responsibility. To perceive oneself as in principle heir to the whole religious history of the race thus far, and the community of which one is a member as in principle the human community, and that to which one gives one's final loyalty as in active relation with all one's fellows, is not to dissolve the question of religious truth but for our day to bring it into focus.

Since other groups in that larger community, as well as one's own, have thought about truth in this realm and about criteria for assessing it and methods for arriving at more accurate discriminations between more true and less, one is helped not hindered also in this matter by opening oneself to their wisdom. (Indeed, is it not intellectually, and not only morally, almost delinquent not to do so?) A salient illustration might be the question with which the West is only beginning, but now earnestly, to wrestle: the truth of myths. On the how and why and what of this, Christian and Muslim theologians have much to learn from the long tradition of, for instance, acute Hindu thinking. Another example that one might pick is the question of pluralism and its intellectual interpretation ('relativism'?): those among us unaccustomed to conceptualising with any degree of rational rigour and critical acumen what is finally involved in 'agreeing to differ' conceptually will find help from those others among us, such as Buddhists and again Hindus and others in the Far East, who have long since worked that one out with much sophistication. Nor can one imagine that the Orient has nothing to learn from Christian or Muslim thought: the imperious significance of history might be one example, and its religious impingement, about which the Western traditions have thought deeply, while some Asian groups are only beginning – but inescapably now – to be self-conscious of major historical change, also in its spiritual ramifications.

I do not regard it as requisite for the thesis of this study to proffer here and now a disciplined epistemology to go along with our new global awareness. Many current Western epistemologies are oriented more to science than to history, more to things than to persons, and are more individualistic than will probably (or anyway should) endure. The task of attaining an epistemological sophistication that will be historically self-critical as well as universalist, is interlinked with, not prior to, our task of attaining corporate critical self-consciousness in the religious realm. In fact, some would hardly be surprised if the comparative study of religion contributed more to the development of Western epistemology than *vice versa*; but the two should go hand in hand. In any case, the striving to understand religion is part and parcel of, certainly not subordinate to, man's general aspiration to truth.

Some among my Western readers might in this regard expect consideration to be given to the question of the truth of transcendence itself, the reality of God. One of the advantages of familiarity with the world history of religion (of man) is that one is then not intimidated by current Western trends of thought that see this as a 'problem'. Rather than feeling called upon to defend the awareness of what some of us call the divine before the bar of modern sceptics' particular logic and exceptional world-view, I am at least equally inclined to call them before the bar of world history to defend their curious insensitivity to this dimension of human life. Seen in global perspective, current anti-transcendent thinking is an aberration. Intellectuals are challenged, indeed, to understand it: how it has arisen that for the first time on this earth a significant group has failed to discern the larger context of being human, and has even tried (with results none too encouraging thus far) to modify its inherited civilisation so. After all, the overwhelming majority of intelligent persons at most times and places, and all cultures other than in part the recent West, have recognised the transcendent quality of man and the world. To be secularist in the negative sense is to be oddly parochial in both space and time, and to opt for what may alas be a dying culture. It is important that we keep in conversation with this group; but important also that we not fall victim to, nor treat with anything but compassion, its incapacity to see.

This incapacity may be linked with that other parochialism which conceived the issue to be between, simply, a nihilistic positivism on the one hand and traditional Christian (or Greek metaphysical) formulations on the other. Both sides of this particular debate can perhaps move forward only if each sees truth in a larger frame.

With regard to the question of truth internally within the

religious field, and among its potentially bewildering diversities, perhaps the primary lesson to be learned is this, if one is to be discriminating but not sit in judgement: that the rigorous and unrelenting search for truth can be combined with a profound respect for others and for variety provided that one recognise the truth that one seeks as to be found not in the history of religion but through it. (Indeed, this is what participants in that history, each for their own tradition, have long been attesting.) Truth, I submit, is a humane, not an objective, concept. It does not lie in propositions. (Propositions are not true or false – *pace* Tarksy and others; to treat them as if they were is parochially possible at best only within a highly circumscribed universe of discourse and a highly limited community of shared prejudgements; also, over a sharply limited period of history.) To it approximate not the propositions themselves but what these mean, have meant, to particular persons, and groups. In so far as truth is apprehended by persons, it is apprehended within history; yet in so far as it is true, it transcends history (and any particular formulation). It is therefore inherently a transcendent as well as a humane concept. It is this fact that allows a student of history to combine a basic respect for, basic acceptance of, others – persons, eras, cultures, groups – not an arrogant sitting in judgement on them, with a basic critical stance for oneself (for ourselves). Far from our being asked to surrender such capacities, the study of the vast variety historically of our human scene, especially in its spiritual forms, requires and carries to new heights our most acute critical capacities. For we look beyond the propositions and symbols and other elements of the various traditions to the persons whom they served, and whom they enable us then to understand, and look beyond even those persons to the truth of which we recognise that they like us were in search (to which they like us were responding), and recognise that to them, unlike to us, that truth, or rather some finite approximation to it, appeared thus and so, the world presented itself in this or that fashion. We are then in a vastly improved position critically, yet charitably, responsibly, non-idiosyncratically, to formulate the truth for us. May a theologian reasonably do less?

A Christian theologian in the era drawing to a close who did not, on a foundation of deep respect, wrestle with both an Augustine and a Harnack, or a Muslim who did not wrestle with both an Ash‘ari and an Iqbal, or a modern theologian in our new era who does not wrestle with all of these and a Chu Hsi and an Aurobindo, would hardly be critical, surely; and hardly likely to approximate the truth very closely in his or her new formulations.

The truth remains transcendent, however; and formulations of it for us that will help us to approximate it as closely as in our day it is our duty and special privilege to attain will once again, as ever throughout history, be particular, historical, contingent. We turn then, finally, to our third heading: the historical dimension of our ideational task. Thus I close as I began, attending to the historical context of our human and religious and intellectual process but hoping that we return to it better equipped to see it and to think it cosmically (theologically, dharmically). We modern intellectuals, as we attempt to give a valid vision of the world a conceptual form today, must corporately and critically be self-conscious of our human involvement in, simultaneously, the historical and the transcendent.

I turn to the historical partly for an historical reason. I have set forth in this study certain views in proffered answer to the question that our human diversity on earth in religious life poses, and that modern developments make urgent. More important than those views is that question itself, and the historical fact that current processes are moving us all towards increasing involvement in it. More important than one lone thinker's attempt to address these issues is that the Church's intellectuals generally, to take the Christian instance, must today do so with a quite unwonted seriousness. Moreover, as I have insisted throughout, the task is collaborative and must be recognised so. A study such as this is valuable, if at all, not only in so far as it may contribute to Christian theological movement in the new direction, but also, and at least equally importantly, in so far as it may prove a step towards Jewish and Muslim and Buddhist and Hindu and secular-rationalist response and mutuality. Part of the newness of our problem is that the significance of any proposed solution has to do with its contribution towards a shareable vision.

Distinctions will not dissolve; rather, in the conceptualisations of responsible intellectuals, those distinctions will survive that men and women wittingly and with reason choose to maintain.

If human life has always been lived in a context with simultaneously historical and transcendent dimensions – the historical ever changing, and religion as the formalised recognition of this double fact – today the historical is increasingly common to us all, so that we not only must but now also may intelligibly think together whether the transcendent too be common for us all, and wherein. The two dimensions continue to interpenetrate in our lives. Thus we today are given a new type of answer to the classical query of what the religious systems of the world have in common. The new answer supplements or undergirds any proffered theoretical reflection; is dynamic and personalist, is historical; has to do with becoming more than with being. For the various religious traditions have now in common the fact that each is being carried by persons who are increasingly involved in the same situations. Muslims, Jews, Buddhists, Hindus, Christians and the others are for the first time being faced with a joint challenge: to collaborate in building a common world. This must be not only the kind of world in which we can all live together, but one also of which we can jointly approve, and to the building and sustaining of which the faith of each of us can effectively inspire.

Those of us concerned with the intellectual and transcendent dimensions of our common life are not insensitive to this historical actuality; and, indeed, some might argue that it may growingly prove more cogent, more revolutionary, more spiritually penetrating than any theory. Yet whether juxtaposition becomes conflict or harmony will depend largely on our theories.

Additionally, even at the ideational level historical development is conducing to the emergence of something that communities may come to have in common, of mighty consequence: namely, for the first time a clear and mutually agreed awareness of their differences. Few know how novel and how difficult this is – and how transforming. We have barely begun to attain it here and there; but as, superseding misunderstanding, it is partially achieved and is acted upon, we begin to see its great significance: for instance, in the West in Catholic–Protestant and Jewish–Christian encounter. Now that Christians are for the first time beginning to perceive Jewish perceptions, rather than to conceptualise Jewish positions (and Christian positions) unilaterally, the internal revisions of Christian theology that flow from the resultant revised self-consciousness are deep. Throughout the world all the various religious communities have historically begun the unimaginably promising venture of becoming authentically aware of each other, and thereby of themselves, and of their several participation in the whole, as we have argued, and aware of their own and the others' participation in the process of unending transition on which we have earlier insisted. For the first time there is for all of us an increasingly common consciousness of the world around us, given by science, and of the total process of our human history, including religious history, and of the fact that this is currently entering a strikingly new phase in all its parts.

In fine, what the religious – and secular – communities of the world have in common historically is an increasingly common awareness of the past, in all its dynamic diversity and cohesion, and an increasingly common involvement in and shared responsibility for an increasingly joint future.

What we have in common transcendently I have tried to adumbrate, but anyway to emphasise. If we cannot posit a theology or philosophy or dharmalogy of comparative religion, we can postulate the conditions out of which it will grow, as the disciplined self-consciousness of our variegated and developing religious – human – life.

Those conditions can and should be developed, and institutionalised. The Christian Church, for example, has already begun falteringly to move, in its relations with other communities at the level of implemented theory, from its erstwhile monologue of proselytising missions to what it now calls 'dialogue', a concept that is in many ways a highly significant improvement but that I personally find on many scores inadequate. I would urge something less occasional, and less polarised. At best, dialogue designates a transition through which one moves to something new. (If dialectic in Hegelian mode suggests – too much, to my ears – antithesis, does one none the less envisage synthesis? In any case, one is changed by serious conversation, otherwise it was not genuine.) As a term I prefer 'colloquy'; partly for its multilateral connotations but chiefly to suggest a side-by-side confronting of the world's problems (intellectual and other) rather than a face-to-face confronting of each other. One might urge 'from dialogue to colloquy' as a slogan within the Church. Primarily, however, as has become apparent, I contend that it is neither rational nor timely (nor Christian) to conceive one's intellectual goals more narrowly. If the Church be serious about its intellectual task for the coming era, it will set up ongoing patterns for comparative theology.

Academically, on the other hand, such patterns already almost exist, and will grow. In Tokyo, Ibadan, Ankara, in Banaras, Makkah, Harvard, departments of comparative religion are in process, and the tendency to avoid the serious questions, through 'objectivity' or otherwise, wanes. The interchange of scholars on visiting and exchange programmes, and the collaborative quality of serious work, grows. The intellectual questions of the meaning of religious diversity, and the meaning of the various traditions, each envisaged within the context of the others and of modern secularity, are being tackled.

Is it legitimate to hope that religious institutions around the world will not leave these questions to intellectuals outside their walls? (Every contemporary Christian theological seminar, for instance, should have a chair for a visiting professor from some other community; or perhaps two, one Jewish and one other. No?)

The historical context has always been relevant, I have insisted, to man's apprehension of God, of truth, of transcendence; and doubly so, to the form of that apprehension, in concepts and other expression. It is relevant today. Our historical situation, it is widely recognised or felt, is such as to make older forms and modes of expression anachronist. It is also, I am contending, such as to make a new apprehension, and a new mode, possible – and right.

The past makes manifest that God participates in human life, in its grandeur and its dismay. Yet He is available to us not in the past, but today. In order to know Him, it helps to know the history of religion, His dealings with humankind; yet our knowledge of Him cannot be that history's knowing, or even way of knowing, but must be our own. The history of man's religious life is that fissiparous, yet not disintegrated, process in which we all, in our separateness, have participated, and through which we have participated in the life of God; but if we would know and understand what we are doing in so participating – in that history and in that life – we must recognise that, as has been the case for each generation but now dramatically more so, our phase is new. And we see it in its place within the whole, world-wide and history-long.

Through Islamic patterns God across the centuries has been participating in the life of Muslims; through Buddhist patterns in the life of Buddhists; through Hindu modes in the life of India; through Jewish forms, also after the first century, in the life, individual and social, of Jews; and some of us know, through Christians forms in our lives. It is through His participation in the religious history of the world (and in the Western case, also the history of the Graeco-Roman tradition) that He has chiefly entered human lives to act in human history. Right now, He is calling us to let Him act through new forms, continuous with the old, as we human beings across the globe enter our strange new age.

Notes and References

CHAPTER 1

1. Wilfred Cantwell Smith, *The Meaning and End of Religion: A New Approach to the Religious Traditions of Mankind* (New York: Macmillan, 1963, and New American Library, 1964; [new edn] London: SPCK, 1978; [same] San Francisco: Harper & Row, 1978).
2. The idea is indeed ambitious, and presumably would be forbiddingly voluminous. As noted below in Chapter 2, I have been groping my way towards a course of this sort at Harvard, beginning with a seminar entitled 'Historical Interrelations among Religious Traditions' on various occasions over the past ten years or so. For others' moves in the same direction, see notes 22–5 below.
3. Tolstoi, *Ispoved'*, written in 1879. It was ready for publication in Moscow in 1882, but an ecclesiastical veto stopped that; it circulated surreptitiously in the country in hectograph form, and was published in Geneva, in Russian, in 1884 by M. K. Elpidine (also 1886, 1888). I have consulted the English translation (*A Confession . . .*)by Aylmer Maude in The World's Classics edition (London: Oxford University Press, 1967 [first published 1921]) and that (*My Confession . . .*) by Leo Wiener, in the Illustrated Sterling Edition of Tolstoy's works (Boston: Dana Estes, 1904); for the Russian text, that in vol. XXIII of the official Soviet edition of the complete works: L. N. Tolstoi, *Polnoe Sobranie Sochinenii* (Moskva: Gosudarstvennoe Izdatel'stvo Khudozhestvennoi Literatury, 1957) pp. 1–57.
4. In the editions just cited (previous note), the story appears pp. 20f., 21–3, and 13f, respectively. The final quotation (given here not exactly as in either translation) is from p. 14 of the original. The exceptional force of the fable for Tolstoi psychologically is made the clearer by his vivid dream three years later (pp. 81–4, 88–90, 57–9, respectively; in the case of the Russian, without the 1882 date).
5. One writer in an article not long ago affirmed, 'there was no European language that did not possess a translation of that work bearing witness to a success perhaps attained by no other legend' – Raoul Manselli, 'The Legend of Barlaam and Joasaph in Byzantium and in the Romance Europe', *East and West* (Rome) VII (1956–7) 333; and another speaks of 'over eighty versions in the principal languages of Europe, the Christian Orient, and even [Christian] Africa' – David Marshall Lang, *The Wisdom of Balahvar* (London: Allen & Unwin; and New York: Macmillan, 1957) p. 5, referring to a Joseph Jacobs study of 1896 that I have not seen.
6. The traditional attribution to John of Damascus was rejected by nineteenth-century scholarship and regarded as disproved. It was championed afresh in

Franz Dölger, *Der griechische Barlaam-Roman, ein Werk des H. Johannes von Damaskos* Studia Patristica et Byzantina, no. 1 (Ettal: Buch-Kunstverlag des Klosters, 1953); but the thesis has won exceedingly few converts. Two versions of the Georgian original have recently been published in English translation by David Marshall Lang, as *The Wisdom of Balahvar* (see note 5) and *The Balavariani (Barlaam and Josaphat): A Tale from the Christian East Translated from the Old Georgian* (London: Allen & Unwin, 1966). The historical transmission of the tale from Georgian, its first Christian appearance, into Greek, thence into Latin, and from these into further languages of Christendom ('from Iceland to Ethiopia, from Poland to the Philippines' – Lang, *Balavariani*, p. 11), is convincingly presented by Lang in his introductory section (pt I, pp. 11–65) of *The Wisdom of Balahvar*, and by Ilia V. Abuladze of the Georgian Academy of Sciences, Tbilisi, in his Introduction (pp. 19–41) to *Balavariani*. Both Lang volumes and (less reliably) the Manselli article (see note 5) give extensive bibliographies of earlier scholarship. It was Lang's work that first put me on to this matter, which seems to have attracted the attention of few other theologians (or even, as he himself notes in *Balavariani*, p. 11, of other comparative religionists).

7. The most authoritative recent survey is the article 'Bilawhar wa-Yūdāsaf' by D. M. Lang in *The Encyclopaedia of Islam*, 2nd edn, vol. I (Leiden: Brill; and London: Luzac, 1960) pp. 1215–17.
8. *Kitāb Bilawhar wa-Būdhāsaf*, ed. Shaykh Nūr al-Dīn ibn Jīvākhān (Bombay: Ṣafdarī, 1306 AH [1888–9 AD]). See also Daniel Gimaret, *Le Livre de Bilawhar et Būdāsf, selon la version arabe ismaélienne*, Hautes Etudes Islamiques et Orientales d'Histoire Comparée, no. 3 (Geneva and Paris: Droz, 1971). This latter provides a French translation of the former, Arabic, work; its substantial Introduction provides also a good synopsis, with bibliography, of work on other pre-Greek versions.
9. See, for instance, Al-Haj Khwaja Nazir Ahmad, *Jesus in Heaven and Earth* (Lahore and Woking, 1952). An account of this work in Robert Graves and Joshua Podro, *Jesus in Rome: A Historical Conjecture* (London: Cassell, 1957) pp. 68–87, elicited from Lang, *Wisdom of Balahvar*, pp. 129f., a 'Postscript' linking the position to our present theme.
10. Parts of the Christian–Arabic version were published (pp. 127–57) and analysed, and the derivation from the Greek demonstrated, in M. H. Zotenberg, 'Notice sur le texte et sur les versions orientales du Livre de Barlaam et Joasaph', *Notices et extraits des manuscrits de la Bibliothèque Nationale et autres bibliothèques, publiés par l'Institut National de France*, XXVIII (1887) 1–166. See also, more recently, Georg Graf, *Geschichte der christlichen arabischen Literatur*, Studi e Testi, no. 118, 5 vols (Città del Vaticano: Biblioteca Apostolica Vaticana, 1944–53) vol. I, pp. 546–8, for a synoptic view; and J. Leroy, 'Un nouveau manuscrit arabe-chrétien illustré du Roman de Barlaam et Joasaph', *Syria: revue d'art oriental et d'archéologie*, XXXII (1955) 101–22.
11. The Buddhist origin was suggested in 1859 by Edouard Laboulaye and demonstrated the following year by Felix Liebrecht. For a synopsis of recent studies, see Abuladze and especially Lang, works cited in notes 6 and 7 above. For the Manichee phase, see the recent work of W. B. Henning, and especially his publication and translation of a recently discovered Manichee version fragment of our tale, 'Persian Poetical Manuscripts from the Time of Rūdakī',

in *A Locust's Leg: Studies in Honour of S. H. Taqizadeh*, eds W. B. Henning and E. Yarshater (London: Lund, Humphries, 1962) pp. 89–98.

12. In the nature of Indian literary evidence, one is in no position to document as specifically pre-Buddhist the use – by Jains or other groups – of this or any other material, except what is found in Vedic, which this tale is not. Scholars differ on the non-Aryan origin of non-Vedic strands in Indian culture, with an increasing tendency to see things so, and in general I myself have long shared this tendency. In the particular case of the 'Man in the Well' story, I have not searched out the matter carefully; but it is certainly common, and early, among both Jains and 'Hindus'. Illustrative of many occurrences is a Jain Prakrit version from the *Samarādityakathā* of Haribhadra, available in English translation, with (non-comparativist) commentary and notes prepared by A. L. Basham, in *Sources of Indian Tradition*, ed. W. Theodore de Bary (New York: Columbia University Press, 1958). Of this work there were two editions, same place, same publisher, same date, which varied slightly; one was in one volume (also published in London: Oxford University Press, 1958), the other in two volumes (also London: Columbia University Press, 1958). The Haribhadra passage is found on pp. 56–8 and vol. I, pp. 53–5, respectively. (The former edition, as the first volume in the series Introduction to Oriental Civilizations, general ed. W. Theodore de Bary, appeared as vol. LIV of the series Records of Civilization: Sources and Studies, ed. in chief Jacques Barzun.) In this instance, for Haribhadra the black and white mice represent not night and day but rather the dark and bright phases of the moon (p. 58; vol. I, p. 55).
13. Cf. preceding note.
14. *Ben ha-m-Melekh wᵉ-ha-n-Nāzîr*. The only copies that I myself have seen are a Lvov (Lemberg) reprint (G. L. Kugel, Lewin, and Co.), 1870, of an Amsterdam edition of the Hebrew. The author's full name: Abrāhām ben Shᵉmû'ēl ben (*or* bar *or* ibn) Hasdai (or Hisdai) hā-Lēvī.
15. For a synopsis of the history, see, for instance, the article of Joseph Jacobs ('J.'), 'Barlaam and Josaphat', in *The Jewish Encyclopedia* 12 vols, general ed. Isidore Singer (New York and London: Funk & Wagnalls, 1901–5).
16. Many matters, of course, many persons, many ideas, were salient in the major development of Gandhi's personality during his crucial London years; that the impact of Tolstoi was among the foremost of these is an impression perhaps not unduly bold. The point comes out in, for instance, his remarking some years later of the person who became his chief Indian mentor that he found him 'higher than Tolstoy in religious perception' (quoted in Hay, p. 16 of the article cited in note 17 below), as it does too in the naming of his 1910 community project Tolstoy Farm (referred to later). It is supported by his own references a couple of decades later in his retrospective *Story of My Experiments with Truth*, which was first published in Gujarātī in the Ahmadabad weekly *Navajīvan*; an English translation by Mahadev Desai was then published serially in *Young India*, and in book form as M. K. Gandhi, *The Story of My Experiments with Truth*, 2 vols (Ahmedabad: Navajivan Press, 1927–9) which has been many times reprinted – for instance, as *Gandhi's Autobiography: The Story of My Experiments with Truth* (Washington, DC: Public Affairs Press, 1948; and Boston: Beacon Press, 1957). See s.v. 'Tolstoy' in index. See also, specifically, Paul Birukoff, 'Tolstoi und Gandhi', in *Fünfzehntes Jahrbuch der*

Schopenhauergesellschaft (Heidelberg: Carl Winter, 1928) pp. 166–70; and Paul Birukoff, *Tolstoi und der Orient: Briefe und sonstige Zeugnisse über Tolstois Beziehungen zu den Vertretern orientalischer Religionen* (Zürich and Leipzig: Rotapfel, 1925) pp. 70–9.

17. For the relatively little recognised fact of Gandhi's Jain involvement, see esp. Stephen H. Hay, 'Jain Influences on Gandhi's Early Thought', in *Gandhi, India and the World*, ed. Sibnarayan Ray (Bombay: Nachiketa, 1970) pp. 14–23, and (Philadelphia: Temple University Press, 1970) pp. 29–38 – although it is possible for a Westerner to read this article without abandoning the standard assumption that being Hindu and being Jain (being 'a Hindu' and being 'a Jain') is an either–or matter, whether for a person, a family, or a culture. The 'Hindu' environment into which Gandhi was born and in which he grew up was influenced, infiltrated, impregnated, by Jain religious and cultural elements – he participated in the Jain tradition – more, and more intricately, than most Western concepts make room for apprehending. Rājchandra (Raychand) Mehtā, Gandhi's spiritual mentor (referred to in the preceding note), had a Vaiṣṇava father 'but [*sic*] his mother was a Jain' (ibid., p. 17), and he grew up to think of himself as Jain; whether Gandhi thought of him (and whether he thought of himself) as Hindu is not clear. There are many sorts of Hindu; that being Jain is one of them, especially in certain areas in Gujarāt, is not to be ruled out *a priori*. The fact is that in India 'Hindu' is fundamentally an alien concept.

18. The impact of Gandhi on his thought and feeling and life began when King was a senior at Crozer Seminary, and developed quickly and deeply; when his long-standing aspiration to visit India was fulfilled in 1959, he made the reverberating remark, 'To other countries, I may go as a tourist, but to India I come as a pilgrim'. On this matter in general, see, for instance, Kenneth L. Smith and Ira G. Zepp, Jr, *Search for the Beloved Community: The Thinking of Martin Luther King, Jr.* (Valley Forge: Judson Press, 1974) pp. 47–70 (ch. 3: 'Gandhi: Nonviolence and Civil Disobedience'). For King's autobiographical remarks, see his *Stride Toward Freedom: The Montgomery Story* (New York: Harper & Row, 1964 [first published 1958]), pp. 66f., 78–85, 194f., etc.; and his *Strength to Love* (New York and London: Harper & Row, 1963) esp. pp. 138f. For his widow's tribute, see Coretta Scott King, *My Life with Martin Luther King, Jr.* (New York: Holt, Rinehart and Winston, 1969) pp. 58, 88, 121, 163, 171–7 (the 'pilgrim' quotation appears on p. 174).

19. More accurately: it has been so, for approximately the most recent 20 per cent of that Church's history, and for much of but not all its community. For the Dominicans, it is favoured by being, rather, the first Sunday in October. In 1571 the 7th was the first Sunday, and the victory at Lepanto over the Turks on that day underlies this choice of date. (In this fact some today might perceive a certain irony, or at least an index of the complexity of Muslim–Christian interrelations historically; see a few lines further on in the text.) The Dominicans traditionally introduced the rosary into the Church; this form of devotion was said to have been revealed to St Dominic by the Virgin, and the Dominican Order has indeed emphasised and developed it more than have others.

20. Bibliographic references must be highly selective. The history of the rosary has been elaborately studied, in its various sectors, Christian and other, and to

some degree also as a world phenomenon. For this last, see Willibald Kirfel, *Der Rosenkranz: Ursprung und Ausbreitung* Beiträge zur Sprach- und Kulturgeschichte des Orients (general ed. O. Spies) no. 1 (Walldorf-Hessen: Vorndran, Orientkunde, 1949). With this it is instructive to compare and to contrast such a work as Franz Michel Willam, *Geschichte und Gebetsschule des Rosenkranzes* (Wien: Herder, 1948), trans. into Eng. by the Rev. Edwin Kaiser as *The Rosary: Its History and Meaning* (New York: Benziger, 1953) – which presents its Part I as 'the first complete history of the origin and development of the rosary' (Foreword). This work means by 'rosary' a Christian prayer; non-Christian use religiously of strings of beads is not regarded – while in the Kirfel work the piety that animates and is animated by such use tends in turn to be underplayed. For one aspect of Islamic usage, as contrasted with that reflected by Muslim devotional treatises, reference may be made to A. J. Wensinck's convenient synoptic historical study from the point of new of an outside observes: 'Subḥa', in *The Encyclopaedia of Islam*, 1st edn vol. IV (Leyden [*sic*]: Brill; and London: Luzac, 1934) p. 492. Specifically on the *nenju*, one may note the pertinent section (pp. 174–7) and bibliography (pp. 255f.) in E. Dale Saunders, *Mudrā: A study of Symbolic Gestures in Japanese Buddhist Sculpture* (New York: Pantheon, for the Bollingen Foundation, 1960). I have found illuminating the following articles: M.- M. Gorce, 'Le symbolisme fleuri de la piété mariale', in *Histoire générale des religions*, ed. Maxime Gorce and Raoul Mortier, vol. IV (Paris: Aristide Quillet, 1948) pp. 52–5 (cf. bibliography, p. 512); P. Sticotti, G. Cardinali, *et al.*, 'Corona', in *Enciclopedia Italiana*, vol. XI (1931) pp. 447–51); and Innocenzo Taurisano, 'Rosario', ibid., vol. XXX (1936) p. 112. For the numbers of beads used at various times and places, one may see, in addition to Kirfel, Eithne Wilkins, *The Rose-Garden Game: The Symbolic Background to the European Prayer-beads* (London: Gollancz, 1969) pp. 54–8.

21. For a compelling exposition of how recent scholarship makes possible and indeed requisite the understanding of mediaeval scholasticism as primarily Islamic, see George Makdisi, 'The Scholastic Method in Medieval Education: An Inquiry into its Origins in Law and Theology', in *Speculum*, XLIX (1974) 640–61.
22. Robert N. Bellah, 'Religious Evolution', *American Sociological Review*, XXIX (1964) 358–74; repr. *Reader in Comparative Religion: An Anthropological Approach*, ed. William A. Lessa and Evon Z. Vogt, 2nd edn (New York and London: Harper & Row, 1965 [1st edn 1958]) pp. 73–87, and in Robert N. Bellah, *Beyond Belief: Essays on Religion in a Post-traditional World* (New York and London: Harper & Row, 1970) pp. 20–50.
23. E. A. Burtt, 'The Future of Religion', *Bulletin of the Ramakrishna Mission Institute of Culture*, XIX (1968) 91–7.
24. Marshall G. S. Hodgson is noteworthy for his posthumous monumental *The Venture of Islam: Conscience and History in a World Civilization*, ed. Reuben W. Smith 3 vols (Chicago and London: University of Chicago Press, 1974); in this work, his synoptic view of world history, to which specific religious and civilisational history is subordinate, shines through but is not explicated. He was at work on a world history at the time of his death, but left it incomplete to the point where it 'apparently cannot be published' (ibid., p. viii; some of his friends hope that it yet will be). An important, explicit, earlier statement is his

article 'Hemispheric Interregional History as an Approach to World History', *Cahiers d'histoire mondiale*, I (1954) 715–23.

25. Trevor Ling, *A History of Religion East and West: An Introduction and Interpretation* (London: Macmillan, 1968; New York: Harper & Row, 1970).
26. Lang, *Balavariani* (see note 6 above) p. 10. As remarked earlier, I owe much to this writer; and the debt is not only for the detail of his wide and deep scholarship. His spirit and vision, also, have served not negligibly as inspiration for my own work here. The point being made is that even so sensitive, broad and significant an interpreter as he has been inhibited, by our Western tradition's lack of appropriate concepts and categories theologically, from appreciating the true import of his own perceptions.

CHAPTER 2

1. There is a problem here in relation to conceptions of divine revelation in verbal form. The term 'Muslim' verbalises a human concept for persons outside the Islamic community; but for Muslims themselves, since the word occurs in the Qur'ān, it is a divine concept. Strictly, then, the sentence in our text (with its word 'human') stands. For Muslims, as for Christians and Western secularists, the concept 'Buddhist' is a human one; and for Buddhists themselves the counterpart Sanskrit concept *Bauddha*, for instance, has not been crucial. (Nāgārjuna would zealously agree with our sentence in the text!) In the Christian case there is a problem in that the term 'Christian' has (has come to have) two distinct, and potentially contradictory, meanings. It may serve as – originally – an adjective from the noun 'Christ' (signifying, then, 'pertaining to Christ'), or as an adjective from the noun 'Christian' (signifying, 'pertaining to Christians'). The one is metaphysical, the other empirical. (Thus, humility is a Christian virtue, Christian smugness is a vice.) More subtly, 'Christian faith' nowadays often means 'the faith of Christians'. The empirical meaning has become predominant in common parlance. Theology uses both, at times ambiguously. Even in the metaphysical sense, the term 'Christian' as used represents inescapably a human concept of the divine, while in Islamic usage the term 'Muslim' is seen as representing the divine concept of the human. (Yet outsiders would say that its meaning in the mind of any given Muslim is again an historical conceptualisation of the transcendent; and Muslims would agree that, although the correct meaning of the term is what God means by it, actual Musalmāns have understood it humanly. Therefore, there is a history of Muslim understanding of the concept.) The matter is further complicated in that in its Arabic metaphysical sense I myself certainly aspire and claim to be *muslim* and argue that all sincere Christians, Buddhists, and the like are so, ideally; this would be the form of the general argument of this book if it were addressed primarily to an Islamic audience. My own tendency in this study is to use all these terms primarily in their historical sense: 'Christian' refers to the Christian sector of the religious history of humankind, 'Muslim' to the Islamic, 'Buddhist' to the Buddhist, and so on. The term 'Hindu' has had no other denotation.
2. 'The Crystallization of Religious Communities in Mughul India', in *Yād-Nāme-ye-Iraini* [sic] *-ye Minorsky*, ed. Mojtaba Minovi and Iraj Afshar (Tehran: Publications of Tehran University, 1969) pp. 197–220.

CHAPTER 3

1. For Muslim readers, this point should be expressed by saying, what is surely plausible, that the Arabic term *dīn* in the Qur'ān is not adequately seen as equivalent to the modern Western (English-language) term 'religion'.

CHAPTER 4

1. Compare Michael Polanyi, *Personal Knowledge* (London: Routledge and Kegan Paul; and Chicago: University of Chicago Press, 1962 [1st edn 1958]), with Karl R. Popper, *Objective Knowledge* (Oxford: Clarendon Press, 1975 [1st edn 1972]).

CHAPTER 5

1. *The Meaning and End of Religion* (see above, ch. 1, note 1).
2. The process of differentiation of those in India who have recently come to be called 'Hindus' began when the Muslims arrived in the country, even though it crystallised only after the Europeans arrived. The Islamic movement introduced into an uncomprehending India the conception of a closed religious system, in due course reified, but the West introduced the concept into Hindu education and thought. Cf. the latter part of my 'Crystallization' article (see above, ch. 2, note 2).
3. 'The Historical Development in Islam of the Concept of Islam as an Historical Development', in *Historians of the Middle East*, Historical Writing on the Peoples of Asia, no. 4, ed. Bernard Lewis and P. M. Holt, (London: Oxford University Press, 1962) pp. 484–502.
4. This shift I have documented and studied at some length in two recent works: *Belief and History* (Charlottesville: University Press of Virginia, 1977); and *Faith and Belief* (Princeton: Princeton University Press, 1979).
5. 'Comparative Religion: Whither – and Why?', in *The History of Religions: Essays in Methodology*, ed. Mircea Eliade and Joseph M. Kitagawa (Chicago: The University of Chicago Press, 1959) pp. 31–58.
6. *Faith and Belief* (see above, note 4).

CHAPTER 6

1. *The Meaning and End of Religion* (see above, ch.1, note 1) p. 139 (1963 edn).
2. Friedrich Schleiermacher, *Der christliche Glaube, nach den Grundsäzen der evangelischen Kirche im Zusammenhange dargestellt*, 2 vols (Berlin: G. Reimer, 1821–22; 2nd edn 1830–1). I have used the seventh edition, a critical version of the second (with modernised spelling *Grundsätzen*), ed. Martin Redeker (Berlin: de Gruyter, 1960). English trans.: Friedrich Schleiermacher, *The Christian Faith*, ed. H. R. Mackintosh and J. S. Stewart (Edinburgh: T. and T. Clark, 1928).
3. *Glaubensweisen*, regularly. See, for instance, section 10:2 (vol. 1, p. 67 of the 7th edn German text; cf. preceding note). Schleiermacher never uses the noun

Glaube in the plural; yet his translators repeatedly present him as speaking of 'faiths' (an example: 'other faiths', at p. 46 of the English, corresponding to vol. I, p. 67, of the German 7th edn). Their term 'religion' often renders his *Frommigkeit*, and even 'the Christian religion' can render his *die christliche Frommigkeit* (section 3:1 – pp. 6 and 15 of the English and German respectively; section 7:3 – pp. 33 and 50; etc.); their 'communal religions' represents his *Gestaltungen gemeinsamer Frommigkeit* (section 7:1 – pp. 32 and 48).

4. Recently, in my *Faith and Belief* (see above, ch. 5, note 4); earlier, in *The Meaning and End of Religion* (see above, ch. 1, note 1). The remainder of the paragraph here in the text synopsises one or two of the developments studied at length in the latter work, and documented.
5. So far as I have been able to become aware, book-titles including such phrases as 'Jewish theology' and 'Islamic theology' occur for the first time only in this century (the latter only by non-Muslim scholars?). In the 'Christian theology' case there seems but one exception to its also being altogether recent. That exception is a work from the early twelfth century, Abelard's *Theologia Christiana*. It has recently been published in a critical edition: *Petri Abaelardi Opera Theologica*, vol. II (Corpus Christianorum, Continuatio mediaeualis, no. 12), ed. Eligius (Eloi) M. Buytaert, (Turnholti: Brepols, 1969) pp. 5–372. An English analysis has been published by J. Ramsay McCallum: *Abelard's Christian Theology* (Oxford: Basil Blackwell, 1948).

   May this unprecedented, and for centuries unimitated, title perhaps be interpreted as not unrelated to his explicit use of the views of thinkers who are not Christians – Greek philosophers and Jews – in his construction of arguments for the theological position, which is then explicitly Christian, that he sets forth? Those others' views he regarded the Church's vision as supplementing but not negating. And may it be interpreted as not unrelated also, perhaps, even to the Church's condemnation (at the Council of Sens, 1140) of his position? In any case, Thomas Aquinas was much more typical when he entitled his *Summa* simply *Theologiae* (for a time it was known also as *Summa Theologica*). The preponderant Christian practice – obvious enough, once one thinks about it – has throughout been to write, and to think, theology: discourse about God. Similarly, Muslims have thought and written *kalām*; and Buddhists have spoken about Dharma, not about Buddhist Dharma.

CHAPTER 7

1. Or one may say, theosophist. See *Essential Unity of All Religions*, comp. Bhagavān Dās, 5th edn (Adyar, Madras: Theosophical Publishing House, 1955 [1st edn 1932]). One may compare Frithjof Schuon, *De l'unité transcendante des religions* (Paris: Gallimard; 1948); trans. into Eng. as *The Transcendent Unity of Religions*, trans. Peter Townsend (London: Faber and Faber, 1953; New York: Pantheon, 1953; [rev. edn] New York and London: Harper & Row, 1975).
2. This particular point is not imaginary. I made the suggestion in my article 'Some Similarities and Differences Between Christianity and Islam: An Essay in Comparative Religion', in *The World of Islam: Studies in Honour of Philip K. Hitti*, ed. James Kritzeck and R. Bayly Winder (London: Macmillan; and New York: St Martin's Press, 1959) pp. 47–59. Various Muslim friends have agreed orally

on this point, and at least one formal agreement has appeared in print. A leading Muslim intellectual of Pakistan (currently Director, National Institute of Psychology, Islamabad) discusses the analogy and remarks, 'This parallel is extremely valuable' – M. Ajmal in *A History of Muslim Philosophy: with short accounts of other Disciplines and the Modern Renaissance in Muslim Lands*, ed. M. M. Sharif, 2 vols (Wiesbaden: Harrassowitz, 1963–6) p. 1115.

3. The text of the lecture as originally delivered read, 'with no chance to sit down with' (and 'have heard or read my first five lectures'). The pressures of preparing the presentation allowed, in fact, no opportunity to consult with Muslim, Buddhist and other friends in time for the delivery; and I have preserved the original presentation virtually without modification (this chapter has been revised less than any of the others). This is so despite the fact that subsequently there has, of course, been time that would have permitted elaborate revision in the light of others' comments had I chosen to pursue that. My decision in favour of the original draft is due to a recognition that to prepare a series of statements that would responsibly and authoritatively reflect other communities' intellectuals' views, and not merely my own however responsible impressions, would constitute a second major step (indeed, series of steps) in the momentous undertaking that this book proposes, rather than being an integral part of this first step. Indeed, I very much hope that not I but those others, not in a few pages each but substantially (and no doubt, diversely), will in fact proffer considered critiques and responses from the communities concerned: accepting, in effect, the invitation that this work constitutes my propounding (just as I hope that Christian theologians will do so). Beyond satisfying myself, through a limited number of careful inquiries in each case, that my brief imaginary presentations here do not appear (at least to some responsible thinkers – not necessarily 'representative', of course) as positively distorting or offensive, however much negatively they may leave out from an adequate response, I therefore allow them to stand; just as I allow to stand the apologies stated above. Yet the invitation expressed at the end of Chapter 6 stands too, and indeed is earnest.

CHAPTER 8

1. This lecture was originally delivered on 2 February 1972.
2. My *Faith and Belief* (see above, ch. 5, note 4).
3. In the Qur'ān (sūrah 16, verse 68) there is a reference to God's according a revelation to a bee; and many Hindus also might be restless at restricting the mundane side of the revelation relation to human beings. Buddhists, also, would not have chosen my concept 'person'; their usual term is *sarvasattāḥ*, regularly translated as 'all sentient beings' (with which compare more particularly the Chinese version, *yu-ch'ing*). This does not affect my argument substantially; and if any of my readers would wish to amend the wording so as to be more inclusive of recipients, I should not quibble. (Nor should I wish to quarrel with the Christian poet's conceit, that evolution has proceeded only because, for instance, some lobster 'reached out and caught hold of the toe of God'.) What I am urging is that revelation is a bilateral concept; that if anything is revelation it is so not in and of itself but only as and when it has some particular recipient.

4. See, apart from items already mentioned, my articles 'The Mission of the Church and the Future of Missions', and 'A Human View of Truth'; also my Taylor Lectures at Yale Divinity School, *Questions of Religious Truth* (New York: Scribner's; and London: Gollancz, 1967). The articles have appeared as follows: the former in *The Church in the Modern World: Essays in Honour of James Sutherland Thomson*, ed. George Johnston and Wolfgang Roth (Toronto: Ryerson, 1967) pp. 154–70; the latter in *SR: Studies in Religion/Sciences religieuses*, 1 (1971) 6–24, repr. in *Truth and Dialogue: The Relationship between World Religions*, ed. John Hick (London: Sheldon, 1974) [US edn entitled *Truth and Dialogue in World Religions: Conflicting Truth-claims* (Philadelphia: Westminster, 1974)] pp. 20–44 (cf. 156–62).

CHAPTER 9

1. *Faith and Belief* (see above, ch. 5, note 4).
2. As the title of the work mentioned in the preceding note indicates, this topic too is explored in that volume; for the Western world, also in my recent *Belief and History*, (see above, ch. 5, note 4).

Index

In this index, the most important matters are deliberately left out. For example, Siddhārtha Gautama, the Buddha, and the Buddhist tradition and community and faith, are mentioned by name at various points; yet the only reasonable entry for them, or for the Qur'ān or Christ or God, or for scientific conceptualisation or interdisciplinary methodology, would be an unhelpful 'passim'. The treatise as a whole is about such matters, from start to finish. Accordingly, we list here certain more specific or in some sense more limited entries.